The Chain
of Curiosity

Also by Sandi Toksvig

FICTION

Whistling for the Elephants

Flying under Bridges

The Travels of Lady 'Bulldog' Burton
(with Sandy Nightingale)

Melted into Air

Valentine Grey

NON-FICTION

Gladys Reunited: A Personal American Journey

The Chain of Curiosity

Sandi Toksvig

SPHERE

First published in Great Britain in 2009 by Sphere
Reprinted 2009 (three times), 2013 (twice)

The pieces in this book were originally published in the
Sunday Telegraph between June 2005 and April 2009.

A CIP catalogue record for this book
is available from the British Library.

ISBN 978-1-84744-345-8

Typeset in Sabon by M Rules
Printed and bound in Great Britain by
Clays Ltd, St Ives plc

Papers used by Sphere are from well-managed forests
and other responsible sources.

MIX
Paper from
responsible sources
FSC
www.fsc.org   FSC® C104740

Sphere
An imprint of
Little, Brown Book Group
100 Victoria Embankment
London EC4Y 0DY

An Hachette UK Company
www.hachette.co.uk

www.littlebrown.co.uk

For Deej

I would also like to thank the following people for their invaluable assistance: Emma Gosnell; John Morgan; Christopher Howe; and Belinda Smith.

Contents

vii

ix

x

Does anyone know why torches never work?

19 June 2005

FORGIVE ME WHILE I ATTEMPT today to write in balanced equations. I have spent the past few weeks struggling to shepherd my sixteen-year-old through her GCSEs, and the science section is starting to get to me. I never did calculations of any kind in my teens. I arrived in this country at the age of fourteen with a smattering of American high-school education, which, my English headmistress declared, doomed me to a life in the arts. Thank God. Neither I, nor I'm pleased to say my daughter (thanks mainly to relentless indoctrination showings of *Singing in the Rain* as a small child), see the point of science. It may be that nitrogen and hydrogen make ammonia and that the process is reversible, but that isn't going to clean my surfaces any faster. (Actually, while we are on the subject of cleaning, can I just say that bleach is the ultimate money-making invention? Here is a product which is sold as something you take home, pour down the toilet and then return to buy more. Genius.) And what about physics, and the endlessly fascinating question: how does a torch work? I have no idea. In our house no torch works. It is simply a carrying-case for dead batteries.

It's Father's Day but I've not sent a card. Partly because I refuse to participate in these artificially generated celebrations and partly because my dear old Dad passed away the week my sixteen-year-old was born. (Happy Father's Day, wherever you are in the ether.) Recently, I came across an old pair of his spectacles and when I put them on I realised that, as luck would have it, his prescription is now an exact fit for me. So I am of an age where I see the world through my father's eyes. (I wear

1

glasses because, as Papa used to say, my arms are not long enough to play a trombone large enough to hold the music where I can read it.)

Still, seeing through my father's eyes is better than seeing through my grandfather's. Grandpa had a glass eye. Actually, that's not quite right. He had two. I'm not saying he was blind. He had two glass eyes for the same eye. One was a perfect match for his working eye and the other was a specially made bloodshot replacement. Upon departing for a good night out he would put in the heavily veined eye and declare that he was going out to party until both his eyes matched. An example to us all.

Eyesight brings me back to science. (Watch and marvel at these small but perfectly formed equations.) It was on this very day, 19 June, in 240 BC that the Greek mathematician Eratosthenes was the first to estimate accurately the diameter and circumference of the Earth. Apparently, he did this by looking at and comparing the lengths of the noon shadows in Syene and Alexandria in Egypt. There is more detail on this but now we are in the murky world of mathematics, for which I employ an accountant called Marvin. Here is another area of study for which I have little patience. The killer for me has always been that two negatives make a positive. I don't have two sheep, you don't give me two sheep, suddenly I have four sheep causing havoc in the paddock. Wait a second, I don't have a paddock. OK, you don't give me a paddock, oh my lucky stars, I have a paddock for those pesky sheep. I had a friend at university who was a mathematical genius but he couldn't wire a plug. One day he arrived in a state of great excitement to declare that he had discovered P, or D, or some other consonant which everyone in his department had been searching for. It was hard to be thrilled. I mean, I didn't even know it was missing.

Good news for dogs and cats. This week has seen the unveiling of the Prince BowMiao range of Italian designer accessories for our furry friends. This includes the usual collection of collars, leashes, jackets and leg-warmers, but also, you will be thrilled to hear, scooter helmets. I haven't the time to explain but I once took a rabbit for a ride on a motorcycle and I have to say the niche market for protective pet headgear never occurred to me. I don't know why but it makes me think about a useless nugget of legal knowledge I have in the back of my tiny mind about two-wheeled transportation. As far as I know, having sexual relations on a motorcycle is not in itself illegal, although you will be done for driving without due care and attention.

Elbow gymnastics and a difficult delivery

3 July 2005

DID YOU KNOW THAT IT is not possible to lick your own elbow? I mention this as a harmless activity to attempt while you are on the phone. Let me confess that I am feeling curmudgeonly: crusty, ill-tempered and possibly turning into a man – it must be the heat. It's the ancient, vexed question of service. For anyone running a large corporation, let me help you out here – service is the act of serving; it is useful labour that does not produce a tangible commodity; a helpful action that may even conclude with the words, 'it's been a pleasure'.

I've spent the week persuading a parcel delivery service to deliver a package to me. As I write that sentence I realise what a simple transaction that should be. They are in the parcel delivery business. They had my parcel. I wanted it delivered. Why, this is like the opening of a Janet and John book on the subject. Sadly, I am a mere girl and fail to understand the complexities of the matter.

What they wanted was for me to collect the parcel from them. As I already have a career, I decided to phone and organise a more traditional arrangement. They didn't like this. 'We prefer,' I was informed, 'to be contacted through our website.' Well, I prefer a man in a smart uniform to bring my goods to the door, but we can't all be picky.

After only sixteen attempts I got through to a computerised voice offering me a million options. I selected one at random and settled down to several hours of inactivity. It was while holding the phone that I began to think about my elbow. Did you know that 75 per cent of people who read the sentence, 'It is not possible to lick your own elbow', will try? The other 25 per cent work for the parcel delivery service and would like you to try for them.

It's been a good week for the Senior Service. The Navy was all at sea on Tuesday re-enacting the Battle of Trafalgar. I never really understood Nelson's career choice. Here was a man who was seasick in the harbour, yet he chose a life on the ocean wave. I have been to sea and can tell you that sea-sickness comes in two stages. In the first you think you are going to die, and in the second you are afraid you are not going to.

For the re-enactment, in the spirit of modern *entente lime cordiale*, it was decided not to refer to the opposing sides as British or French, but as Red and Blue. What a sensible concept. After all, with actual fighting, you could have someone's eye out. I think turning conflict into a team game is a thought ripe for development. Why not have a reality show where the contestants battle it out over world affairs? Never mind about G8 and the big concert, here is a way to engage the public's attention. You have a red and a blue team of celebrities. If you win you get given, say, Switzerland, while if you lose you become opposition leader to Robert Mugabe.

This week it was announced that a British cruise company is launching the world's first holiday devoted to laughter therapy. Apparently, you set to sea and laugh all the way round the Med, something last done by Julius Caesar. Forget shuffleboard. Here there is 'laughter yoga' and, indeed, here I draw the line. Not only can I not lick my own elbow, I can't even do a forward roll. I do a rather fine Swiss roll but only if the Aga isn't acting up.

Back to the Navy. One day Winston Churchill visited a naval base and was taken to an area where there were a lot of sub-merged wrecks. Churchill watched as the system located a target and a depth-charge was dropped. After a few seconds, there was a huge underwater explosion. Several pieces of wreckage came to the surface, including a door emblazoned with the letters 'WC'. 'The navy always knew,' Churchill quipped, 'how to pay proper compliments.' Now that's what I call service.

Tell me, what is the point of swimming?

31 July 2005

ON THIS VERY DAY IN 1955, Marilyn Bell of Toronto, Canada, at the tender age of seventeen, became the youngest person to swim the English Channel. This is the sort of feat that can only provoke one response – why?

I've never really understood swimming as a leisure activity and, certainly, deciding to go the distance encased in goose fat seems to border on mental instability. I have always viewed swimming as more of an anti-drowning device than a pleasurable recreation. I mention all this because we are packing for our family holiday and within the week the cry, 'Come on in, the water's lovely!' will bounce off the pleasingly dry walls of our temporary abode.

My deep lack of interest in this area was founded in the local baths we attended when I was at boarding school. Here a positive viper's nest of verrucas resided as we broke the ice once a week to take the plunge. There were three skill groups, A, B and C. It will give you some idea of my lack of ability that within a month of my joining, the sports mistress had added group F for my benefit.

Some years ago when I set to sea with John McCarthy to circumnavigate these isles, the age of our vessel brought fears of enforced swimming to the surface. We visited the life-jacket company Crewsaver and were fitted with the latest flotation devices. I still have the business card of the executive who attended to us. His name? I kid you not – Will Drown.

I spent part of this week avoiding water aerobics. A friend took me to a health farm for the day and there seemed to be an opportunity for water-based gymnastics every five minutes. Instead, I ran to the treatment centre. (OK, I didn't run. Let's not go mad here.) Many young women dressed in pseudo-medical white coats were in attendance, none of whom could conclude a sentence without a rising inflection. They did this in voices with an astonishing high pitch. Indeed, if two or more of them spoke at the same time, I swear dogs began to gather in the garden. In addition, everyone seemed to have lost the letter G off the end of any available therapy. There was WaxIN, RelaxIN and, of course, TannIN.

I opted for a facial, and lay down to be encased in cucumber. 'What is your regime?' the young woman enquired. It was a question that had never occurred to me. I didn't think I had a regime. I wondered if Robert Mugabe had ever had a facial and been asked the same question. 'I wash my face with water,' I managed. Not any more apparently. I came home with twenty-eight different products and no longer do WashIN. I do RehydratIN.

I don't know that I shall go again. Much better to follow the advice of my comic hero, Lucille Ball. 'The secret of staying young,' she once declared, 'is to live honestly, eat slowly – and lie about your age.'

While we are awash with liquid, there has been an artistic tragedy at the excellent Ways with Words festival at Dartington Hall in Devon. The artist Wayne Hill had been displaying his latest work, *Weapon of Mass Destruction*, at the annual literary jamboree. The piece consisted of a two-litre clear plastic bottle filled with melted Antarctic ice. You will be way ahead of me in realising the true artistic significance of such an item, but, sadly, some ignoramus thought it was just a . . . well, bottle of water. The £42,500 art gem was not only taken but has probably been drunk. Mr Hill was quoted as saying, 'It looked like an ordinary bottle of water, but it was on a plinth, labelled, described and in the programme of the whole festival. It was very, very clear what it was – a work of art.' Some people are such philistines.

Oh, one more thing about water and sport. I don't need to tell you that the Women's World Water Polo Championships took place this week in Montreal. I'll save you the remarks about the skill of the horses and simply heap praise on the Hungarian goalie Patricia Horvath, who apparently played like a demon. She saved shots from every angle, even stopping a couple with her forehead. I'm back where I started. Anyone else feel the question 'Why?' coming up?

No towels or television – what stoics
we are

7 August 2005

I SEND YOU A POSTCARD from the Dodecanese group of islands. Dodecanese means twelve, yet there are thirteen main Dodecanese islands. Trust me, this is not a hot spot for the pedant. I'm on holiday and to be honest I am struggling with the entire concept. It is not just the horde of screaming toddlers, who would rather be anywhere except abroad with sand up their double-lined nappy, who are interfering with my escape. My great-aunt is also on my mind. She was a milkmaid who lived in the Danish countryside. When she got married her new husband took her to Copenhagen for a week. Upon her return, none of the other milkmaids wanted to know what the far and distant capital city was like. They all wanted to know what it was like to have a week off.

The family and I have come to the Greek island of Rhodes for a week to escape milking the cow of rainy routine. We are very happy, but aspects of the sojourn require me to recall some of the finer points of the great Stoics. I stand cheek by jowl with the birthplace of Colossus, one of the Seven Wonders of the Ancient World, yet I am preoccupied with the minutiae of existence. It has taken four days to wrest swimming towels from reception and we're still working on a bottle opener.

There is something about proximity to the Mediterranean that briefly makes a promise seem enticing. No Greek or Italian wishes to disappoint, so they provide some future guarantee which sustains until the inevitable moment of actual disappointment. I remind myself that Rhodes was the birthplace of rhetoric and when the manager asks if there is anything he can do, no answer is required.

The television stands idle in the room, its promised connection another myth. Until then, it makes a useful resting place for drinks and high-factor sun cream. We are cut off from news and scan the turquoise sea, just like the ancients, wondering whatever did happen to that nice Helen from Troy. Like the average Rhodian of a thousand years ago, I have no access to books or the great Alexandrian library that is the internet. I can't, therefore, check who it was who said there was no future for the television, composed as it is of half a Greek and half a Latin word. I like this twilight of knowledge. I imagine it will be like this when I am old. I shall sit in a chair which has wings to prevent me falling out, and half remember detail. I've tried to learn a little Greek but my mind resists. Somewhere in the back of it I still have the Swahili for 'Tell the servants not to put treacle in the carburettor' and I may have reached my linguistic fill. For the moment I sit in the shade safe from the pen of the ever-ready pedant.

The first joke books came from Greece. The Greeks loved a good gag. Indeed, Philip the Great of Macedon paid a social club in Athens to write down its members' witticisms. There the Oscar Wilde of his day held court while, no doubt, Dorothy Parker stayed home with the donkey. *Philogelos*, or the *Lover of Laughter*, was written in the fourth century. It has 265 jokes of which 102 are about pedants.

I remind myself to edge away from pedantry as we set out in the hire car. It has no licence plates, but then there seem to be no police. The kids quickly tire of playing 'spot the moped accident' as we drift from cove to cove, swim in the medicinal waters of Kalithea and dip shared spoons in rich yogurt draped in honey. I tell the kids about the world's first car-boot sale when the people of Rhodes sold the siege equipment abandoned by Demetrius Poliorcetes, whose attack failed in 305 BC. The

11

Rhodians sold his warmongering detritus and built a statue to the sun god instead.

We drift and the winding route takes us to the city of Rhodes. 'Ha!' I cry, 'All roaming leads to Rhodes!' There is silence. From the back of the car my son clears his throat. 'They can't have had a car-boot sale,' he declares quietly. 'They didn't have any cars.' Pedant.

I only wanted to be an astronaut for the boiler suit

14 August 2005

THIS WEEK I'VE BEEN FOR a trip down memory lane, which, with the way my synapses have been working, can be a bit of an uncertain enterprise. The landing of the space shuttle under the firm command of Eileen Collins brought back childhood dreams of life as an astronaut. If I am completely honest, I may well have found some of the initial attraction to be related to fashion. Who among us could not hide a multitude of physical imperfections in one of those all-in-one suits? My journalist father covered all the Apollo space missions. Indeed, I have the curious distinction of having watched Neil Armstrong step out onto the moon while I stood inside Mission Control next to his secretary. I loved it and the only things that came between me and a career in the stars was an inability to comprehend science and a fear of flying.

Much of my dislike for aviation stems from the associated language. I don't like to depart from somewhere labelled 'Terminal' and I hate the idea of a 'non-stop' flight. Sadly, for the first female in space, her trip was both non-stop and terminal. Laika the Russian dog was the first living being to orbit the Earth in space. She blasted off inside Sputnik II in 1957 and proved that animals could survive the rigours of space travel. Unfortunately, it was a one-way ticket and she died before anyone could think how to bring her home or see if the RSPCA had a view. Today things are rather more sophisticated and I imagine there is in-flight entertainment and everything. If you look at the NASA website there is actually a section called 'Upgrades'. Maybe if you click on it you get a wider seat.

*

In the untidy office of my mind strange facts lurk and loom when least expected. Today's date reminds me of heady celebrations as we mark the end of the Boxer Rebellion in China on 14 August 1900. Who could forget the happy oriental scenes as once again Chinese men took to the street wearing celebratory Y-fronts? I can also delve into my mental recesses and tell you that there are two streets in the UK named after Stalin, that the glue on Israeli postage stamps is certified kosher and that Mel Blanc, who was the voice of Bugs Bunny, was allergic to carrots.

I have a mind like a steel trap for this kind of trivia, but none of this helps me remember where I left my glasses. If I added up all the minutes in the week when I stand in the centre of a room trying to recall where I was going and why, I could probably find the time to learn even more. I suffer a kind of daily vagueness which up until now has been slightly worrying. This week, however, cheering news for anyone with mildly dysfunctional neurons. On Tuesday, a Macedonian gentlemen named Ljubomir Ivanov, who is only thirty-five and frankly has no excuse for being forgetful, took a driving holiday with his wife. He happily chugged across Europe until he got a phone call in Germany saying he'd left Mrs Ivanov at a petrol station in central Italy. Apparently, she usually sits in the back seat and he didn't see she wasn't there until six hours after filling up.

More bad news for my recall abilities – scientists say that being fat can lead to dementia. I have decided, however, to throw caution to the winds and proceed with my all-cream-cake regime. It seems to me that the fatter I get, the fewer places I will go and so the less I will have to remember.

Apropos of nothing in particular, I met a woman this week with hair of a platinum hue the like of which I've not seen since I last caught a Jean Harlow film during a prolonged period of insomnia. The bottle blonde (several bottles I warrant) was

14

working as a personal assistant. When I asked her what she had previously done for a living, she replied, 'I was a trophy girl-friend.' I love this idea. I plan to become one myself. I have long suspected that I would end up on the shelf, but I had no idea it might be as a trophy.

Why our guinea pig is looking glum

28 August 2005

THERE WAS A CURIOUS THEME in the news this week as we discovered that testing kids in this country has allegedly become easier, while testing animals is now almost impossible. GCSE results were out on Thursday and I spent the early hours of the morning eating my cardigan with anxiety as we awaited my oldest daughter's grades. I spent much of this past spring treating her like a goose on a pâté farm as I force-fed facts into her. Indeed, I spent so long at it that I went from knowing nothing whatsoever about chemistry to finding myself bringing up the periodic table as possible dinner party conversation.

On reflection, I thought sixteen-year-old studying seemed tougher than I remembered. I mean, even the title of the exam has four letters compared with the one 'O' in my day. My lovely girl did well, only to be told by educational know-alls that it has all become easier anyway. She doesn't care and has embarked on a round of heady celebrations. The joy is only marginally marred by the despondency of our guinea pig, who finds his farm holiday has been cancelled and he is not to be tested at all.

Fireworks in the gender war – two university professors (both male) claim to have tested 80,000 people (male and female) and discovered that men are more intelligent than women. One of them, Professor Lynn, claimed that this was because men had bigger brains. He failed to mention that men also wear bigger shoes, which must explain why they so often put their foot in things.

One litmus test of boy brain power might be to look at the

academic results of the current crop of world leaders. The White House website proudly states that George W. Bush graduated from Yale University in the 'top 85 per cent of his class'. The top 85 per cent? Am I missing something or does this mean that he was 15 per cent away from the bottom? Tony Blair, of course, got a second from Oxford and a third at the Bar, and it is difficult to know which organisation was nearer the correct mark in their assessment. Still, be fair, he is sorting out terrorism in far-flung places. Now all he has to do is have a little look at letting it happen round agricultural establishments in Staffordshire.

On the subject of great minds, the Nobel Prize-winning biochemist Albert Szent-Györgyi (not an easy name for an autograph) once submitted his findings of a new sugar molecule to a noted scientific journal. As the mother of a child with a chemistry GCSE, even I know that all sugars end in '-ose'. Szent-Györgyi felt ignorant about the actual structure of his discovery and wanted to call it 'ignose'. The editors of the sober publication thought this was frivolous and asked for another suggestion, to which the eminent scientist submitted 'Godnose'. In the end he was quite right about his own ignorance. It turned out he had found vitamin C and not sugar after all. Could happen to anybody.

For some, the great test of the week has related to the thwack of leather on willow at Trent Bridge. Cricket is the game that separates the native Brit from the late interloper onto the pitch such as myself. As I understand it (and frankly I don't), two teams, dressed in identical colours, battle it out for several days over a small pot of ashes and it is hugely exciting.

To the baffled outsider the Ashes competition has all the hallmarks of some kind of quaint post-cremation entertainment in which rival family members vie for the remains of a particularly loved one. Personally, I think if you want to make a display of saying goodbye you can't do better than the firework option. At a cost of about £1,500 you can now have the dust of a dearly departed incorporated into a specially modified rocket and send them off with a bang. The top-of-the-range option is apparently a spectacular show of rockets, star shells, aerial mines and Roman candles. I don't know what the bargain basement deal is – perhaps a sparkler and a quick whizz round a Catherine wheel.

Here I am, making an exhibition of myself again

18 September 2005

AS YOU READ THIS, ACCOMPANIED, I fondly imagine, by the heady scent of a fresh cafetière of Blue Mountain coffee, think of me, prostrate and in some pain, on the floor of the British Museum. No, I'm not recreating some strange homage to *The Da Vinci Code* or expressing a longing for a bit part in *Midsomer Murders*, but taking part in the annual Young Friends sleepover. Once a year my kids and I enter the portals of the Egyptian collection as night is falling and lay out our bedding in preparation for a night where Mummies lie among the mummies.

Each year has a different theme – Vikings, Gladiators, Egyptians – but the routine is the same. Fun and games, followed by several sleepless hours as I lie victim to a faulty Li-Lo that puffs up nicely on contact with the pump only to lose the will to live with a surprising suddenness around 2 a.m. As dawn breaks I will inevitably point out with wonder that we are lying beneath the Rosetta Stone, that 2,000-year-old legend that provided the key to hieroglyphics. My young lad will nod and ask if I brought breakfast.

Spending a night on a stone floor is all part of a desperate, modern parenting desire to provide a broad education. I usually go with my friend Kari and her son. 'Remind me why we do this?' she groans as she slips gin and tonic into a Thermos flask. 'Ah,' I reply smugly, 'I read an old Persian proverb which reminds us that "History is a mirror of the past, and a lesson for the present".' Kari nods. 'Yeah. I know a proverb,' she says, 'Money isn't everything, but it definitely keeps the kids in touch.'

Over the years at the museum, we have, among other things, built longships, battled Celts, mummified each other in loo roll and learnt that no white English person over forty should be permitted to belly dance. This year we are wandering through the country that has always been known to its own people as Iran but which we, because of some hideous misunderstanding, called Persia. It is a wonderfully rich and diverse culture, but I can't stop thinking about the lovable old Shah of Persia, a man not noted for his social graces.

Apparently, during a royal visit to London in 1889, the Shah found himself in a crowded room with the Prince of Wales. He asked the Prince whether the women in the room were all his wives, and then suggested that Wales have them beheaded and find prettier ones. Despite this, the Shah was rather taken by the Marchioness of Londonderry, whom he promptly attempted to purchase.

There's a surprising amount of sex in museums. A lot of my time is spent explaining away appendages on ancient fertility symbols that only the boys seemed to have noticed. Ancient or modern, nothing much changes. It was only a few years ago that Madame Tussaud's announced that the company had found it necessary to use glue to 'fix' one of its most popular wax figures. 'Every time we passed by,' a curator explained, 'Bill Clinton's zipper was undone.'

It is, of course, likely that we will emerge from the museum after ten hours of Persian culture, only to have the boys talk about the cool laser light one of the others used to find their way to the gents. Kids don't always seem to comprehend our best efforts to educate them. I am reminded of the Sunday school class who were asked to draw pictures of their favourite Bible stories. The teacher admired many sheep and angels and then she came to a small boy who had drawn four people on an aeroplane. She asked him which story it was meant to represent. 'This,' he replied, 'is the flight to Egypt.'

The teacher nodded and pointed to the four people. 'So, who do we have here?'

'That's Mary, Joseph, and Baby Jesus,' replied the boy.

'And the fourth person?' asked the teacher.

'Oh, that's Pontius the Pilot.'

Metaphors at dawn in a war of words

25 September 2005

I'VE GONE A BIT JAPANESE this week, so bear with me while I arrange these verbal stones into a peaceful path of prose. This week my latest novel took part in a Japanese bidding war. I don't like the idea of any of my offspring taking part in conflict, but if they must then a literary one would be the preferred option – adverbs at dawn and no firing your metaphors till you see the whites of the enemy's pages.

Anyway, somebody won (to be honest I didn't take sides) and now a story set during the Second World War about a small Danish boy dealing with occupying Germans will be translated into Japanese. (If you haven't read it, I hope it doesn't spoil it if I tell you that the Germans don't win in the end.) I've never been to Japan and I realise that I have an image of the place entirely made of fragmented stereotypes – a land of big wrestlers, small women and an awful lot of flower-arranging on fast trains.

As I am now clearly set on the road to becoming a Japanese national treasure I realised this won't do, so I checked out this week's top stories in Japan. So far, I've learnt that the Bulgarian Sekiwake Kotooshu is doing well in the Sumo (Bulgarian?), the prime minister is having trouble with the post office and, last Wednesday, a fifty-two-year-old police sergeant in Ebina used his bare hands to catch a 1.1 m long crocodile in a tributary of the Sagami River. As soon as I have more I'll let you know.

Speaking of arranging stones in a pleasing manner – this week marked the anniversary of the auction of Stonehenge. It was sold on 21 September 1915, to one Cecil Chubb for

£6,600. It seems that old Cecil (where, oh, where are the young Cecils?) happened upon a property sale at the Palace Theatre in Salisbury, where Messrs Knight, Frank and Rutley were advertising 'Lot 15. Stonehenge with about 30 acres, 2 rods, 37 perches of adjoining downland.'

'I'll get that for the wife,' thought Cecil, ever mindful of the difficulties of buying that elusive gift for a loved one. Anyway, it seems Mrs Chubb didn't care for it. I don't blame her. Many women prefer something smaller in the rock department and, frankly, how many of us would know what to do with two rods and all those perches? Cecil gave the place to the nation and the rest is a history of tea-towel concessions. (Sidebar: The Chubbs made their money from owning an asylum. It's the only place I can think of where the gift of one of those hideous signs, 'You don't have to be mad to work here . . .' and so on, might be appropriate.)

I have an American friend who collects novelty teapots and I have just bought two for her birthday. One is shaped like a lighthouse and the other one is a ballerina from whom the tea pours in a most surprising manner. Now that I am practically Japanese I realise that I need to rethink the whole gift concept, which brings me to a Japanese businessman called Koji Fujii. Mr Fujii sells lucky charms to give as tokens of one's esteem.

It seemed to him that: 'Everybody wants to have a little piece of luck for himself, especially nowadays. At the moment the only news people hear is bad. From a poor economy, to scandals in politics and war.'

I agree with him, but I'm not sure about his choice of product. Inspired by the fact that the words for 'luck' (koun) and 'poo' (unko) are similar in Japanese, Mr Fujii sells three-inch gold-plated lumps of, well, to use an archaeological term, coprolite (human excrement).

'People like products that are humorous and look nice,' he claims, and so far more than two million of these lumps have been sold. Many, you'll be pleased to hear, with funny faces painted on them. Do let me know if you're interested.

This weekend I'm having dinner with my fellow writer, Stella Duffy. I shall mention a bidding war and suggest we play literary duel – stand back to back, walk ten paces, turn around and hurl a pause.

Just now, my concerns seem utterly poultry

2 October 2005

I was going to have a crack at the Government this week but heckling, even from this distance, seems a dangerous activity so, as a tribute to my cowardice, this week I bring you – chicken news. The world's chicken population is more than double the human population, yet how often do they get a fair share of the headlines? Well, in St Petersburg, Florida (land of the hanging chad) this week, the front pages were cleared to cover a hideous chicken wing assault on a police officer. Officer W. D. Nesbit stopped Beverly Anne Campbell, sixty-one, for going the wrong way up a one-way street. She responded by attacking W. D. with a plate of chicken wings and a two-litre bottle of Coke that she happened to have about her person. (I can't drive with so much as a coffee and find her ability to have a lethal buffet at the ready immensely impressive.)

She has been charged with assault and battery – the first presumably relating to hitting the man in blue and the second to the provenance of the chicken.

As the daughter of a foreign correspondent I spent much of my childhood on the American campaign trail. In those days being on the stump was often referred to as the 'rubber chicken circuit'. Chicken was the staple meal whichever state you were in and whatever time you turned up. A fellow named Christian Herter was running for a second term as governor of Massachusetts. Many miles are covered in these campaigns and one day he arrived late and famished at a church barbeque. Herter was an unassuming man and he took his place in the queue, where a woman served him a single piece of chicken. Herter politely enquired if he might have a second piece. The

25

woman shook her head. By now the governor was tired and decided to pull rank. 'Do you know who I am?' he demanded. 'I am the governor of this state.' 'Do you know who I am?' the woman replied. 'I'm the lady in charge of the chicken. Move along, mister.'

This week I met the ultimate free-range chicken. She was called Tikka and she has travelled the length and breadth of the country. Martin Gurdon is a motoring journalist who wanted to write a travel book. These days such an endeavour requires at the very least some kind of gimmick – travel with a fridge, on a camel, on a camel with a fridge or, in this case, in the company of a live chicken. The book is called (and here's where you see years of writing experience not being wasted) *Travels with My Chicken*. I think it is rather mean on Tikka, who after all didn't choose to go, and should, at the very least, have got her name in the title.

The world of the motoring correspondent strikes me as relentlessly macho and so the idea of Mr Gurdon journeying with a hen party seems rather pleasing. Hitting the road with livestock is hardly new. I belong to the University Women's Club in London, which has a rather pleasing 'No Goats' rule. Apparently some member from the West Country kept turning up with her goat and in the end, as the chairwoman told me, 'We had to make a rule. It kept making a frightful mess in the dining room.'

Before the world knew that what we all longed for was 24-hour rolling news, Ted Turner set up CNN. It was known in the business then as Chicken Noodle News, although I don't recall a single soup-related item. As a tribute to those balmy days when waiting a day or two to garner information gave time for actual reflection, here is a showbiz chicken story. Did you know that before the actor Brad Pitt became famous he earned a living as a costumed chicken at the El Pollo Loco restaurant? I've never come across a costumed chicken but I did once meet a man dressed as a Twiglet in Sainsbury's.

And finally an obligatory chicken joke.

Q: Why did the chicken cross the road?

A: He'd been heckling at a conference and . . . (No, I haven't the nerve.)

A pride of big women and the prejudice of men

9 October 2005

I'VE BEEN IN THE PRESENCE of so many brilliant literary women this week that I feel about as articulate as a lorry. On Thursday I had a half-hour chat with Alice Walker, who wrote *The Color Purple* and changed the view of women's writing for a generation. She was hideously jetlagged but, instead of diving into her hotel minibar, she managed an analysis of early black writing that someone ought to publish as a crib for A-level.

I also played the narrator of a new musical of Louisa May Alcott's *Little Women* at the Drury Lane Theatre. I love this book not just for the story but also because Ms Alcott wrote it for money. Her father was a philosopher who owned an orchard. Philosophy not being a big money-spinner, the Alcotts spent an awful lot of meals trying to find new ways to serve apples. Anyone who writes a book just because they fancy a slab of pie will do for me.

Louisa and Alice both made me wonder whether boys and girls have a different attitude to the whole game of words. I have a brilliant male friend who refuses to write the novel I know he could. He writes cracking columns, great journalism and even riotously funny shopping-lists but he will not settle down and churn out the 60,000 or so words that would make the great book which would amuse us all. The reason, he claims, is that he cannot write *The Great Gatsby*. I tell him that's OK, somebody already did. But to this particular boy the field of novel-writing is awash with competitive testosterone and he won't even put his kit on.

*

I once did *Call My Bluff* with Jeffrey Archer (I'm not proud, it's just a fact). He cornered me in the corridor before the television recording and wagging a finger at me declared, 'I've been watching you and I know how to win.' 'Good for you,' I replied, trying to remember what it was that had made me think it was just supposed to be fun.

In a bid to spend my week with every Alpha female in London, I also spent an evening on stage with Professor Lisa Jardine, Sue MacGregor, Jenni Murray and Kate Mosse (the author, not the one with the challenging lifestyle) introducing the Best of the Best of the Orange Prize for Women's Fiction. (A prize which Lord Goodman once said was pointless as there hasn't been a good woman novelist since Jane Austen.)

Before the announcement of the winner, we discussed the ten brilliant books in the running, with the panel saying clever things and me providing the Coles Notes to the proceedings. Andrea Levy was announced as the winner, and she promptly got up on stage and talked about how good all the other books were.

During the course of the week, I added Pamela Stephenson, Gloria Hunniford and Joanne Harris to my list of chats. They all had new books out and none seemed even to know that there might be an element of competition. I was also supposed to meet Maya Angelou, but sadly she was poorly. Just as well because I know I wouldn't have been able to help myself asking – 'Why does the caged bird sing?'

Literally exhausted, I headed off at the end of the week to watch *Signs of a Diva* performed by the deaf actress Caroline Parker. Caroline plays a deaf woman obsessed with the great women singers – Billie Holiday, Dusty Springfield, *et al.* – and signs to some of the greatest tracks ever laid. Speaking with her hands, she was the most articulate of all.

I'm not saying it's right, but women do seem to have taken a lot of this writing business lying down. Which brings me to the news about cervical cancer. Apparently, there may soon be an injection instead of having to undergo the dreaded examination. I do think females could have been a bit more vociferous in their reactions to this ordeal. I can't believe that if a man had ever been told to lie down and relax while a nurse came at him with the Eiffel Tower in her hand, an alternative wouldn't have been found sooner.

Why has no one asked me to go topless before?

30 October 2005

THERE WAS A CERTAIN FRISSON last month when I was asked to pose topless for a photograph. Admittedly, it was for my mammogram but nevertheless I stood there, squashed between two cold plates, and wondered why it hadn't come up more often. I've been in show business for thirty years and you would have thought that at some point a part would have required me stripping off for the sake of art.

Actually, in art a nude is correctly called a 'pity', mainly, I think, because the Victorians thought it was a pity that the model didn't have any clothes on. I've never been publicly naked and on the whole I rarely use bad language, and I've been trying to decide why. It's not that I am puritanical, it's just that the nudity thing has never come up and I find the English language far too rich to spend my time dwelling on a couple of Anglo-Saxon expletives.

This week I took the brood to see the new musical *Billy Elliot*, which is a jolly tap-dancing affair in which a young lad from Durham escapes to the world of ballet in London. He does this mainly, it seems, to get away from the incessant swearing. I've never heard such a cascade of cursing. I asked my eleven-year-old what he thought. 'I've heard all the rude words before,' he said sagely. 'Just never without other words in between.'

On the subject of rudeness, I met the author Lynne Truss this week. Having sorted out grammar in her book *Eats, Shoots and Leaves*, Lynne has moved on to consider rudeness in her new work, *Talk to the Hand*. Basically, she's against it but feels it's rather a lost cause.

31

Personally, I find speaking bluntly tempting but impossible. How often I have held back with a clothing shop assistant who is fulfilling the shop part of her title by being present in the establishment but who has no notion of the assisting section. As she ignores me and focuses acute attention on a hangnail, I long to blurt out, 'I came in here to slip into something more comfortable. I didn't know it was going to be a coma.' But I don't say a word. I can't. Four years at boarding school left me with an unshakeable need to carry a fresh linen hankie, an admiration for sturdy pants and an ingrained streak of manners.

Now, don't think that I am joining Tony Blair in his campaign to restore 'Respect'. I'm not a fan of the fella and think he should tidy up at home first. I mean, invading someone else's country without checking your facts first is very rude and I should be jolly cross with my kids if they ever tried it.

There is something thrilling about someone who doesn't worry about social niceties and speaks their mind without an edit facility. The Houses of Parliament used to be blessed with many such blunt speakers, among whom few could surpass Ted Heath for speaking his mind. When Mr Blair paid tribute to the late Father of the House, he admitted that, 'Ted was very blunt in his manner.' He recalled arriving as a new MP in the mid-1980s, and meeting Sir Edward for the first time. The old MP asked the fledgling Blair which party he belonged to and, on hearing the answer, boomed: 'Well you don't look like it or sound like it.' How thrilling to hear the truth so entirely naked.

They say manners maketh the man, but in my case my salvation tends to be my eyesight. I was once on a Tube train late at night when a young man sitting opposite pointed to his crotch and demanded, 'What do you think of that?' Thinking he might be showing me some interesting point in a book, I replied, 'I'm sorry, I can't see anything small without my specs.' He fled at the next station and it was only when he got up that I realised he hadn't been carrying a book at all.

Seven, a number you can count on

6 November 2005

AH, THERE YOU ARE. It's always a worry when you move home that your friends won't be able to find you. Welcome to Seven, my new writing pad. Seven. It's a nice number, not rushing too fast to the front, but not lagging at the back either. Numerologists say the number seven represents analysis, understanding, knowledge, awareness, studiousness and meditation.

This, I feel, doesn't quite cover it. Indeed, thinking about the number has become something of an obsession this week. Did you know that there are seven types of combs on chickens (rose, strawberry, single, cushion, buttercup, pea and V-shaped)? That there are seven species of bear and it takes a lobster about seven years to grow to be one pound? Mice, whales, elephants, giraffes, and humans all have seven neck vertebrae; it takes seven years to make Swiss grating cheese; Diana, Princess of Wales was Humphrey Bogart's seventh cousin and the opening-day queue at the first McDonald's Drive-Thru in Kuwait City was seven miles long. I don't know why I like such facts. Perhaps it suggests that life is not as random and chaotic as the daily grind would suggest. Did you know that during a twenty-four-hour period, the average human will exercise seven million brain cells? Really? How come these people never serve me in shops?

Once you start it's difficult not to see the number everywhere. Seven deadly sins. Actually, there used to be eight, including an old favourite of mine – acedia, which is the sin of apathy – but Pope Gregory the Great trimmed the list to seven and couldn't be bothered to put that one in. Seven natural wonders of the world, seven wonders of the ancient world and there

33

are seven centres for recycled toothpicks in Kulang, China. OK, that last one is a bit strange. I can't imagine the call for one toothpick recycling plant let alone seven, but apparently it's big business for Kulang. People bring in used toothpicks and get paid 50p per pound.

While we're abroad, can I just highlight my concern about a general geographical knowledge survey conducted recently by the National Geographic Society? It quizzed groups of eighteen-to twenty-four-year-olds from nine nations, and the United States, policeman to the world, came last. One in seven of the US high school and university graduates could not find their own country on a world map.

The Americans may not be great shakes at geography, but there is still great work going on in their universities. In 2003, the world-renowned computer expert Selmer Bringsjord, at the Rensselaer Polytechnic Institute in upstate New York, unveiled a computer program called Brutus 1. Bringsjord had spent seven years developing software that enabled the computer to write short stories. Now, you might think that the development of a PC that could put me out of work would be a worry, but no. There is a glitch. 'Brutus 1 is only the first version of the program,' Bringsjord explained. 'It is a good imitator of styles that we feed into it, but so far it can produce only 500-word stories written from a male point of view about betrayal in a university setting.'

On the story front – I'm pretty sure Snow White had seven vertically challenged friends, so that there was one for each day of the week, but why does the week divide up like that? In less complex days, people's time was split according to retail opportunity. So the Roman 'week' was the *nundinae*, nine days counted inclusively from one market day to the next. In today's world of twenty-four-hour shopping, this would make the calendar a little tricky. The Babylonians believed the number seven was sacred, partly because they thought there were seven planets in the solar system.

Me? I blame the moon. The four phases of the moon are roughly seven days in length. I remember an anthropology professor at university holding up an antler bone on which twenty-eight markings had been scratched. 'This,' she said, 'has often been thought of as man's first attempt at a calendar.' We wrote this down. 'I would ask you to think about such a statement,' she continued. 'What man needs to know when twenty-eight days have passed? This, I would suggest, is woman's first attempt at a calendar.'

I'm on a roll now. The average raindrop falls at seven miles per hour; it takes seven people to make a water-polo team and, even though there were only six manned lunar landings, there are seven Apollo lunar landers on the moon. (Apollo X didn't land, but they dropped their lunar lander as some kind of test.) Did you know that there have been seven saints named Gerard? Heaven. Seventh, obviously.

Down with heels, hurrah for bras

13 November 2005

I WOKE UP THIS MORNING feeling cross with Catherine de Medici. I know she's been dead for more than 400 years but I'm good with a grudge. While I am being annoyed, let me also be unkind and tell you frankly that she wasn't a looker. The truth is she was a plain child with a big nose, and her husband, Henry, married her for political reasons. Now I've never had that happen to me, but I can imagine it doesn't make you feel too special on the day.

Anyway, she was Italian and wanted to make a splash at the French court. I've never even made a splash on the netball court, but Kate and I do have something in common. We are both, or rather I am and she was, 5 ft tall. Apart from getting chest passes in the face on the aforementioned netball court, lack of height has never bothered me. Getting things off high shelves is what boys are for – and I have one of those. C de M, however, decided to defy her genes and invent the high heel. As if this were not bad enough, she went on to ban thick waists and confine women to 350 years of the corset. I curse her every time I have a black-tie function to attend and heels to dust off.

This week I have two such wretched functions. It's all right for boys. They let the moths flutter from their dad's old tux, spit on their shoes and they're ready to rumba. Isn't it time we invented an all-purpose garment that looks good with flat shoes for women? No one ever says to a man at these events: 'Weren't you wearing that last time?' or 'Oh no, how embarrassing, we've both turned up in the same thing.'

*

I temper my temper with two pieces of gratitude. It was on this very day in 1913 that a former socialite, Mary Phelps Jacob, fed up with underwear confinement, patented the first modern elasticised brassière (it's French for upper arm, apparently); and hurrah for the First World War. OK, this one is a bit strange. In 1917, the US War Industries Board called on women to stop buying corsets – which apparently freed up 28,000 tons of metal. I love the idea of the Hun being subdued by raining stays.

Which reminds me of the Battle of the Stocking. My children are haphazardly descended from the Stewarts of Appin. These were fine Scots who went to battle under the Banner of the Stocking, or *Bratach na Mogan*, a tribute to the bravery of their women. One day, the men were off in the hill of Bunrannoch, doing whatever it is that occupies men in hills, when the homestead was attacked by a band of raiders. The women didn't have any weapons, so they took off their stockings, shoved stones in them and used them as cudgels. I think the attackers must have been shocked to the core because they ran off without so much as a free haggis. There was a time when the stocking was a useful stand-in for a broken fan belt, but I much prefer it as a weapon of mass destruction.

I once met the curator of underwear at the Victoria and Albert Museum. I was in search of the correct method for attaching a merkin. If you don't know what that is, I'm fairly confident it is information you can live without. I spent a happy afternoon rummaging through some surprising cardboard boxes and it reminded me of the Musée du Slip Belge, or Belgian Underpants Museum, which may or may not still be in the town of Schaerbeek. I visited it years ago and I have no idea if this display of underwear from Belgian luminaries (whoever they may be) is still in existence. I tried to check on the internet, but all the sites were in French, and if you have the page automatically translated, Musée du Slip Belge comes up as Museum of the Belgian Slipway – which strikes me as something much seedier.

Let us move swiftly on to genuine culture. It's St Augustine of Hippo's birthday. He was born in 354, in Numidia in North Africa. St A of H was the eldest son of St Monica and a Pagan Pa – which, I feel, must have caused tension at the dinner table. Augustine was a fella keen on writing *bons mots* to God, of which my favourite has to be: 'Give me chastity and continence, but not yet.' I like the Hippo part of his name. I don't know whether he was allowed to choose his own animal, but I think it would be a good way forward for us all. In future, kindly address correspondence to St Sandi of Shih Tzu.

The long march to Christmas

20 November 2005

THIS WEEKEND MARKS THE beginning of my Viking forebears' Yuletide revelries. Those fine, bearded, blond fellows would start about now and carry on until 7 January. Presumably, the rest of the year was then allocated to getting rid of the headache. About this time, I get a stirring in my DNA to light the Yule log, start wassailing and invade Norfolk.

You may well think it is a little early to be writing a Christmas column, but the timing of these things is critical. Any earlier and I would look a fool, any later and I might find you've already got one. I also take this time of year very seriously in a truly Scandinavian way. About now, I start making the ginger biscuits, polishing the candle holders for the tree and sewing my own Christmas cards. Indeed, I had thought to hand-embroider this week's piece for you, but it was the devil's own job finding that much matching thread.

For anyone who thinks I have suddenly gone off on some religious bent, trust me that a lot of the celebrations have nothing to do with any faith whatsoever. We mark 25 December only because Pope Julius I got fed up with everyone making such a fuss over the winter solstice; hanging a wreath on your door actually salutes Strenia, the Roman goddess of health; we light the tree in order to shelter the woodland spirits who have no protection in winter; 'Jingle Bells' was written to celebrate American Thanksgiving and Santa Claus was invented by Coca-Cola.

These days, some people can get a little uppity about celebrations, but it was ever thus. Did you know that the old song *The Twelve Days of Christmas* is actually a coded catechism song for Catholics? Between 1558 and 1829, being a Catholic in England wasn't good for your health, so a chap named Drennon wrote the song as a kind of secret message. Apparently, the two turtle doves represent the Old and New Testaments, the three French hens equal Faith, Hope and Charity, and so on. The lords a-leaping are the Ten Commandments, which I think is a refreshing take on a long list of don'ts.

It seems a good seasonal fit that the real St Nick came from Turkey. It would be about this time in Victorian days that turkeys bound for the holiday table would be on the march from the much-invaded Norfolk. Apparently, the only way to get these doomed creatures to market in London was to make them walk. They would set out about now, wearing tiny boots made of sacking or leather to protect their feet. I don't know why. I've never thought of the turkey foot as a delicacy, nor did the prospect of a career as a bird cobbler ever arise at school. Geese, however, did not have boots. That would have been silly. The farmer just slapped tar on their feet and sent them, presumably goose-stepping, on their way.

Long before fowl filled our Agas, the traditional Christmas dinner was a boar's head prepared with mustard. A boar is a substantial item, so we are talking about a fair old amount of condiment. The story goes (and who am I to prevent the spreading of ancient rumour) that the custom of eating boar began in the Middle Ages. Allegedly, there was a menacing boar and a university student with a book of Greek philosophy (a mincing bore).

Now you might not immediately think of Socrates or Plato as a potential weapon, but, according to tradition, the boar charged at the student and he, responding in an academic manner, rammed his Aristotelian treatise down the creature's throat. It choked to death on the finer points of thought,

40

whereupon the student cut off the boar's head and brought it back to his college. The moral here is to approach all wildlife philosophically. (Did you know that Christmas trees are edible? I don't recommend it, nor do I have a suitable recipe but, apparently, the needles are a good source of vitamin C.)

Christmas for me also marks with sadness the day the great W. C. Fields died. The legendary comic was a lifelong agnostic and, having been so scathing about his existence in this life, he also claimed he was unconcerned about the next. On his deathbed, however, a friend of his visited and found Fields thumbing through the Bible. The friend was bemused and asked what the dying man was doing. 'I'm looking,' he declared, 'for a loophole.'

A storm in a coffee cup

27 November 2005

THEY SAY IT'S GOING TO be bitter this winter so I've been checking the forecast in my coffee. Ever since 1987, when Michael Fish told me I could sleep safe from stormy conditions and a tree promptly fell through my house, I have taken barometric matters into my own hands. Each morning I pour out a fresh cup of Java and settle down to check its steaming surface. The small bubbles that drift across the top are very clear – float towards the rim of the cup and it's wellingtons and pacamacs all round. Float to the centre – it's going to be fine. Float in great lumps – the milk's gone off and I'll have to go out whatever the weather. It's all to do with pressure in the air, apparently. Strictly speaking Mr Fish was right, of course. It wasn't a hurricane in '87 but an 'intense North Atlantic depression'. I suffer with black days myself but never so intensely that I plunge a quarter of the country into darkness.

According to NASA and many a news report, the world's most violent weather occurs in the United States of America. In a typical year, the colonies have about 10,000 violent thunderstorms, 5,000 floods, 1,000 tornadoes and several hurricanes. Of these tempestuous events I like the tornado which spun through El Dorado, Kansas, on 10 June, 1958. This had nothing to do with Dorothy and the land of Oz but was the one where the storm pulled a woman out of her house and carried her sixty feet through the air. She landed with minor bruising next to an old LP. When she glanced at the label she found it was *Stormy Weather*.

*

While I'm humming along you might like to take a moment to pay your respects to one of my fellow Scandinavians. Anders Celsius, he of the Celsius temperature scale, was born in Sweden on 27 November 1701. I'm an old-fashioned girl and still convert everything to old money. Thus I can't help but tell you that, had Mr °C been alive today he would have been 204, which in Fahrenheit would be 399.2000367200037°. Suddenly I see that Celsius is easier because that last figure would be hell to mark on a cake. Anders, rather pleasingly, had his own problems with the scale. Apparently, when he first thought of it he decided to do the whole scheme upside down. Thus freezing equalled 100 degrees and things boiled at zero. He was a distinguished fellow and no one liked to say this might not be the best way forward so they waited until he died to flip the whole thing round.

If the simple coffee method of forecasting is not for you and you want to take your predicting a little more seriously, then, at a very rough estimate, you would have to do about ten billion mathematical calculations per day. This must have been a headache during the pre-computer days of the abacus. According to Marco Polo (not a phrase that I have had cause to write before), Kublai Khan, the thirteenth-century Mongol emperor and all-round good egg, had 5,000 resident court astrologers calculating away. Part of their job included the somewhat hazardous task of predicting the weather. When asked why there were so many of them, the emperor explained that guessing incorrectly often led to 'early retirement'.

Early retirement is now a long, distant dream for most of us. My only hope of claiming those words for my own is the occasional early winter departure up the wooden hill to Bedfordshire with a box of tissues and a honey and lemon tea. Thanks to recent research by the Cardiff Centre for the Common Cold we now know that standing around in a chill can lead to what women call a cold and men claim to be the flu. The onset of the cold season reminds me of my father's favourite cure for the sniffles:

1. Get into bed with a glass of whisky and a hat.
2. Place the hat on the left bedpost by your feet.
3. Keep drinking until you can see it on the right bedpost.
4. In the morning, have coffee and check to see if the weather makes it worth getting up.

From bad to verse

4 December 2005

COME, MY PEOPLE, AS I unlock my word-hoard and travel with you through tribes and nations across the earth.

What do you think? I woke up this morning and instantly decided to change my writing style. As inspiration I picked the seventh-century Old English poet Widsith but, apart from that opening sentence, I have to say it is not going well.

Widsith's work is full of people called things like Hrothwulf and Hrothgar, who repulse the Vikings (it doesn't say how but I'm guessing table manners) and then hew a lot of things in order to face up to Heorot Heathobeard's army. These are not matters that come up very often in my daily sojourn. The most H-related trouble I have on a daily basis is haemorrhoids and, apart from telling you that things in that department are probably going from bad to verse (sorry), there is nothing poetic about it.

I've been inspired to seek the change (not an ambition for many women of my age) by a chance meeting this week with a poetry boy band. Aisle 16 are just like any other boy band – floppy hair, hopeful grins and a careful selection of personality types – the intense one, the chunky one, the cheery one and the one awash with sexual ambiguity who does most of the talking. Unlike the world of manufactured pop, however, these boys write their own material and then dazzle with virtuoso displays of verse-speaking. I had forgotten how much I like poetry and how wonderful it is to hear it spoken by heart.

To be honest, I'm not sure if I've done well choosing Widsith as my mentor. The fact is that the whole of Old English poetry is preserved in just four manuscripts, which either suggests historical carelessness or that maybe I should pick something more popular.

Today is the anniversary of the passing, in 1123, of the great poet Omar Khayyám. He was born in Nishapur, Iran, and originally named Ghiyath al-Din Abu'l-Fath Omar ibn Ibrahim Al-Nisaburi Khayyámi, but as soon as he opened a checking account he changed it to plain Omar. In Persian, Khayyám means 'tentmaker' and if we all did as directed by our surnames, Omar might have ended up working in an Iranian branch of Millets. Instead, he went on to write that great poetic masterpiece, the *Rubaiyat*.

The word *'rubaiyat'* just means 'quatrain' and I am guessing that there were others around at the time, because everyone calls it *The Rubaiyat of Omar Khayyám* just in case anyone got confused at the till. He wrote several hundred of these quatrains, but in his life also found time for multi-skilling. He is apparently well known for inventing the method of solving cubic equations by intersecting a parabola with a circle. Thank goodness for that, because it wanted doing.

There used to be, and indeed may still be, a Pennsylvania Supreme Court Justice called Michael Eakin who had a penchant for delivering his opinions in a bit of a *rubaiyat*. He was once dealing with a woman called Susan Porreco, who brought her husband to court over the quality of her engagement ring. She had discovered that the ring was not the top-notch item she had been led to believe and she felt this was sufficient to void their pre-nuptial agreement.

In his ruling, Eakin opined,

'A groom must expect matrimonial pandemonium,
When his spouse finds he's given her a cubic
    zirconium

Instead of a diamond in her engagement band,
The one he said was worth twenty-one grand . . .'

Berated by the Chief Justice for his poetic leanings, Eakin declared, 'You have an obligation as a judge to be right but you have no obligation to be dull.'

Did you know that the boxer Muhammad Ali was once asked to lecture on poetry at Oxford University? Or that a poem written to celebrate a wedding is called an 'epithalamium' and that a writer of inferior poems is called a 'poetaster'?

Perhaps there is a new career ahead for me as an epithalamium poetaster with a cracking right punch. Actually, I learnt quite a lot of poetry at school and can still do the whole of Gray's *Elegy* if anyone is short of entertainment for a wedding or bar mitzvah.

Please sign this elephant

11 December 2005

I HAVE A FRIEND WHO used to sign Christmas cards for a now deceased member of high society. His signature was rather better than hers and we were thrilled the other day to see a sample of his work for sale at a ridiculously high price.

Autograph-gathering is a curious phenomenon. I have often wondered at the tenacity of the people who hang around stage doors and then inevitably miss the big star because most celebrities look like nothing on earth without a wig on.

This week, however, both my son and I turned into signature stalkers. I met my childhood heroine, Julie Andrews. We chatted, she was charming and I thought I was pleasingly cool, until I found myself overwhelmed with a desire to get her to sign something for me. Anything – a scrap of paper with a pencil, a bar of soap with a quill, a passing elephant with a paintbrush . . . In the end, she signed my programme with a felt-tip. I'm fairly sure I danced home.

A few days later, I took my eleven-year-old, tennis-obsessed son, Theo, to the Masters Tournament in London. Having paid a fortune for seats, we then spent the bulk of the evening running up and down corridors trying to catch John McEnroe. We came home triumphant, with the fellow's monicker scrawled across my boy's rucksack.

Not one letter of the autograph was discernible. It's a good job McEnroe can play tennis, because he has worse penmanship than a doctor with a prescription pad. 'Who's scribbled on your bag?' asked his sisters in horror. 'That's John McEnroe's autograph,' replied Theo, smugly. 'Yeah, right,' sneered his older and wiser siblings. I didn't show them Julie's. I didn't think they'd be impressed.

I have, in my time, brushed with the very fringes of fame and people do ask for autographs at the most astonishing times. I was once utilising a public convenience where the door had a faulty lock. As I went about my business, the door burst open and a woman stood framed in the doorway. 'Sorry!' she boomed and hurried to shut the door.

Two seconds later, the door banged open again to reveal the same intruder. 'You're that Sandi Toksvig. Can I have your autograph?'

For the great stars it must be truly trying. There is a wonderful story about the actor George Arliss being mobbed by autograph-hunters at Charing Cross station. Arliss was the first British actor to win an Academy Award for Best Actor and, in his time, he had an enthusiastic following.

Finding there was no escape from his fans, he turned away and saw that he was standing in front of the left-luggage office. He enquired how much it would cost for a large parcel, paid his money, leapt over the counter and checked himself in. It was a method he confidently recommended, as he put it, 'to other picture stars in railway stations'.

Anyone who has dipped into these pages before will know that I have a relentless fascination with history. Indeed, I often wonder how different the world might have been if George Bush had read just one picture book about the past.

Apart from today being the birthday of the Venetian blind (so many jokes occur, but we must move on), it is also the anniversary of the erection of the world's first, and possibly only, monument to a pest, in 1919. Here is fame of a different sort and proof, if proof were needed, that there's nowt so queer as folk.

The people of Enterprise, Alabama, had had their cotton

crops completely destroyed by the boll weevil, a 6 mm beetle enjoying a vacation from Mexico. The infestation led to the introduction of the peanut as an alternative crop, after which life – and cocktail parties in particular – improved ever more.

In gratitude, the locals raised a bizarre statue in the centre of town of an Athenian woman draped in flowing white, holding a black boll weevil above her head, while fountains play below.

Sadly, over the years, not everyone has appreciated this fine display and, on several occasions, the sculpted beetle has been stolen by boys making pests of themselves. Here, we can only hope that the local headlines read: See No Weevil.

Cinderella, I know how you feel

18 December 2005

THERE ARE TWO SNOWMEN IN a field and the first one says to the second one, 'Can you smell carrots?' It's panto season and, yet again, I find I have not been booked for so much as the back end of a horse.

Chum after theatrical chum is busy giving their Dick or dealing with those pesky babes, while I can merely dream of going to the ball. My lucky friends are fully occupied following in the great British tradition of sexual innuendo delivered by men in tights all hoping that the girl in the end will get, well, actually . . . the other girl.

Political correctness leaps from the window as they gather on stages across the country to teach yet another generation the value of a social stereotype: 'Every Christmas I get an awful pain that stays for a week. Then my mother-in-law goes back to her own home.' Ba boom. Up and down the country the same collection of routines – The Ghost, Busy Bee, and so on – will be cobbled together to make an evening's entertainment. The only concession to modern times is that the brilliant 'My dad died in Baghdad, my dad did' routine is almost certainly unperformable.

I was in pantomime only once, twenty-four years ago at the Orchard Theatre, in Deptford, Kent. I played the world's youngest Fairy Godmother, with Wendy Richard as Dandini and Dickie Henderson as Buttons. It was terrible, but I consoled myself with the thought that being in a turkey at Christmas is entirely appropriate. Nevertheless, I loved it and each autumn I feel a slight sense of frisson that yet again I may be called to don the fishnets. So far . . . nothing.

*

51

Most pantos are a bumper time for regional theatres. Indeed, for some, it is their only sell-out season. We should therefore take a moment to empathise with the playwright W. H. C. Nation. Mr Nation might have hoped that his surname suggested great throngs of people but, sadly, he holds the dubious distinction of having produced the pantomime that attracted the smallest audience in recorded history. His Christmas piece, *Red Riding Hood*, took to the boards of Terry's Theatre in London at the turn of the twentieth century. Apparently, only two people turned up to watch and they did so from high up in the gallery. I can only imagine that the moment for dividing the audience in two for the singalong was a less than fulsome success.

On a theatrical note, we mark today the passing of Sam Wanamaker, the American actor and the inspiration behind the stunning Globe Theatre in London. I bought flagstones with my children's names on in order to be part of this great enterprise. I took my eldest to look around. 'Imagine,' I said enthusiastically, 'what it must have been like to see *Hamlet* when it was brand new, and no one knew what was going to happen at the end.' My daughter looked at me quizzically and said, 'Mum, I don't know what happens at the end, so don't spoil it.'

I took to the stage for the first time in some years the other night for a charity evening. I had forgotten what a silly way it is to make a living. An actor friend of mine describes performing as 'being a grown-up but still playing at shops'. Despite this, I am due to hit the road next year with a new show starring myself and my friend, Bonnie Langford. Neither of us has any need to scare ourselves stupid in this way, but we follow in a long line of theatrical addicts who just can't give it up. I've been trying to think of something spectacular to give the show some extra pizzazz.

Who can forget, for example, the 1936 Metropolitan Opera

season in New York? The Australian soprano Marjorie Lawrence was making her debut as Brunhilde in *Die Götterdämmerung*. Traditionally, Brunhilde either heads off to her fiery immolation at the end leading an old nag or handing the equine extra over to some groom. Marjorie, however, was a game girl, and charged off, legs akimbo, through a ring of real flames.

No one had tried this before and it is fair to say that the audience felt they got their money's worth. I suggested it to Bonnie and her response was less than civil.

The great leading lady Ethel Barrymore once said, 'For an actress to be a success, she needs the face of Venus, the brains of a Minerva, the grace of Terpsichore, the memory of a Macaulay, the figure of Juno – and the hide of a rhinoceros.'

Absolutely. The only question is: can we find a rhinoceros willing to tour?

Everything's shiny in my empire

8 January 2006

SOME PEOPLE DECIDE TO CHANGE their lives when an earth-shattering illness or event occurs. I thought I'd avoid all the attendant grief and do it before. So, this year, I decided to throw caution to the wind and start my own media empire. At present, it consists of me and 400 rather nicely embossed calling cards, but I have high ambition. No longer will I sit watching television and crying, 'What were they thinking?' One day, others will be watching television and crying, 'What was Sandi thinking?'

I'm a week in and, thus far, self-employment is going well. My study has never been tidier, I have fought with no one over whose turn it is to make the coffee and I am fairly confident of making the short-list for Employee of the Month. The downside, of course, is the quality of the gossip. There's a limit to how many times I can look at myself in the mirror and reveal something inappropriate. I took a pleasing three days to cross-reference the three diaries I got for Christmas (three kids – three diaries) and spent some time perfecting my signature as director of my fledgling company.

These are the good things. Sadly, I've also developed the early stages of some kind of stationery mania. I made the mistake of ordering paper from an online company and it sent, by return, the fattest catalogue of office-supply possibilities I have ever seen. Paper clips of every size; envelopes, buff and white, with and without windows; neat little holders for brochures, and my latest purchase – a laminator. This marvellous device will laminate anything. Indeed, since I put the dog through it he looks fantastic. He just stands all shiny in a corner and never bothers me for a walk.

*

In the past, I have mostly worked with a team of people and I am a tad anxious that I shall become lonely. My great heroine Dorothy Parker once had a small office within the Metropolitan Opera House in New York. This may sound grand but, apparently, it was a dingy cubby-hole and no one visited. One day the management sent an artisan to paint Parker's name on the door. She told him it was spelt 'GENTLEMEN', and thereafter received a stream of callers. Parker always said a woman didn't need much room to live in. Just enough space, she remarked, 'to lay a hat and a few friends'.

It hasn't taken me a nanosecond to realise that I loathe the paperwork of self-employment. Things arrive for my 'urgent attention' and I instantly develop some form of catatonic state. Then, a friend of mine recommended a filing system perfected by the First Earl Alexander of Tunis, the man who commanded the evacuation of Dunkirk during the Second World War. Having overseen such a massive piece of organisation you would think he would be adept at all things managerial. The truth is he had a unique method for dealing with unfinished business. At the end of each working day there was always a stack of unopened letters left in his 'IN' tray. These he would simply transfer, unread, into his 'OUT' tray, from which they would be returned to the sender. Alexander thought the system was splendid. 'It saves time,' he explained. 'You'd be surprised how little of it comes back!'

Being a woman without deadlines means that I also have time to read more of the daily papers than before. I call this 'keeping up', or 'putting my finger on the pulse', or 'touching the zeitgeist' when, in fact, it is a bad habit that is leading to yet more deplorable behaviour. I never realised how many possibilities there were for sending away for free videos on 'walk-in' baths, uPVC conservatories or incontinence pants in a wider fitting.

I've filled in every form that has passed through my hands. The trouble is it is not my name and address that I put down. I am ashamed to say that, instead of replying to an urgent request, say, from the council, to reveal my recycling data, I find out the name of the person directly responsible for this irritating correspondence and send them something suitable – a medically proven, non-invasive cure for piles, for example. Or to the director of the company who wanted to know if I wanted my sixteenth-century barn pebble-dashed and/or double-glazed – a free booklet on *Living with Incontinence*. It is appalling behaviour and I am deeply ashamed. Perhaps the best thing is to report myself to the boss in the morning.

Baton-twirling's a risky pastime

15 January 2006

I AM RETURNED FROM A quick foray to the American Colonies and I'm afraid I bring grave news. It seems that cheerleading injuries are on the increase. Last year, more than 200,000 young cheerleaders had to attend a medical facility with a cheerleading-related injury. I had no idea. What's happening to the world? Now you can't even wave a pom-pom without personal risk.

I went to high school in America and, when I was a child, cheerleading was quite near the top of my list of 'Dumb things girls are supposed to do'. At the pinnacle was baton-twirling in a marching band. This struck me as immensely stupid. Indeed, on the one occasion that I stole Rita Offenbach's baton and tried silver-stick tossing myself, the thing struck me so forcibly I nearly had my eye out.

Apparently, cheerleading has come on since my day. Gone are the days of simply rhyming the name of your football team with the word 'Ra'. We have, it seems, entered an era of cunning stunts. According to the National Center for Catastrophic Sport Injury Research (a name that could give your tongue a stress fracture), cheerleading is now the number one cause of serious sports injuries to women.

I would find this deeply depressing were it not for an active campaign for the practice to be redesignated from its category of 'Just Plain Silly' to a 'Body Skill' and then, in the future, to 'An Actual Sport'. I still can't say I'll get involved. The truth is I can't even do a forward roll. Indeed I would go so far as to say no roll is worthy of the name without a sausage in it.

*

Good news, in case anyone was worried, on American intelligence. Amid allegations of possible illegal surveillance of American citizens inside their own country, Dan Burton of Indiana, the Republican member of the House of Representatives, has decided to do something positive. He has introduced a bill to rename the FBI's huge headquarters, known as the J. Edgar Hoover building. Washington is awash with edifices named after the great and the good but, on reflection, there are those who wonder if the former director's name puts the Federal Bureau of Investigation in the best possible light.

The little that is known of Hoover's life makes fascinating reading. Eavesdropping was second nature to him, and his main contribution to the civil rights movement was using the bureau to discredit Martin Luther King. Then there are the urban myths about his cross-dressing, homosexuality and 'passing' as white while actually being of African-American descent. A lot of this is probably nonsense. The fact that he never married and spent forty years holidaying with the associate FBI director and confirmed bachelor Clyde Tolson just means he was lucky to find a friend.

Meanwhile, other notables such as Ronald Reagan and George H. W. Bush are having their names put up on airports and the like. This leads one to wonder what the present president will have named after him. In a desperate attempt not to be too political, I'd like to suggest a pretzel factory. As for Bill Clinton, all I can think of is a dry cleaner's.

I had an encounter with the American medical profession while I was away. I was on holiday with a friend who is remarkably creative about illness. This is a person who could get malaria in the Antarctic. We were in Cape Cod and it was cold. We went walking in a large nature reserve. We were the only people for miles around walking anywhere. We wandered through the marsh grasses and tried to think what twitchers see in bird-watching. We saw a red bird. It was very nice but I was entirely content not to know it by name.

The following morning my friend complained of an itch. Being kindly, and with a Brownie badge in first aid, I had a look. The itch was alive and quietly sucking on my friend's back. Its head was buried deep beneath the skin while its abdomen swelled, like Nicholas Soames after a good lunch.

It was a deer tick. A parasitic creature that lives in the summer. It was January. Nobody gets deer ticks in January. We went to the doctor, who had a white coat and a pleasing resemblance to Dick Van Dyke. If anyone is interested it costs $148 to have the head of a tick disengaged from your epidermis. I returned to the UK to find the press feasting on the recent Lib Dem debacle. I don't know why but, suddenly, the $148 seemed cheap.

For the love of a pickled cucumber

22 January 2006

I'VE GOT QUEENS ON MY mind at the moment. Before you think I'm heading off into a pink polemic, I'm talking about the ones with crowns and countries of their own. Last week, I was broadcasting on the subject of coinage and I was given a Maria Theresa thaler. This is a beautiful silver coin which was common currency in the eighteenth century and from which we get the corrupted word 'dollar'. I've been carrying it in my pocket as a talisman and this has given me time to examine MT's portrait. She was not a looker and, indeed, from her profile one might suspect she was a girl who, at weekends, was given to a check shirt and a sensible shoe.

Clearly, being a monarch is not a beauty contest, which reminds me that today is the anniversary of Queen Victoria's death. To mark the occasion, you'll be pleased to know, I'm wearing black, I've covered up the piano legs and shoved my son up the chimney. Victoria was quite a girl, but not someone you'd want in the front row of a comedy show, partly because she wasn't a great one for a gag, and partly because her English was poor. Her mother was German and mildly overbearing.

When Victoria was young, Mama trained her to keep her chin up by sticking a sprig of holly under her collar, a technique that would make anyone lose their humour. VR was eighteen when she came to the throne and you get some idea of her maternal relationship when you learn that her first royal act was to have her bed moved from her mother's room to the first one of her own.

What she did in her room is her own business but it certainly wasn't reading Dickens's *Oliver Twist* under the covers because

60

she was advised it dealt with 'paupers, criminals and other unpleasant subjects'. She stayed away from most of her subjects and never did learn to speak English fluently.

She, Albert and the children all spoke German in the home. I like the idea of the family gathered round the fireplace reading improving works aloud in a Teutonic tone with a small piece of foliage shoved down their fronts. Nevertheless, VR has some pleasing aspects. She used cannabis to relieve her monthly indisposition and drank whisky mixed with claret, a concoction that might make anyone think the piano legs were looking a bit on the sexy side and needed covering up.

Victoria is known for having been obsessed with her husband. Indeed, Benjamin Disraeli refused to see her on his deathbed, in case she asked him to take a message to Albert. Her devotion, however, slightly paled this week in the face of a Croatian widow and her pickled cucumber. Vera Dudas, who is seventy-three and comes from Duga Resa, is a widow. She doesn't quite have the gilded buildings of Victoria to commemorate her deceased husband, Pavao, but she has something unique – a cucumber which she says was pickled by her mother-in-law when her late husband was born in 1930.

Vera believes that this seventy-six-year-old vegetable is the world's oldest pickled cucumber and has submitted it for inclusion in the *Guinness Book of Records*. 'Unfortunately, the cucumber has survived longer than Pavao,' said Vera. 'I remember my entire married life when I look at that cucumber; it was with us everywhere we ever lived and through all our experiences – good and bad.' Naturally, she has insured the item and this may be the only time in my life that I would be keen to read a policy document.

We Danes are partial to a pickled cucumber, although I've never looked at one and thought about marriage. We tend to consume it with pork. This brings us to a dilemma that has at last been sorted out. What if you were eating your pork and pickle during a power cut? How would you find your food? No problem. Scientists in Taiwan, and not a moment too soon, have created pigs that glow in the dark. 'There are partially fluorescent green pigs elsewhere,' (there are?) said Wu Shinn-Chih, the assistant professor of animal science at the National Taiwan University. 'But ours are the only ones in the world that are green from inside out. Even their hearts and internal organs are green.'

Apparently, they used jellyfish genes to help create the animals, who are going to help with stem-cell research. I like pigs. They are bright creatures. I often wonder whether the Old Testament instruction not to eat pork was less the word of God and more pigs trying to outsmart us.

A whole world in a five-foot room

29 January 2006

IT'S TAX RETURN WEEK AND, despite spending several hours with my accountant trying to decide what I might have spent £4.95 on in October 2003, I'm surprisingly cheerful. It's a procedure that puts a spring in my step as I embrace the fact that calculating year-end returns is not what I do for a living. It's not that I think being an accountant is a bad thing. It's just not my thing.

Indeed, this week my work has allowed me to have more fun with my clothes on than ought to be allowed. I've been acting in a radio play and rarely have I spent a headier couple of days. Standing in a five-foot-square room in Bristol, I managed to have sex in a carriage, was publicly whipped four times, swiftly followed by a rather charming cup of tea in eighteenth-century Philadelphia. The actors were, as ever, delightful and, as ever, there wasn't one who didn't live in the land of anecdotage. We would crunch across a small tray of gravel to create a bustling market place when the red light was on, and then instantly launch into our favourite Googie Withers story when it was off.

You might think that, with all the modern entertainment gadgets available, the wireless was on the wane. But not so. More than ninety per cent of the British public tune in to a radio programme at least once a week. In my house, we have it on like aural wallpaper. I'm biased, but I think Radio 4 is worth the entire licence fee. Where else would you get a six-part series on the history of the duffel coat alongside an in-depth analysis of what might be up with your hydrangeas and a soap opera where tractors play a critical role?

I think we forget how big radio was in its early days. In 1936 Jean Harlow (originally named Harlean Carpenter, which I like rather better) was starring in a radio play called *Madame Sans-Gêne*. Miss Harlow was playing opposite the then box-office heart-throb, Robert Taylor. Crowds of people queued for seats at the Music Box Theatre in Hollywood to watch the recording, and several hundred had to be turned away. The overflow audience were desperate to see the stars and broke through the police cordon and crashed into the theatre, where the drama was being broadcast live. The thunderous interruption was perfect, as the drama at that moment required the rendition of a riot.

Exactly seventy-six years ago this month, George V broadcast to the world, and he did so not just through wires, but via the body of a man called Harold Vivian. The King was at the House of Commons to welcome some international delegates and his words were due to be broadcast to America. As his Majesty was about to speak, the control operator, the said Mr Vivian, noticed that a critical wire had broken. He picked up the two ends and held them together in his hands, thus allowing the sound of the King's voice to pass through him and on to millions of transatlantic listeners.

Radio has many applications other than news and entertainment, which brings me to the unlikely question: what do Viagra and radio have in common? Other than the obvious answer that both might keep you up at night, the manufacturer of Viagra has announced that tiny radio transmitters are to be added to the shipments sent to chemists to thwart counterfeiting. The notion of a combination drug that enhances your sex life while providing accompanying music is almost too much to bear. (Although I suspect if you could hear Wogan at the same time that might rather dampen the tone.)

*

On a personal note – I lost my faith in my fellow man this week when my car was broken into in our fair capital city for the second time in a month. Other than a burgeoning relationship with the glass-replacement people, and a realisation of the intellectual challenge some policemen find in taking notes, the only good thing to come out of this is that I haven't lost my sense of irony.

I can't say the crooks did well. Among the items taken was a bag of unwashed pants heading for the launderette. The only possession stolen that I bemoan was a Folio edition of a book written by Henry Mayhew, the original founder of *Punch*. I suspect the drug-crazed thieves won't appreciate it, but the title of the work was *London Characters and Crooks*. If anyone gets offered a copy for a fiver at a car-boot sale, do let me know.

Radio Diva – the station just for me

5 February 2006

I'M NOT TECHNOLOGICALLY MINDED. One hundred and forty-five years ago today, a Cincinnati fellow called Samuel Goodale patented the moving-picture peep-show machine. The customer dropped a coin into it, cranked a handle on the side and soon had a flickering idea of what the butler had found so engaging. I still think that's ingenious. Despite more than a quarter of a century of appearing on television and radio, I have absolutely no idea how any of form of broadcasting works. I feel I am in the mindset of the woman I was visiting when my mobile phone went off. 'Isn't that clever?' she said, 'How did the caller know you were here?'

I saw my first colour television in 1967 when we moved to America. The gargantuan mahogany box had a flap at the front which you pulled down to reveal three light bulbs – one red, one green and a blue. These combined to create a wash of colour across the picture that made even the Lone Ranger look mildly jaundiced. Having come from Denmark, where a typical evening's black-and-white television viewing consisted of the news, read at 7 p.m. by my father, and a short feature on indoor bicycle racing followed by close-down, we marvelled at it.

Given my history of technical ignorance, imagine my astonishment this week to have come across something called the Music Genome Project. Via the internet (www.pandora.com), you can now create your own, tailor-made music radio station without the annoying adverts and chatter – and it's entirely free.

You type in the name of a favourite artist – say Barbra Streisand. The computer picks one of her songs and tells you that the music you like 'features mild rhythmic syncopation, meandering melodic phrasing, mixed acoustic and electric instrumentation, a clear focus on recording studio production and a prominent rhythm piano'. And, then, the computer wanders off to find you some more. I've discovered two singers of whom I'd never heard, but who I think are fantastic. I've named my station Diva Radio and it reminds me of Mr Goodale's peep-show machine. I crank up my box of tricks and have entertainment that is just for me. Extraordinary.

The other technical area I have trouble getting to grips with is flying. Nothing about sending two tons of metal up into the air makes sense to me and I am an appalling passenger. This week I have several flights to make and it makes me think of Maxine Dunlap. Maxine was the first woman glider pilot. This strikes me as entirely insane. Being in a plane is bad enough, being in one without an engine is, frankly, pushing your luck.

On this day in 1931, she was airborne for the first time. It was only for a minute, which can't have been good for duty-free sales. I shall think about her as I take to the skies. I shall focus on brave women, such as Baroness Raymonde de Laroche of Paris, the first licensed female pilot, and the first aeroplane passenger, who gloried in the name of Miss Pottelsberghe de la Pottery.

While we are praising women of the past, I have to mention that it was also today in 1953, that my heroine, the comic genius Lucille Ball, received the first of her many television Emmy Awards for the sit-com *I Love Lucy*. At its peak, two-thirds of America tuned into the show. In 1952, Lucille Ball's actual pregnancy was incorporated into seven episodes without ever once using the words 'pregnant' or 'pregnancy'.

I have an *I Love Lucy* doll that I prize, as well as an exclusive Action Man of the former Iraqi Information Minister

Mohammed Saeed al-Sahaf, known as 'Baghdad Bob'. You pull a string and he says amusing things about the infidel, but I fear my tasteless toy is about to be outdone.

An American firm is launching a talking, 12 inch Princess Diana doll. She has jointed ankles, a button that releases sixteen phrases in her actual voice and, in the true sign of a well-researched product, she bears the title of the 'Princess of Whales' (sic). The company produces a number of these tiny Tussaud's tributes with the voice of the person represented, although I thought Moses and Jesus sounded suspiciously similar. The George W. Bush doll comes with a Certificate of Authenticity, which is probably more than can be said for the real thing. I cannot imagine who would want such a thing, but I'll let you know when mine arrives.

I wonder if the Danes will ever be the same

5 February 2006

THE DANES HAVE A WORD that doesn't translate into English – *hyggelig*. It means to be cheerful, comfortable and cosy with friends and family. It suggests candlelight, rather beautifully prepared snacks and beer. It is a state of being that most Danish people aspire to on a regular basis. They will invite you over to *hygge* on any excuse. It is how I think of Denmark – a peaceful land of bicycling natives with cheerful demeanour who have tended, by choice, not to take centre stage in world politics.

To understand the attitude of the Danes there are a couple of pieces of history that are useful to know. The country has prided itself for centuries on its policy of religious toleration. It was back in the seventeenth century that King Christian IV first invited European Jews, persecuted elsewhere, to settle in Denmark with complete freedom to trade and to practise their religion.

In 1814, long before many other countries, Denmark granted the descendants of Jewish immigrants full equality with all other citizens. It was an act that came to the fore in the Second World War when, despite Hitler's best efforts, fewer than two per cent of Danish Jews were taken to the concentration camps. In a heroic action over ten days, the Danes rose up and saved their Jewish brothers and sisters.

This is the country that I was born in. A land that prided itself on the fundamental principle of equality for all its citizens. Indeed, the sense of being no better than your neighbour was set down in a list of fictional commandments by the novelist Aksel Sandemose, and published in his novel *A Refugee*

69

Crosses His Tracks, which is set in the imaginary Danish village of Jante. The village was governed by Janteloven, the law of Jante. Among the rules were those which stated: 'You shall not think that you are something'; 'You shall not think that you are wiser than us'; and 'You shall not think that you are better than us'.

Of course, Sandemose made up these laws but, in a way, they reflected a Danish attitude: a core belief in the commonality of man; a sense that Denmark belonged to all Danes, no matter what their position in the social hierarchy.

Over the years, Denmark did not spend much time trying to colonise the rest of the world. There was, of course, that small Viking foray into Norfolk, and they did have Iceland, the Faroe Islands and Greenland – but I don't think anyone fought them over it – and, for some reason, they once held half the Virgin Islands.

Despite these ventures, the issue of immigration has, until recently, not been huge. It is not as though there were swathes of folk in foreign lands longing to come home to the Danish fatherland. The history of immigration to Denmark is recent and short, and today immigrants and their descendants make up only about eight per cent of the Danish population.

In the later part of the twentieth century, the Danes went about building a welfare state that would enable everyone to be *hyggelig*. It became a very attractive place for refugees, and immigrants from Turkey, Palestine, Pakistan and the Middle East were warmly welcomed on humanitarian grounds.

The Danes are proud of their country. There is hardly a house that couldn't or wouldn't fly the flag on a national holiday. Last week, that same flag that was being burnt by angry Muslims the world over.

The Danes like their country's image of fairy-tale castles and Hans Christian Andersen; a favourite poster for Copenhagen is one that shows a policeman stopping the traffic to allow a mother duck to cross the road with her brood. Perhaps they expected the new residents to find Denmark as pleasing as they did. There was almost a belief that you could transplant anyone from abroad and turn them into instant Danes.

What seems to have surprised Denmark is that many of the people arriving in need of relief also wanted to bring their own culture. They did not want to be Danish in the way the Danes did. Even today it is estimated that, instead of assimilating, ninety-five per cent of third generation Turkish/Danish males import their spouses from Turkey.

Meanwhile, odd political coalitions began to emerge, some of which wanted to close down what they saw as the 'free-for-all' buffet Denmark provided for anyone who wanted it. In 2002, prime minister Anders Fogh Rasmussen's centre-Right coalition needed the support of the Right-wing DPP party and, as a consequence, a series of tough immigration measures were passed, which left some Danes and many Europeans reeling.

Following the publication of twelve cartoons in a national newspaper, Denmark now finds itself an unlikely frontline in a clash of cultures between Islam and the West. It is important to remember that the cartoons were printed not to poke fun or to ridicule but on a point of principle. Kåre Bluitgen, the Danish children's writer, wanted to write a book about Muhammad, but was unable to find an illustrator willing to submit drawings for fear of violent attacks by extremist Muslims.

Depicting Muhammad is against Islamic law, but that is not the law of the land in Denmark. The newspaper *Jyllands-Posten* (an unlikely candidate for a lead role in international relations) invited twenty-five cartoonists to stand up for what it said was the right of free expression. Twelve illustrators responded and, last September, the drawings were published.

It has taken some time and some considerable misinformation by extremists for the matter to boil up as it has done this week. The prime minister has refused to censor *Jyllands-Posten* because the Danish government does not have the power to tell its people what they may or may not print.

Now we find ourselves in the bizarre situation in which mobs threaten Danish businesses across the globe, but few news outlets show the cartoons that started it in case they cause offence. Censorship is here, and I wonder if the Danes will ever feel really *hyggelig* again.

Bingo, an answer to poverty

12 *February 2006*

I can often be heard to say that, while wisdom is supposed to come with age, in my case age seems to have come on its own. The fact that I can often be heard to say it is, I suspect, another sign of age. It makes sense to me that a lot of extremists are very young. They find it easy to be confident that they are right because they don't know any better. Once you are old enough to know better you can't remember how it was that things used to seem so certain.

I find the world more and more confusing. I was in Berlin this week (a misunderstanding over the route the number 38 bus takes from Victoria station) and, in the absence of English reading material, I purchased a copy of the *International Herald Tribune*. In it I found a large advertisement for a global financing company which apparently intends 'to eliminate poverty in the world'. About time, I thought. I read on to discover that by providing money to assist with organic agricultural development in places no one else has thought of, I could not only save my internal organs and those of poor farmers by growing better food, but also yield a ten to fifteen per cent profit per year. 'It's really good business,' declared the ad, 'to enjoy profit while eliminating poverty.' This notion has never occurred to me. Indeed, I've been foolish enough to think that helping the poor meant giving money away. Here, at last, was someone with the sense to see others' misfortune as a chance to earn a buck.

I was reminded of Trudi, the bag lady in Lily Tomlin's one-woman show, *The Search for Signs of Intelligent Life in the Universe*, written by Jane Wagner. Trudi had been successful in advertising but is driven to the streets after suggesting to a snack-food company that they market their products to the Third World. As she says, 'These countries got millions and millions of people who don't even know where their next meal is coming from. So the idea of eatin' between meals just never occurred to 'em.'

The other idea that may not have occurred to them is playing bingo for food. I was once researching the old game of 'two fat ladies' and went to play on the south coast. I sat next to a woman who was on holiday. She and the family were staying in a caravan park and, while the kids frolicked on the beach, she played bingo for cans of beans, bags of potatoes and, on a Tuesday, a whole chicken. I always have a slight twinge about bingo, for it reminds me of Johann Friedrich von Struensee, who was executed in 1772 in Denmark for crimes against the state. Denmark is struggling in the popularity stakes at the moment, as did Struensee when he was alive. His offence? Well, there are those who say he invented bingo. The fact that he also locked up the king and had a child with the queen probably didn't play that well in court.

Still, playing bingo for food is, I think, more civilised than fighting for it. Today is the anniversary of the defeat of the French by the English in 1429 at the Battle of the Herrings. I like a battle that does what it says on the tin. Basically, there were herrings (300 coachloads to be precise) and everybody wanted them. I can't imagine being that desperate for something piscine, though I did once have an incident over a sprat with a very disagreeable woman at the wet fish counter in Sainsbury's.

In the interests of détente, however, I don't wish to dwell on victories over other countries. Today, we should embrace all things French. It was exactly twenty years ago today that the Channel Tunnel treaty between Britain and France was signed and twelve years ago that a group of walkers trekked through the tunnel for charity, thus becoming the first humans to walk from France to Britain since the Ice Age. Of course, if the railways keep up their excellent record of service it can't be long before walking becomes the preferred option.

I love the French and, here again, my age is showing. I think the concept of the nap after lunch is horribly neglected in this country, and so too is a sense of reality from our politicians. Charles de Gaulle had a political career that lurched from one crisis to another, but he knew what to blame. 'How,' he exclaimed, 'can one possibly govern a country that has 350 kinds of cheese?'

I'll have a triple axel on ice

19 February 2006

I'VE BEEN SPENDING A LOT of time at the ice rink. Not on the ice, you understand. I like ice, but only if it's bumping into a slice of lemon. Despite my Scandinavian roots, I have no intention of slipping about on the stuff. My friend Bonnie Langford has been participating in a celebrity ice-dancing competition on ITV; at the same time she and I have been putting together our new stage show. This has meant rehearsing hilarious comedy sketches five feet away from the great Christopher Dean of Torvill & Dean. Like a child on holiday abroad, I now have a smattering of the sport's *lingua franca*. I know a good triple axel when I see one, and I wouldn't draw breath if someone attempted a quad salchow. So I've been watching the Winter Olympics with real interest.

I began with the figure skating but soon began pressing the remote control to reach the more arcane activities, such as the housekeeping-on-ice event known as curling, the insane chuck-yourself-down-a-hill-on-a-tea-tray, and my favourite: jumping off a ninety metre wooden hill while wearing skis. In the 1988 Winter Olympics in Calgary, Matti Nykänen of Finland took three gold medals in this event but all I can remember is the plasterer from Cheltenham known as Eddie 'The Eagle' Edwards. Here was the true Olympic spirit – a man with almost no sporting skill who flapped his arms in mid-air for balance and then complained he couldn't see anything because his glass-bottle spectacles steamed up during take-off.

Not being of a sporty disposition myself, I like the sense of not taking any of it too seriously. My favourite Olympic champion of all time was the American swimmer Eleanor Holm. During her damp career she broke six world records and won twenty-nine US backstroke titles. She also won the 100 m backstroke title at the 1932 Olympic Games and was en route to the 1936 games in Berlin when she became the first athlete ever disqualified for substance abuse. Bored while on the boat to Germany she had taken to sipping champagne and shooting craps. Disqualified from competing, she went on to party her way round Berlin and memorably commented that 'Goering was fun. Lots of chuckling. And so was the little one with the club foot', who turned out to be Goebbels.

Part of the attraction of watching the Olympics is seeing athletes who are so highly trained for their particular discipline that they have difficulty in walking normally. This is particularly true of the speed skaters. Eric Heiden won five gold medals in the men's speed-skating events during the 1980 Winter Olympics in Lake Placid. Here was a living Popeye figure with a waist of thirty-two inches and thighs of thirty inches each. One can only imagine that he had his pants specially made.

I have even gone so far with my interest as to choose my favourite contenders in the tea-tray competition. Anne Abernathy, otherwise known as Grandma Luge, is the oldest woman ever to compete in the Olympic Winter Games. She is in her fifties and this is the sixth Olympics for which she has sprayed on some Lycra, laid down on her back and hurtled down a mile of ice at 85 mph. During her career she has had countless broken bones, twelve knee operations and one severe brain injury. It's enough to make my view of ice only pairing with lemon seem sensible.

The lunacy of some of these events reminds me of the man who brought ice skating to dry land. In 1760, Joseph Merlin, a Belgian who was famous for making violins and harpsichords, moved to London. He was so keen on ice skating that he wanted to do it indoors and was the first person to roller skate. Unfortunately, his skill at invention was not matched by sporting prowess. He revealed his new toy at an elegant masquerade. Dressed as a minstrel he made a spectacular skating entrance on to the dance floor while simultaneously playing the violin. Unable to stop, he continued headlong into a full-length mirror, demolishing it, his violin and his nose. Marvellous. I think there may even be an official sport in that.

By the way, the 360-degree curve in a luge track is known as a *kreisel*. I'm starting to worry that the whole thing is taking up too much of my time.

Counties of Britain – Surrey

19 February 2006

I WAS NOT BORN IN Surrey nor did I spend my early years in this quintessentially English county; yet it weaves in and out of my life like a leitmotif. Indeed, without wishing to be morbid, it is the place where I intend to have my crematorium sweepings flung to the four winds.

I'm not the first person, foreign to these shores, who has made Surrey their home. Take to the Pilgrim's Way and climb up the wooded slopes of St Martha's Hill, south-east of Guildford, and you come upon the crossing of the Downs Link and the North Downs Way. From here you can walk east to Canterbury or south to the sea. St Martha's church stands alone on the summit with spectacular views across the county. In the cemetery lies the grave of Yvonne Arnaud.

Who? I hear you cry. Arnaud was a French actress who died the year I was born. The principal theatre of Guildford is named after her. What brought her to these Surrey hills? Perhaps, like so many others, she fled the smoke of London and landed in the nearest patch of green.

Odd to think I live in a place that was once fortified against the Danes. 'Surrey' just means 'south region'. The Venerable Bede spelt it 'Suder Ge' and in *The Domesday Book* it was 'Sudrie'. But however you write it down, it has always been recognised as an accessible garden for London.

They say people have been living in Surrey for more than 500,000 years. Indeed, the oldest preserved dwelling in Britain was discovered in Abinger. Of course you didn't get much of a house for your money before 3,000 BC mainly because of those pesky ice sheets. By the time of the Mesolithic period, however, south-west Surrey was packed with folk all living in hope of that one day a train would take them to the capital.

There is no question that the countryside improves as it drifts south out of London and escapes the hinterland of architectural horror. There is little to please the eye of those passing through Croydon or Purley. Here concrete, the car and the route to Ikea are king. But it is not just the traffic or the tower blocks that depress. It is in many of the county's theatres that you will find the tumbleweed blowing. Where once great and original drama trod the boards, now tours pass through entertaining senior citizens. How Sybil Thorndike would have wept.

Through the filthy windows of a suburban train Surrey often looks manicured to within an inch of its life; a place of arboreta, parks and gardens. In fact the landscape is more interesting than that. I'm not a geologist but even I can spot the changes; from the forested Weald in the south to the wild heathland around Hindhead and Leith Hill; the chalky bits of the North Downs and then all the undulations that weave it together. As you pass through the villages their names present history before you: Pyrford, the ford marked by pear trees; Horsley (East and West) the horses clearing, and so on.

Many of the old roads still follow strange winding routes, far too narrow for modern life. These tell you something of the people and their preoccupations. Maps of the triangle formed by Woking, Leatherhead and Horsham clearly show a network of tracks heading south to the summer pastures. These were not people trying to connect with each other. Perhaps this ancient sense of distance from one's fellows still characterises some of the small villages. During the great storm of 1987, I lived in a tiny Surrey hamlet down the road from the local Conservative MP. I never saw him after the winds brought down every large tree in our road. Mind you, I didn't see many of the neighbours either. Everyone kept to themselves and muddled along. Yet, despite a certain sense of aloofness, Surrey has been home to early liberal attitudes and to the arts. Woking has the oldest purpose-built mosque in Britain and my favourite building in Surrey is the Watts Chapel in Compton. It was designed by Mary Watts, wife of the Victorian artist, George Frederick Watts. The chapel is a montage of Art Nouveau, Celtic, Romanesque and Egyptian influences. Mary believed in social improvement through the arts and she opened her home for clay modelling classes – the resulting building is astonishing.

The county is full of surprises. I remember as a child being taken into a wine bar in Reigate no bigger than an old sweet shop. We passed through a back door and down steep brick stairs into a network of caves hand-dug out of the sand. It was only after I moved to Surrey that I discovered how much my ancestors would have appreciated these caverns. My maternal great-great-grandparents, James Fisher and his wife Eliza Jane Windsor, pulled pints at the Greyhound in Guildford, while my great-grandfather, Field John Jackson Trickett, was the publican at the Fox in Kingswood.

Today we don't have innkeepers in the family but there are a lot of writers and journalists, which brings me to the part played by Kingswood in the early days of Reuters news agency. Pigeons were brought there from London by train and released with messages. This system, coupled with the invention of the telegram, allowed Reuters to deliver information quicker than anyone.

Perhaps there was some kind of DNA calling when I decided to settle in Surrey. Today, I live in a converted barn that was built around the time Henry VIII was first thinking marriage might be for him. It is beautiful and ancient. Very Surrey in fact.

Did the Greeks tell the first joke?

26 February 2006

A PRIEST, A RABBI AND an imam walk into a bar and the barman says, 'What is this? A joke?' I was driving past the latest protests against the infamous Muhammad cartoons last week when it occurred to me that we could all do with a good, shared laugh. There's something very healing about an explosion of laughter, but the trouble is we all have quite different views about what constitutes a genuine cracker and when it would be appropriate to tell it. I remember there was a period after 9/11 when the *New York Times* wrote great invectives against ever finding anything funny again. Oddly enough, it was today in 1922 that the French newspaper, *La Revue Mondiale*, slammed into Parisians for dancing to jazz music as, it said, it detracted from the post-World War reconstruction; and it was today, in 1945, that the US instituted a nationwide curfew on entertainment to conserve energy.

People have needed to laugh ever since someone sat round the first camp fire and said: 'Have you heard the one about the three-legged bison?' I have a Navajo kachina doll that sits on my desk. He is called the Watermelon Clown and by all accounts there are things his role model can do with fruit that would make your sides ache. The Pueblo people call their clowns *kashari* and revere them for relieving them of the burden and stresses of daily life. Apparently there was one, Agapito of San Ildefonso, who could keep you chuckling for five hours straight, which makes the average twenty-minute set of a stand-up comic seem rather paltry. Being a *kashari* is regarded as a semi-religious calling and someone whom the people cannot do without.

You get official clowns as far back as 3000 BC in Egypt, but the joke itself seems to be a Greek invention. There are those who say that Palamedes crafted the first gag, but then he also gets credit for inventing numbers, the alphabet, lighthouses and the practice of eating meals at regular intervals. Certainly the oldest collection of jokes is the *Philogelos*, or 'Laughter-Lover', a Greek collation from the fourth or fifth century AD. The jokes have not survived well and there are a couple about lettuce which, unless you're up on the whole lettuce and sexual malfunction belief, might not have you roaring.

Jokes vary depending on the cultural context. I was doing a one-woman show to an older audience in St John's Wood last week. In the interval the organiser asked me if I could tell a Jewish joke and I remembered the following: A grandmother has taken her grandson to Coney Island, the beach area in New York, and bought him a hat and coat. As they stroll along the beach a freak wave hits the boy and carries him out to sea. The grandmother is distraught and gets down on her knees to plead with God for the child's safe return. Just then a second wave brings the boy right back to her feet. She clasps him in her arms, looks up to God, and says: 'He had a hat!'

Is that funny to everyone? I think so, but then I've reached the stage of finding a lot of so-called entertainment completely bewildering. There is a new reality TV show in Holland called *Pimp My Life*. It's made by the Dutch Evangelist Broadcasting Union, who sound like they ought to know better. Basically the producers find a homeless person and thrust him into a week of luxury – limo, new clothes, fancy restaurants and hotels. They then give him a week to turn his life around, find a job and a place to live, and, 'After that, the tramp must do it on his own.'

In the interests of world understanding, here is a Navajo joke. A woman is driving in Northern Arizona when she sees a Navajo woman hitch-hiking. She stops and picks her up. As they chat, the Navajo woman notices a brown bag on the front seat between them. The woman driver nods and says: 'It's a bottle of French wine. I got it for my husband.' The Navajo woman is silent for a while and then sagely says, 'Good trade.'

By the way, Joke 114 in the *Philogelos* is missing its punch line. The joke goes – 'Seeing a eunuch, an Abderite asked him how many children he had. The eunuch replied that he had none, since he lacked the means of reproduction. Retorted the Abderite . . .'

Suggestions on a postcard please.

Lovers, poets and amorous nuns

5 March 2006

I HAVE BEEN TO VENICE for the carnival and returned rather dampened round the edges. I had fondly imagined it might be a salacious sojourn of wandering the streets incognito in search of libidinous excitements. As I drifted down the Grand Canal on a rusting *vaporetto* wearing nothing but a cape, a tricorn hat and a come-hither look in my eye, I came across not unbridled passion but, instead, a sobering lesson in the ephemeral nature of fame.

The word 'celebrity' is perhaps the twenty-first century's most misused epithet, so it is hard for us to imagine the true nature of superstardom that attached in the past to such people as Marie Taglioni. To the unknowing, Ms Taglioni may sound like a decent Italian main course, but in the nineteenth century her renown as a ballet dancer was so great that a pair of her toe shoes were sold for 200 roubles, then cooked and served in a sauce that was eaten at a dinner for fanatical balletomanes with cast-iron stomachs.

Venetian guide books will tell you that she 'collected palaces along the Grand Canal', which makes her sound both rich and more sensible than anyone whose life has focused on stamps. The truth is more pedestrian. In her middle years she had a liaison with a Russian prince, who was more than a decade her junior. Alexander Troubetzkoy presented Marie with the Casa d'Oro, a fifteenth-century Venetian *palazzo* that would make anyone willing to stand *en pointe* for an hour or two. Stuck for a few quid, she began a programme of light marble removal that included eight balconies and a stairway. (These she sold to the American art collector Isabella Stewart Gardner, and you can see them in the collector's old place in Boston.) Her DIY palace renovations were to no avail. In the end, the prince did what toy boys do and married Marie's daughter, and the dancer ended her life destitute, giving deportment lessons in London.

Her fall from grace, however, pales into insignificance when you put it alongside the biopic of Giacomo Casanova. The eighteenth-century erotic hero claimed to have slept with 120 women, although not, I think, on consecutive nights. He was arrested in Venice in 1755, partly because people thought he was a magician and partly because he owned a copy of Pietro Aretino's book on sexual positions. (Unavailable on Amazon.)

Aretino was the first man to make a living from writing pornography and Casanova may have been among the first to get into trouble over it. He was sentenced to five years in the dungeons of the Doge's Palace. In true romantic style he managed to escape down the Grand Canal with his friend, Father Balbi. What is less romantic is that he ended his life toothless, ridiculed and poor as a librarian in Bohemia.

Of course, the true sexual hero of Venice has to be Lord Byron. Here was a man who could be called many things, but certainly not fussy. His menu of amorous possibilities was pleasingly *à la carte* and all-inclusive – women of all classes, boys and, if it was raining and he couldn't get out, siblings. Byron claimed to have out-Casanova'ed Casanova by sleeping with 200 Venetian women in the one year.

Apparently he liked to swim home after an evening's liaison. He would jump in the canal and paddle along with a candle in order to avoid being hit by a passing gondola. Byron did at least die famous and a hero, but he had had a rotten childhood, what with the club foot and the alcoholic governess who made sexual advances when he was nine.

*

86

Sex seems to have been a root cause of trouble in a lot of Venetian history. Robert Browning's son, Pen, bought the glorious Ca'Rezzonico with his American heiress wife, but that can't have been a happy marriage as she left him to become a nun.

Not that nuns were immune from the Las Vegas lure of Venice in the past. It wasn't uncommon in eighteenth-century Venice to see nuns in low-cut dresses fighting for the honour of serving as mistress to a visiting papal nuncio.

I thought I would go to Venice and return sated and inspired. Instead, I am back worrying that I ought to plan a bit more for the future. The poetic hero thing seems unlikely, so if anyone wants deportment lessons or knows of a job going in a library, would you let me know?

It's all chaos, in theory

12 March 2006

AT THE RISK OF GIVING you a headache on what may be your only day off – why is there such a thing as 'chaos theory'? This strikes me as an ill pairing of words, akin to the marriage of 'Polish' and 'cuisine' or 'Flemish' and 'humour'. Surely if things are inherently disordered, then spending a lot of time looking for some underlying system to explain it is absurd. Yet, it is a quest for understanding that I entirely identify with. Not being either very scientific or religious, I long to discover that there is some eternal plan that will one day be made clear – presumably having been delivered by four horsemen. Meanwhile, I spend my time squirrelling away little nuggets of anecdotal evidence that suggest we are all working to some mathematical or systematic concept.

Take the whole issue of composers and their ninth symphonies. Beethoven hadn't written a symphony for ten years, then he penned the groundbreaking *Ninth* and dropped dead. He heads a long list of the moribund with nine symphonies to their credit – Schubert, Dvořák, Vaughan Williams. The fear of this nine-only syndrome so worried Mahler that he sat down to a tenth and promptly lost the beat. Bruckner tried to cheat by calling his first two symphonies 00 and 0, but he too died while creating his ninth. The only composer with any sense was Sibelius. He stopped after eight and lived for another thirty-three years.

I know there are people in the world who find order in mathematics and certainly we can all see how pleasing it is that $111,111,111 \times 111,111,111 = 12,345,678,987,654,321$.

Nevertheless, my organisation of the world through numeracy

88

stops there. I am as likely to believe that Douglas Adams was right in *The Hitchhiker's Guide to the Galaxy* when he declared that the ultimate answer to the mysteries of life and the universe is '42' as any other number.

Consequently, I was thrilled when scientists in Cambridge first worked out one of the fundamental keys to determining the age of the Universe – the Hubble Constant. After three years of calculation, they found the answer was forty-two. Sadly, they have now changed the range to between fifty-seven and seventy-eight, but for a brief moment everything made sense.

If I can't find the answer in maths, then I sometimes seek order in happenstance. One of my favourite stories concerns Gracie Fields's musical director, Harry Parr Davies. He was en route to the US on the *Queen Mary* when he leant over the ship's rail and lost his only pair of glasses. He couldn't rehearse without them, so Gracie went to see if there were any for sale in the shop. Along the way, she noticed a sign being pinned up that read: 'Found, a pair of spectacles. Apply purser.' Gracie asked if Harry could try them, and they turned out to be his spectacles. The man who had found them had put his hand out of a port-hole on a lower deck to see if it was raining – and the glasses had landed in his palm.

That, of course, is nothing compared to what fell on the Danish tenor Lauritz Melchior. As a penniless music student, he was sitting in a garden in Munich learning a new opera. He had just sung the words, 'Come to me, my love, on the wings of light,' when, as he said, 'there was a flutter, a flash of white, and there, sitting at my feet, was a beautiful little creature who had dropped right out of the blue'. It was Maria Hacker, a Bavarian actress working as a stunt girl, who had parachuted out of a plane and landed practically in Melchior's arms. The two were married for thirty-eight years.

Or how about this – on 5 December 1664 a ship carrying eighty-one passengers sank in the Menai Strait. Only one person survived – Hugh Williams. Move on to the same spot on 5 December 1785. Another ship, this time with sixty passengers, sank. Once again the man pulled from the sea was one Hugh Williams. 5 December 1860 – down went another boat and, once again, Hugh Williams was the survivor. Now I know it's a common Welsh name but still, if you live in the area, you might think it a useful moniker for a sailor.

Why do I seem obsessed with all this? Well, I should like it if life were not based on chaos. If there really were some theory that explained the unexplainable. This week we said goodbye to the funniest woman I ever met. Linda Smith was only forty-eight, and it just doesn't make sense.

On the phone to my 5,823,206 pals

9 April 2006

I'VE BEEN THINKING OF PHONING someone I don't even know. Whether this constitutes the early onset of a form of stalking dementia, I don't know, but it's not my fault that I am being constantly encouraged.

There is a new phone system called Skype. It is entirely free and, once it is downloaded onto your computer, you can call anyone in the Skype directory, anywhere in the world and talk to your heart's content. While I am writing this there are 5,823,206 people who are currently online, available for free conversation. Sadly, I only know one and she's getting a bit bored with me ringing and saying, 'Isn't this amazing?'

This leaves me with what's called the 'Skype me' option. This is a list of people who don't know you, but are willing for anyone to call out of the blue and have a chat. All you know about them is their online name, which country they are in and what language they speak. The rest is pot luck. Some do provide further details. Ryan – 'Skype meh' claims to live in 'Minnesoooota'. He is also happy to reveal that he was born in 1986, which makes him nineteen and possibly too young to be a good speller. There is a Canadian Skype master; a Chinese-speaking person in Andorra; Ed Whitton in Brisbane wants me to Skype him sideways and someone in County Armagh says 'Skype me, bite me', which is probably something my mother would warn me about.

I can't really think why I am tempted. I'm not much good on the ordinary phone as it is. I tend to mumble a response and then hang up. I disconnected our answering machine and have been known to take several decades to respond to something urgent. There is, however, a curious frisson about ringing someone unknown in, say, Atlanta and asking whether the old Georgian law that forbade tying a giraffe to a telegraph pole or street lamp still holds true.

The Americans reckon the average Westerner spends a year of their life on the phone (and that may just be getting through to the satellite television helpline). The British were reluctant users. When it was first mooted here, the Post Office chief engineer felt it would be of little practical value. 'The Americans have need of the telephone – but we do not. We have plenty of messenger boys.'

Actually, I like the idea of messenger boys. How pleasing to have some slight fellow in a pillbox hat bringing me a folded *billet-doux*. I fear that my temptation to Skype the unknown is part of a terrible conspiracy to stop communication between people who actually know each other. Perhaps we should go back to the days of 1878 when Emma M. Nutt became the first American female telephone operator.

Her legacy echoed in my Danish childhood. There was no dial on our wooden phone. My father would turn the handle and wait for a fearsome woman to connect him to our single-digit number. These women were buffers to the rest of the world and no one ever got through them trying to sell double-glazing.

Today is the anniversary of, in 1859, one Samuel Clemens getting his licence as a river-boat pilot on the Mississippi. Of course, he went on to greater fame as the writer and humorist Mark Twain. In 1890 he sent out the following Christmas greeting, which really has to be the last word on the whole phone business.

'It is my heart-warmed and world-embracing Christmas hope and aspiration that all of us, the high, the low, the rich, the poor, the admired, the despised, the loved, the hated, the civilised, the savage (every man and brother of us all throughout the whole earth), may eventually be gathered together in a heaven of everlasting rest and peace and bliss, except the inventor of the telephone.'

I think I've decided to stay silent for the moment. My father used to answer the phone by barking our surname. Something hardly anyone does any more. As it happens, Toksvig is a corruption of Danish for 'small burial ground by the river' and it describes where we hail from. I used to think it was rather fine to have such a descriptive moniker, until I came across a Maori hill in New Zealand called *Taumatawhakatangihangakoauauotamateaturipukakapikimaungahoronukupokaiwhenuakitanatahu*, which translates as 'the place where Tamatea, the man with the big knees, who slid, climbed and swallowed mountains, known as a land-eater, played on the flute to his loved one'. The minute anyone tries to Skype from there I shall be on the blower.

Give us chocolate – and women rule

16 April 2006

IT'S EASTER SUNDAY AND I'M puffed out. I've been blowing eggs, which sounds as if it ought to be a racier occupation than it is. My children and I always decorate the Easter breakfast table. We have small, moulting chicks, who come out year after year and stand among a few coloured eggs laid at the feet of a frankly demonic-looking bunny. I like things with tradition. It wouldn't be Easter without several hours spent getting blown egg out of my hair.

Sadly, my babies have now moved beyond the age where they enjoy an Easter-egg hunt. But I have discovered a marvellous thing about getting older. My memory is so bad these days (about the only thing I retain well is water), that I can hide my own eggs and still get hours of fun out of the game. I realise that I must be of comparable middling years to the vicar who conducted services at my boarding school. I still relish his Easter-holiday declaration, 'As we head for the spring recess, let us ask Matron to come forward and lay an egg on the altar.'

Today is, of course, also a day for chocolate. I have to say I'm not a huge fan. I can never look at the confection without thinking about the actress Janet Leigh being murdered. You will recall the scene in Alfred Hitchcock's *Psycho*, when Anthony Perkins (as the Oedipally challenged Norman Bates) takes against Janet's hygiene habits and stabs her in the shower. The whole scene lasts just forty-five seconds, but took seven days and several gallons of chocolate syrup to shoot. Back in the heady days of black and white, it was the texture and not the colour of things that mattered and, apparently, chocolate syrup is just the right consistency for blood heading for a plug hole. I

94

don't think the film scared me when I was young, but it did put me off ice-cream sundaes for a while.

I don't know why I am not a chocoholic. Apparently, most women are. According to scientific studies, seventy per cent of women claim they would rather have chocolate than sex and, presumably, the remaining thirty per cent are not married. It's all down to a chemical called phenylethylamine. You can either find it in chocolate, or your brain produces it when you fall in love.

Instinctively, humans must have known this long before anyone ever set the stuff to melt over a Bunsen burner. During the eighteenth century in Central America, many mountain villages had a ban on anyone under the age of sixty consuming the stuff. I guess they wanted the women under sixty to keep their men happy and not have seventy per cent drifting off to some cocoa club.

Even in the heady presence of chocolate I would suggest, however, that women tend to have the upper hand. There is a lovely story about the great Quaker, social reformer and cocoa manufacturer George Cadbury who, sometime in the early twentieth century, was hosting a visit to his chocolate factory by King George V and Queen Mary. Cadbury was leading the way through the factory with the Queen, while his wife, Elizabeth, followed with the King. It was very cold but George took his hat off as a sign of respect. Queen Mary was a kind soul and kept asking him to put it back on, but he declined. Anxious about the chill, she repeated her request, but still he remained bareheaded until, finally, Elizabeth Cadbury boomed from behind, 'George, put your hat on,' and he did.

If the science of chocolate or eggs has taken your fancy, you might want to know that it was today, in 1705, that Queen Anne knighted one of history's greatest scientists, Isaac Newton.

95

Newton's First Law of Motion, also known as the Law of Inertia, is that the natural state of objects is not at rest. Anyone who has a small boy will know this to be true, but you can test it with eggs. Take one hard-boiled and one raw egg and spin them both. Put your hand on the hard-boiled one and it will stop spinning. Apply the same pressure to the raw egg and then let go. The egg will start to spin again because the liquid inside is still spinning.

Do you care? Probably not, but paint the eggs pretty colours first, eat a great slab of chocolate and you may find it will keep you occupied for hours.

On the subject of remembering things – I cannot for the life of me recall where I stored the Easter bunny. I wonder if the children will believe me if I say he couldn't come, owing to a bad hare day.

Waxworks? I just glaze over

30 April 2006

I WAS HAVING CANAPÉS WITH Gandhi this week who, despite having been dead for some years, was looking in good shape. He didn't eat much, partly because I don't think chicken on a stick was his thing and partly because he was made of wax. I was attending an event at Madame Tussaud's, where I spent most of my time muttering 'Who on earth is that?' Not because the waxworks weren't life-like, but because my finger is so far from the pulse that I have no idea who anyone in the public eye might be. I was there to host the event and amuse, but, faced with so many famous faces moulded into life-size effigies, I began to feel like a celebrity candle-end.

There was a model of Madame Tussaud herself. She was not a looker but she must have been a game girl. Born Marie Grosholz, she learnt wax-modelling from her mother's employer, a doctor called Philippe Curtius. Marie grew up to become art tutor to King Louis XVI's sister and went to live at the royal court in Versailles. Along came the French Revolution. Not many people will have seen this as a tourism opportunity but Marie went back to Paris where she and Curtius spent their days picking heads out of the guillotine basket which included Marie's old royal art students. She would sit with them on her lap while the good doctor sculpted away. Apparently the waxing technique hasn't changed over the years, except of course for the great football legend Pelé, who I believe received the first Brazilian.

I don't know whether Marie would have thought of herself as a feminist but she left her husband, François Tussaud, to tour

97

her wax collection to Britain. That was back in the 1820s but times move slowly and women are still chipping away at gaining entrance into the world.

This week saw the first mixed lunch of that splendid charity, the Lord's Taverners. I didn't realise they had never asked women to their spring lunch before and thought the word 'Mixed' on the invite meant there might be some vegetarians. I was there as the first ever woman speaker and was amused by the number of men who were discomforted by being forced to bring their wives to what has for more than fifty years been a stag-do. There was one old boy who was immensely solicitous to his spouse. 'What can I get you, sweetheart?' he said, 'Are you all right, darling?' and 'Another drink, my angel?' I asked him how long he had been married and he replied, 'Thirty years.' I said how lovely it was that he showered her with so many endearments. 'Yes,' he replied, 'to be honest I've completely forgotten her name.'

Marriage, of course, is tricky. I was reminded of the story of a husband who was berated by his wife into having a health check-up. She went with him to the doctor's and after the screening the doctor asked to see her on her own. 'Your husband,' he said, 'is suffering from an extreme stress disorder that could kill him. In order to prevent this you need to prepare him three nutritious meals every day, you must never disagree with him, never nag and make sure you make love to him on a regular basis. If you do all that for twelve months he might recover.' The woman thanked the doctor and went to join her husband. 'What did the doctor say?' he asked. The wife shook her head and replied, 'I'm afraid he said you're going to die.'

The two events I attended both had splendid intentions – one to promote English tourism and the other to raise money for sporting opportunities for both able and disabled children. There is a certain formality to these occasions and I always worry that I will offend without meaning to. This is particularly true when I know nothing about the principal subject of conversation – which at the Lord's Taverners was cricket. I've never been to a match but thought of a friend who was taken to Lord's. She was bored to tears, but an hour in, a batsman gave a tremendous swipe and knocked the ball out of the ground. 'Thank goodness they got rid of it,' she sighed. 'Now we can all go home.'

The lunch was great fun and many much-needed funds will go to help disadvantaged kids get some exercise. It's just a shame that the monies aren't provided as a matter of course. When asked what he thought about Western civilisation, Gandhi replied: 'I think it would be a good idea.'

Mad aristos and English women

23 April 2006

FOR REASONS I CAN NO longer recall, I spent an inordinately large part of last weekend chasing canoeists along the Thames. An otherwise sober friend had decided that paddling 125 miles in the Devizes-to-Westminster marathon was a good idea and I, in an otherwise unsober moment, apparently agreed to go along as 'support'.

I certainly wasn't getting in the boat. I once paddled 1,700 miles down the Zambezi and I can tell you it leaves you with a condition I can only describe as trench bottom. It put me off water for years, but I didn't mind the idea of driving alongside someone else and chucking them bananas while they panted and I didn't. I know heavy breathing is supposed to be good for you, but if I ever reintroduce it into my life, I do hope it won't be through sport.

The Thames, however, is an independent devil and, in most instances, refuses to follow the road. I rarely saw water, my friend or any paddlers at all. What there was, however, was a glorious slice of English eccentricity. Grey-haired women organisers in woollen hats boomed instructions, using clipped accents and a volume one usually finds bred only in draughty castles.

At Marlow, a man wearing a mayoral chain over his blazer had four people to tell him the precise moment when he should press a buzzer for the next start, while men called Tarquin moved 4×4s into place to pick up the camping stove Camilla had used to great effect the night before.

Once I finally tracked down my elusive chum, I wasn't allowed to see him, as the camp was 'in seclusion', to avoid, presumably, the rush of supporters bearing steroids. So, a weekend spent lost in the countryside supporting someone I didn't find until the end and then wasn't allowed to see.

It was no more eccentric, of course, than the fact that, today, England celebrates its patron saint, who was possibly a Roman soldier, who allegedly slayed a dragon to save a Libyan princess and certainly never set foot on English soil. He is supposed to have died today in 303 or 307 (the year, not a hotel room) by being beheaded in Palestine.

It was King Ed the third who, in 1348, introduced the battle cry 'St George for England', ignorant of the fact that George was set to be patron saint of Venice, Genoa, Portugal and Catalonia, and had quite a cult in Russia and Ethiopia.

It is said that the Queen has a hood ornament of George slaying the dragon placed on every car she sits in. I had a hood ornament once, but only after a misunderstanding involving a bicyclist and a faulty pelican crossing.

While we're being so English, today is also the birth (1564) and death (1616) day of old Will Shakespeare. The coincidence of his dying on his birthday suggests he may have been what we in show business like to call 'tired and emotional' when he went.

Shakespeare, who couldn't spell his own name, brought us words that are now in common parlance – 'hurry', 'bump', 'eyeball' and, inexplicably, 'anchovy'. He was also the first person, other than royalty, to appear on a British stamp. He did not, however, manage to do as much for eccentricity as this country's aristocracy.

Did you know that the one-foot measurement is based on the length of King Henry I's arm? He decreed that the standard foot should be a third of the length of his arm – 12". Just think, if his arm had been 42" long, then a foot would be 14" and I wouldn't even manage to be 5 ft tall.

And who can forget Squire John Mytton, his hiccups and the nightshirt? Incensed by a bout of hiccups, the Squire decided to 'frighten away' his malady by setting fire to the nightshirt he was wearing. It took two men to put out the conflagration and the Squire was appallingly burnt, but apparently very satisfied with the result. I know this because I have an ancient copy of Edith Sitwell's wonderful *English Eccentrics* which, in my library of several thousand books, I laid my hand on instantly. No one else would have found it, for my filing system defies logic and is sensible only to me.

The glorious portrait of Edith on the front made me long to be both English and eccentric: a mad woman who chases phantom rowers across '. . . this sceptred isle, This earth of majesty, this seat of Mars, This other Eden, demi-paradise . . . This precious stone set in the silver sea, This blessed plot, this earth, this realm, this England . . .' Thanks, Will.

Bare buttocks in the grass, please

7 May 2006

LAST WEEK, AND I DON'T think it made all the papers, the Dutch prime minister, Jan Peter Balkenende, admitted he was boring. Mr Balkenende (hardly a man for first-name terms) is a member of the lower chamber of parliament, known as the *Tweede Kamer*. How perfect that a man who has the self-confessed charisma of a small soap dish should belong to a house named after a fusty gentleman's jacket.

The Dutch PM made his statement as a sort of awkward confession, but I thought it was marvellous. How Tony Blair must wish he had a DPM who had opted for a bit more of being glazed over, rather than gazed over.

In present times, there seems to be a notion of life as a permanent state of entertainment, diversion and stimulation. I can't recall the last time I heard a parent say to their child, 'Here's an old loo roll and a washing-up bottle, now go and play.' Boredom has been around for ever. The Danish philosopher Søren Kierkegaard called it 'the root of all evil'. Wordsworth said it was a 'savage torpor' and Chekhov wouldn't have had a career without it. I think it is a lost art form and we ought to campaign to bring it back.

I was in Holland a couple of weeks ago for the Dutch publication of my last book. (Please don't be impressed, but I am now officially an international author.) A marvellous event was held in a theatre in Rotterdam, where young people read relentlessly from what was allegedly my work. It could have been Double Dutch, for all I know, so I settled back in my seat in complete contentment. I was exactly where I was supposed to be, I had no idea what anyone was saying and, for a small hour, I sat undisturbed by anyone.

I allowed my mind to range over what I know about the Dutch. My only knowledge of the *lingua franca* is the name of a dish of varied beans called '*blote billetjes in het gras*', which, as far as I recall, translates as, 'bare buttocks in the grass'. I've never tried it and bemoan the lack of Dutch restaurants in the UK where one might attempt such a sensual order.

There is, of course, as I found out at lunch, a reason why Dutch cuisine has failed to take the world by storm. Nevertheless, the people of the Low Country have given the world other blessings – the microscope, the pendulum clock, roller-skating, Wall Street, a court ruling allowing self-employed prostitutes to charge sales tax, and Father Christmas.

The latter is a curious fellow. In Holland, old St Nick has a servant called Black Peter. Peter is the one who actually drops the presents down the chimneys. If, however, your child has been naughty, he puts them in a bag and takes them to Spain. The fact that the Dutch consider this a punishment suggests they and I have booked with the same tour operators.

I had many misconceptions about the Dutch. I thought they would be a quiet people, but I had clearly based this on childhood images of Anne Frank, who, of necessity, said very little, and Vincent van Gogh, who didn't hear all that well. The people I met loved a laugh and weren't shy about speaking out. I was sorry that I couldn't engage in banter with them.

Perhaps I should have developed a system of communication such as the one Steven de Souza, the screenwriter and director, used when filming *Street Fighter* in Thailand. The film's hundreds of extras all spoke different languages. De Souza developed a system of numbered cards: 1 meant you were happy, 2 meant you were sad and 3 meant get in your boat.

*

Anyway, I enjoyed sitting silently. I was once interviewed by a lad of about twelve from a local paper. 'Where do you get your ideas from?' he asked. I told him there was a website called Ideas R Us and, tragically, he wrote that down. The truth is, ideas catch you up during traffic jams, they drift in on the lapping water of a cooling bath and even occasionally pop up while standing behind someone who has dared to take six items into the 'five items or fewer' shopping queue.

For the Catholics, boredom, or acedia, was one of the seven deadly sins but, in fact, in Greek it means 'caring free'. The Hindus and Buddhists think of it as a gateway to spiritual enlightenment so, as it's Sunday, let's drink to torpor, ennui and sloth. I have my own system of cards ready – 1 means I'm sleeping, 2 means go away and 3 is for more sherry.

Feed the cat, and you risk your neck

14 May 2006

FORGIVE ME IF I BEGIN by whingeing, but I am in some pain. For some reason, lately, I have suffered a series of what can only be described as middle-class injuries. My thumb has a laceration inflicted from grappling with a lobster dinner – despite being dead, the lobster won; my forefinger is practically septic from the burn I received while instructing my son on the safe way to deal with fondue; and the back of my hand is in agony after I inexplicably managed to pinch it as I locked the door to the ladies at the Dorchester Hotel in London.

I don't feel any of my wounds could have been predicted, but then accident statistics suggest a host of other activities that I had never imagined might lead to a four-hour wait at Accident and Emergency. In 2003, 3,000 people suffered a lesion from a non-powered hand-tool, 2,718 needed medical treatment after striking against or being struck by sports equipment, three people in the UK were bitten by crocodiles and four needed treatment after accidental suffocation and strangulation while lying in their own beds.

The world is a dangerous place and you can never predict where trouble lurks. More people are killed annually by donkeys than in plane crashes. Having travelled both by donkey and chartered airliner, I can't decide whether or not that is comforting.

Today is the anniversary, in 1976, of Keith Relf, the former vocalist with the Yardbirds, being electrocuted by his guitar. Being killed by a donkey, which is, after all, a sentient if stupid being, is one thing; having musical instruments turn on you is deeply disturbing. Mr Relf bore no responsibility for his early demise, unlike the American rock musician Terry Kath, who shot himself in 1978 after uttering the words: 'Don't worry – it's not loaded.'

With the more bizarre accidents there is often no blame attached. There was a New Zealander called Peter John Robinson, who, one morning in 2001, was feeding his cat, Piper. As he did so, he slipped and fell, knocking himself out. Sadly, he landed face down in Piper's water bowl – and drowned in the inch and a half of liquid.

Where blame can be attributed, then there is surely no finer example of being hoist by your own petard than the death of the American chemical engineer Thomas Midgley, in 1940. Midgley was an inventive fellow, but it's hard to say whether his passing was not a blessing to the planet. He discovered that petrol burnt better if tetraethyl lead were added, leading to generations of us having toxic lead in our systems.

In 1930, he developed Freon, a non-flammable gas which was splendid in fridges and aerosol cans and, later on, in the destruction of the ozone layer. In 1940, Midgley sadly got polio and couldn't walk. Undaunted, he came up with a rope-and-pulley invention that allowed him to get out of bed without assistance. Sadly, he died suspended in mid-air, strangled by his final invention.

Not all accidents end at the funeral parlour. My favourite story of things slipping from the hand occurred at the wedding of the mayor of Leningrad's daughter, in 1980. Grigory Romanov wanted the best for his child and, as a senior member of the Soviet Politburo, he was able to get it. For the celebrations, he managed to persuade the director of the city's Hermitage museum to lend him Catherine the Great's china tea set. It all went well, until one guest got to his feet and accidentally dropped one of Catherine's cups. The other guests took this to be a signal for a toast and, in a traditional gesture of good luck, they all rose to their feet and hurled the entire service into the fireplace.

It is the unexpectedness of accidents that makes them so fascinating, such as the death of the stuntman Bobby Leach, who survived going over Niagara Falls in a barrel and died after slipping on orange peel. Today, the notion of a simple accident is outdated. Television ads show ignorant people falling off ladders and sliding across newly polished floors, for which they then receive compensation.

I realise that I should stop suffering and start suing. I shall be instructing my solicitors, Freeman, Hardy and Willis, to pursue all lobster-pot manufacturers, hot-oil salesmen and the concierge at the Dorchester, as soon as possible.

So, what would da Vinci make of it?

21 May 2006

I n the midst of the current troubled
T imes, when you would think that
S o many political, sociological or
N ation-defining events are in the
O ffing, it is curious, even tragic,
T hat the world focuses on trivia.
E veryone it seems has got Da
V inci fever. Wishing to fit in and
E ver mindful of the desperate
N eed to keep my finger, even
A t a distance, on the pulse of
G eneral trends, I have decided to
O ffer this week's prose as an
O pen piece of code. Crack it and
D a reason why Da Vinci himself
B elieved Tom Hanks was destined to
O pen the mysterious world of
O pus Dei to everyone will become
K lear.

OK, I was doing well until I got to the letter K. I am bemused by
the obsession with *The Da Vinci Code*, the secret world of
Opus Dei and what Ruth Kelly wears when she attends a meeting. There is a strange tendency for the population to believe
that clever people like to encode their thoughts in order to
maintain their edge.

Sometimes, this is true. In 1610, Galileo Galilei, the Italian
astronomer, physicist and Queen lyric, believed he had discovered

two moons orbiting another planet. He encoded his finding in the anagram: smaismrmilmepoetaleumibunenugttauiras. The German astronomer Johannes Kepler believed Mars had two moons, and spent weeks deciphering Galileo's nonsense until he finally cracked it as '*Salve umbisteneum geminatum Martia proles*' ('Hail, twin companionship, children of Mars'), thus confirming, he believed, his own prediction.

In fact, his Italian colleague had written nothing of the kind. Galileo's secret message was '*Altissimum planetam tergeminum observavi*' ('I have observed the most distant planet to have a triple form'), which related to his mistaking the rings around Saturn for moons. This proves two things: 1. Even the brightest and the best make mistakes; 2. You can take any group of letters and turn them into endless Latin sentences.

It also suggests that code-crackers may bring too much of an agenda to the table. They may simply feel satisfied when they decipher the message that they believed was there all along.

When Germany occupied Denmark during the Second World War, the noted Danish physicist Niels Bohr managed to send a telegram to his friends in England. In it, he explained that he was safe and concluded with the request to inform others 'and Maud Ray, Kent'. There was a consensus that this must be code and, eventually, the latter part of the message was deciphered as: 'Make uranium day and night.' In fact, Maud Ray was the name of Bohr's old English governess, who lived in Kent.

I wonder what Leonardo himself would have thought of the latest brouhaha. Admittedly, the man was a genius, the prototype of your regular Renaissance fellow but, frankly, also a bit of a dabbler. It was rare that he finished one thing before cracking on to the next. If there is a Da Vinci code, then this man with mild attention deficit disorder would never have finished it. I know there are fashion points involved, but I have often thought that the reason the *Mona Lisa* has no eyebrows is that the artist got distracted and moved on to something else.

If the wretched Dan Brown circus does make you decide to visit the Louvre, you might want to take a close look at the *Mona Lisa*. It was stolen in 1911 by Vincenzo Peruggia, an Italian house-painter. He kept it with him in a hotel room for a year before it was returned.

There is something delightfully French and laid-back about this story. Peruggia stole the painting on a Monday morning, but no one noticed until just after twelve on Tuesday. It tells you everything you need to know about the public that more people visited the museum during that year to stare at the blank space than had ever been to see the painting.

There are those who believe that the real work of art was never returned and the tiny portrait now hanging behind bullet-proof glass is a fake. Perhaps Peruggia painted it by numbers, and if you add those numbers up it will reveal a code that . . . dear God, I think I'm being infected.

Harris tweed and goats on leads

4 June 2006

MY FAVOURITE FARMING JOKE IS the one about the three-legged pig. A city slicker visits a farm for the day and is amazed by the speed with which a pig, challenged in the leg department, is able to negotiate the farmyard. 'That's quite an animal,' says the city-dweller. 'Indeed,' replies the farmer, 'that pig saved my life. There was a terrible fire here last year and the pig managed to open the barn door and get all the animals out before pulling on the bell rope by the front door to wake the household.' 'Gosh,' said the guest, 'is that how he lost his leg?' The farmer shook his head. 'No, but a pig like that, you don't want to eat all at once.'

I mention this because it is county show time and there is hardly an agricultural county within reach that hasn't been providing its populace with a chance to check out the chickens and place an overdue order for a combine harvester. Attending one of these events made me realise how little I know about the farming world and how misguided I've been in thinking Harris tweed had gone out of fashion. We entered through a gate marked 'Sheep and Goats', which immediately struck me as strange, because I thought the idea was to separate them.

People in white coats were parading goats on dog leads, while an otherwise elegant woman was poking about at their bottoms. No doubt it was in the hind quarters that she might identify a winner, but to the non-cognisant it looked over-familiar. Sadly, we had missed the sheep judging but my twelve-year-old son and I went and looked at the prize-winners. A fourth-prize ewe stood disconsolately, penned beside the less-than-thrilled winner. They looked identical and led me to wonder what cloning would do for the annual fair. Perhaps it will come down to personality and the poor animals can have their nether parts left alone.

Sheep always make me think of Winston Churchill. Today, as it happens, is the anniversary of his 'We shall fight on the beaches ... we shall never surrender' speech to the House of Commons in 1940.

After the First World War, Churchill had said he was going to devote himself to painting, which he loved. He once visited the office of the *Time* magazine publisher Henry Luce, who had one of Winston's landscape paintings. 'It's a good picture,' Luce declared, 'but I think it needs something in the foreground – a sheep, perhaps.' The next day Luce was upset to get a call from a Churchillian minion demanding the return of the painting.

Luce thought he must have deeply offended the great man, until a few days later, when the artwork was returned with the addition of a single sheep grazing in the foreground.

My boy went off to enjoy amusement rides too rickety-looking for me to find amusing, so I had a wander. There were vague echoes of Churchill in the poultry tent, where signs warned me that 'Careless talk costs birds' lives'. The world of the chicken-fancier, it seems, is fraught with tension and the merest slip of a home address might lead to some rival not taking the fair route to a rosette.

Experts abounded and there was much talk of breeding. I left feeling I could never make another 'crossing the road' joke again. I headed for the local radio stand, where at least I would understand what was going on. A large whiteboard proclaimed the day's attractions and began with the words: 'Why not have a go at Reading.' Suggesting a pop at the county seat of Berkshire seemed bizarre. Why, it was the town where Jane Austen went to school, it was once the home of the world's largest biscuit factory and the place where the first, albeit badly

113

spelt, English song, 'Sumer is icumen in', was penned. It was only after a moment's irritation that I read the next line of the notice – 'the news'. Why not have a go at reading the news? The English language is a tricky beast.

While I was rummaging in the car-boot sale of information that is my mind, I recalled that a chicken at top speed can get up to 9 mph, while a pig can manage 11 mph. I don't know who found that out or whether thoughtless chatter was involved. There was an Elizabethan champion of science who died while trying to come up with a better way of keeping food in those pre-fridge times. He caught a severe cold while attempting to preserve a chicken by filling it with snow. His name? Francis Bacon. Why is that so pleasing?

Why I can't stomach bare chests

25 June 2006

A MAN GOES TO SEE the doctor in a desperate state. 'Doctor,' he begs, 'you must help me. I'm under such a lot of stress, I can't stop losing my temper.' The doctor settles back in her chair and says sympathetically, 'Tell me about your problem,' to which the patient replies – 'I just did, didn't I? You idiot!'

I was once asked to appear on a television programme called *Grumpy Old Women*. I declined on the grounds that, these days, forty-eight is the new youth and I also like to think I have a sunny disposition. This notion has, however, been disproved in the latest spate of warm weather. It's not that the heat makes my temper rise, but that rising temperatures bring out the worst in some men – their stomachs.

When I was a child growing up in America in the 1960s, grown men were rarely seen without at least two top garments – a shirt and, beneath that, a white singlet. In summers of intense heat fathers, in the privacy of their own gardens, might sometimes have been seen sweating over a barbecue in the said undergarment. Never was flesh completely bared to the public gaze. Nowadays, however, I can hardly approach the fresh-fish counter at a supermarket without standing beside some fellow parading his collapsed stomach muscles and concave chest to every loyalty-card holder in the place. Perhaps I live in a particularly muscle-challenged area, but so far I have not seen an Adonis among them.

I've thought about carrying a small mirror with the notion of presenting these bold breast-barers with a view of themselves, while continuing to silently rummage through the root-vegetables. The trouble is, I don't think it would make any difference and I am appalled that it makes me grumpy.

Then, I depart from my provision store of choice and find myself ranting about people who think the indicator on their car is an optional extra. And what about perfect strangers who call out to you in the street, 'Cheer up, it can't be that bad'? How annoying is that? How do they know how bad things might be? Have they just been cut up on the high road by an unattractive naked person who refused to indicate where they were going?

I feel I am following in the footsteps of that other grumpy old woman, Favell Lee Mortimer. Her Victorian work has recently been republished as *Mrs Mortimer's Bad-Tempered Guide to the Victorian World*. It is based on her trilogy of travel guides for children, which take your breath away with the breadth of their crabbiness. Mrs Mortimer rarely left home, yet she cuts entire civilisations down to size with cantankerous prose that makes Attila the Hun look like a UN representative.

The Portuguese, she declares, are 'indolent, just like the Spaniards'; the Welsh are 'unclean'; the Zulus are 'a miserable race of people' and the Italians are 'ignorant and wicked'. As to what she has to say about the Jews and Catholics, I find it impossible to repeat. It reminds me of the tetchy vicar who, feeling the charitable donations to his pet mission were not going well, put up a sign reading, 'I've upped my pledge, now up yours.'

The people of the American Appalachian mountains still use the word 'ill' in its fourteenth-century meaning of 'bad-tempered' and I think they are right. Developing, for example, a rage against the free offers on the internet for a computer cursor shaped like a smiley face is surely not the sign of a healthy mind. When matters take a downturn, I try to think about things that, by comparison, show I have nothing to be upset about.

What about, for example, what happened to the seal-rescuers of the *Exxon Valdez* oil spill in Alaska in 1989? After the environmental disaster, these kindly folk spent about £90,000 rehabilitating two seals. After much care and concern, the animals were released back into the wild. The applause from onlookers was halted only when, a minute after the release, both seals were eaten by a killer whale.

Back to the doctor. A man arrives at the clinic covered in bruises. 'What happened?' asked the doctor. 'Well,' says the man, 'I was sitting at home when the doorbell rang. I opened it and there was a 6 ft tall cockroach who punched me and ran off. The next night the cockroach rang again, kicked me and ran off, and last night he reappeared and there was another attack.' The doctor nodded and said, 'Yes, there is a nasty bug going around.'

Please don't come up to me in the street and tell me you've heard it. If you've no shirt on, I can't legislate for my response.

School reports: could be better

16 July 2006

HOW WONDERFUL THAT THE NON-SPORTS fans among us can breathe a sigh of relief that, for a while at least, we don't have to be plagued by middle-aged men with testing hairstyles telling us why a 4-5-1 formation is not all it's cracked up to be. Time for some of us to settle down to the annual fun of reading our children's school reports. Not, I have to say, that they are as amusing as they used to be. In these days of hypersensitivity, reports are now written by computer program and with a vagueness of meaning that suggests staff have half an eye on the law courts.

Thus, where a child whose sole intent is to emulate the diplomatic skills of the French football captain, Zinedine Zidane, might once have been accused of thuggery, bullying or at any rate being 'a disruptive influence', today's report would refer to his behaviour with the splendid euphemism of 'challenging'.

This word is the absolute pearl in today's report-speak created entirely from a list of approved and appropriate phrases. Personally I think swimming the Atlantic is challenging, but you can't be too careful. If research is correct then being a thug is in your DNA and no teacher wants to meet the irate parental source of the 'challenging' behaviour.

From this year's offerings, pretty much all I can tell you is that my three kids have good attendance, but I probably guessed that as I haven't been tripping over them in the house during the day. What is missing is the fortune-telling aspect of the all-knowing teacher, who could dismiss you and your entire future in the blink of an eye. Personally, I will never forget Mrs

Rochester, who was adamant that, at the age of twelve, I was never going to be academic and recommended that my parents consider agricultural college. My father, bless him, laughed for about a week.

Mrs R was following in a great tradition of dismissing a proportion of students to the woodpile. Thus Sir Isaac Newton, genius in mathematics, optics, physics and astronomy, was described by his masters as 'idle' and 'inattentive' and Sir Winston Churchill, voted by the public as the greatest Briton of all time, was characterised as being 'a constant trouble to everybody and is always in some scrape or other. He cannot be trusted to behave himself anywhere. He has no ambition.' John Lennon was 'certainly on the road to failure' and Roald Dahl, one of the world's most popular children's authors, was famously accused of being 'incapable of organising his thoughts on paper'.

What I want the reports to include, of course, are words like 'potential tycoon' or 'budding business mogul' but admittedly that may be hard to spot.

Today, as it happens, is Orville Redenbacher's birthday, or rather it would have been if he hadn't popped his clogs in 1995. 'Popped' is the appropriate word, for Orville was – and I have never come across this trait in anyone else – a popcorn tycoon. From his earliest days on a small corn farm in Brazil, Indiana, Orville had a passion for popcorn. He experimented with thousands of corn hybrids, looking for the miracle kernel. By the time I was growing up in the US, the white-haired, skinny Redenbacher in bow-tie and thick glasses was selling his Gourmet Popping Corn on television. Popcorn is huge in America, and Orville's home county, Clay, has an annual popcorn festival where last year thirteen skinny, bow-tied people competed in the Orville Redenbacher Look-Alike Contest. You can read all about it in the local paper, which carries the curious masthead of *The Brazil Times*. Here you can also learn that more popcorn is sold in cinemas during scary films than any other genre. Perhaps there is something about a romantic comedy with Meg Ryan that doesn't require either sugar or salt.

Just in case you were wondering, the bit of popcorn that we eat is called the endosperm, but I bet even Redenbacher would have had a problem with that as a marketing name.

Popcorn brings me to a woman called Heather Ross and her underpants. Heather is in the panty business and her company, Munki Munki, sells women's undergarments with a difference. They are decorated with a cartoon complete with a scratch-and-sniff panel designed to remind them of their favourite men. This year you can buy handyman (cedar), BBQ guy (tangy BBQ sauce), mower man (fresh-cut grass), and cowboy (hay). I bemoan the loss of last year's couch-potato-man pants, which smelled of popcorn. I have no idea what Heather's school report predicted for her but I bet she was challenging.

I'd go to any lengths to avoid swimming

6 August 2006

I LIKE TO THINK THAT I have an insatiable desire for knowledge, but every now and then I learn something that frankly I could have done without. Did you know that, even as you sit reading this, more than a hundred million micro-creatures are swimming, feeding, reproducing and depositing waste just behind your lips? The idea that an entire colony of living beings is treating my mouth as an open-air lido for summer fun I find deeply disturbing. Add to that the staggering statistic that the average human in one lifetime produces enough spittle to fill two swimming pools and you may start to think about putting up miniature signs in your cheeks urging 'No running, petting or diving.'

Today is the eightieth anniversary of the first American woman to swim the English Channel. Gertrude Ederle managed it in 14 hours, 39 minutes, breaking not just the equilibrium of several jellyfish but also, as I understand it, the men's speed record. I once met a man who had swum the freezing waters of the Bering Strait and I asked him the same question I would have put to Gertrude – why? Surely there was a ferry with a buffet service that would have done just as well.

There are instances when I see the point of swimming – for example, to avoid unnecessary drowning. Some creatures have no choice. The tuna has to keep swimming at all times. Apparently, without a continual flow of water across its gills, it suffocates.

I see the point of swimming for the tuna, but even in these balmy summer days I am not sure humans were meant to be aquatic. In 1927, when the Hollywood director Cecil B. DeMille was making his epic *King of Kings*, he was worried that the actors who were to play Jesus and Mary might do something to compromise their holy screen image. His two stars, H. B. Warner and Dorothy Cummings, were required to sign contracts in which they undertook not to be seen doing any 'un-biblical' activities. These included playing cards, visiting night clubs, riding in convertibles and swimming. It would seem that DeMille's Christ could walk on water but not get in it.

I have friends who swear by swimming. They will tell you that swimming a quarter of a mile is the exercise equivalent of running one mile. I have to say that that information doesn't encourage me, as I don't fancy doing that either. Not long ago I met a world champion swimmer who was immensely fit, but had no conversation whatsoever, which was not really surprising. Swimmers spend a lifetime devoted to a sport where everyone sticks to their lane and whose key lesson is how to avoid hitting your head on the tiles as you get to the end of the pool.

To be fair, there are aspects of competitive swimming that I enjoy. Who could fail to have lost their hearts to the swimmer from Equatorial Guinea nicknamed 'Eric the Eel'? Eric Moussambani represented the aquatic hopes of his nation in the 2000 Olympics on the wildest of wild cards. He had first dipped into a pool just eight months previously and had never seen one that was full-length. He won his 100m freestyle heat by default when his fellow competitors were disqualified for false starts and he completed the final in twice the time of everyone else.

Sadly, some of the more esoteric aspects of pool competition have disappeared over the years. In 1900 the second modern Olympic Games were held in Paris and included underwater swimming. Competitors got two points for each metre swum underwater with an additional point for every second they stayed below the surface. Tragically, Denmark's Peder Lykkeberg only managed second to local boy Charles de Venderville. Peder stayed underwater longer but managed a shorter distance. It is hard to imagine the tension in the crowd who were watching an event that no one could see.

Just out of interest: on average, sardines live to be fourteen years old, which brings me back to my view that swimming is fundamentally about staying alive in water. There was a millionaire who had a twenty-first birthday party for his daughter. He filled the pool with alligators and told all the young men present that anyone who swam a length could have either his daughter or a million pounds.

One fellow did just that and as he left the pool the amazed millionaire asked, 'What do you want most? The money or my daughter?'

'Neither,' replied the swimmer. 'I want the guy who pushed me in.'

Don't let a lack of talent hinder you back

13 August 2006

THE OTHER DAY, I FANCIED going to the south of France. I was halted in this enterprise only by my failure to plan ahead, and the large body of water in my way when I reached Brighton. Ever one to turn the clouds of calamity into the sunshine of surprise, I opted for the next best thing – cream tea at the Grand Hotel.

There is something inexorably soothing about interrupted travel plans being replaced by the dabbing of clotted cream off summer shorts with a linen napkin. Sated, I returned to my car only to find someone had placed an advertising flyer on my windscreen. It asked, 'Have you got what it takes to be a star?' and then proceeded to provide the website address that would provide me with the '1st step 2 success', if not, obviously, the first step to spelling ability. It claimed to be the 'world's first truly interactive and diversified talent site', through which I might become 'the best talent of 2007'.

The word 'talent' was everywhere, and it made me stop and think. These days, hardly anyone refers to stars as having talent. Frankly, the modern celebrity usually has no discernible skills, is discovered by chance and is often marked out only by an inability to sound consonants clearly.

It reminds me of Desi Arnaz, who for years was the on- and off-screen husband of the genius Lucille Ball. Despite spending years in America, he never mastered English fully and his thick Cuban accent made the words 'recognised talent' come out as 'recognise Stalin'. Of course, these days recognising Stalin on television would probably be all you had to do to win a million pounds.

*

124

Even in the acting game, things have changed. Gone are the days when a thespian with the help of a versatile make-up box and sixpenny collection of moustaches could turn their hand to any character. Today, it is less about acting and more about resembling. I once got the part of Charlotte Rampling's assistant in a film because she was playing a member of the European Parliament and my Dad happened to be an MEP. As the great French dramatist Henri Bernstein said, when he visited Hollywood in the 1950s, 'Genius and geniuses every way I turn. If only there were some talent!' These days even the joy of the talent portion of beauty pageants is a rare beast. I once took part in the annual frog-jumping competition at the Calaveras County Fair in California, where I had the great pleasure to meet that year's Miss Calaveras, crowned for her outstanding talk on the role of the tractor in agriculture. This year, Kaileen O'Brophy clinched the crown with a dance from the Hansel and Gretel ballet, which sounds a lot less fun.

So reluctant is the modern world to distinguish anyone via a talent ranking that, at the other end of the scale, we don't even produce true awfulness. As a fan of the singing of Florence Foster Jenkins, a woman with little notion of pitch, rhythm or indeed a recognisable note, I do at least love the person who aims for notoriety in a field for which they have no discernible aptitude.

It is time, for example, to restore the late lamented Amanda McKittrick Ros to her rightful place in the literary canon. Once admired by both Mark Twain and Aldous Huxley, she was a writer of such awfulness that anyone who has ever read a book can only stand back and admire. Who can surpass her musing upon the inspirational Poet's Corner at Westminster Abbey:

Holy Moses! Take a look!
Flesh decayed in every nook, Some rare bits of brain
    lie here,
Mortal loads of beef and beer.

I will tell you only that her ode to Easter begins, 'Dear Lord, the day of eggs is here,' and leave you the joy of discovering the rest.

I don't even mind if someone's talent is obscure – an ability to read barcodes or distinguish a make of car from the sound of its door slam. There's an American group called the Beat Box Boys, whom I haven't seen but, apparently, their act involves one man beating boxes while another rips duct tape off a fat friend. About 100 years ago there was a man called Le Pétomane, who could pass wind to the tune of 'The Marseillaise'. He was so popular that Parisian audiences had to have medics on standby to deal with the hysteria. That is talent.

Inspired by the word, I went home and accessed the flyer's website, but it is still under construction. I suspect this suggests not only that I shall not become the best talent of 2007, but that the organisers, in their quest for skill, should have started in the IT department.

It's all just one big arcade game

27 August 2006

JUST IN CASE YOU WERE thinking of going out today, may I remind you that it was exactly nine years ago that a camel, minding its own business at Knowsley Safari Park, Merseyside, was killed by lightning. The chances of this happening are apparently slight. You are about as likely to be fried from above as you are to go to eternal rest by falling out of bed.

Indeed, I can go one further and tell you that in America there is a higher probability of meeting your maker via legal execution than by lightning strike. I think this says more about the American judicial system than it does about the vagaries of weather. Nevertheless, however unlikely the event, I would feel bad if I hadn't warned you.

It would seem that every minute of every day there are about 1,800 thunderstorms threatening camels and the rest of the Ark with lightning somewhere on Earth. For reasons I can't fathom, most casualties occur on a Sunday afternoon. My suspicion is that this is because it is a time when the bulk of golfers are adamantly lifting metal sticks above their heads in defiance of good sense.

Coming across the demise of the Knowsley camel reminded me of unlucky Major Summerford. The major was a good British egg who fought at Flanders. Sadly, in February 1918, he was knocked off his horse by a flash of lightning and paralysed from the waist down.

He retired and moved to Canada. Six years later he was fishing when, bam, more lightning, and his entire right side was paralysed. Summerford spent two years retraining himself to walk, only to be dashed once more by a bolt from above in the summer of 1930 that finally scuppered all movement. He died two years later and was laid to rest. Four years after his demise his tombstone was destroyed by lightning.

The study of lightning is called keraunopathology and, according to keraunopathologists, eighty per cent of all people hit by lightning are male, because men are five times more likely than women to be struck by a bolt from the blue. (I have read that in Britain two women were killed in 1999 by lightning conducted through the underwiring in their bras, but that claim hasn't, as it were, been upheld.)

Generally, I don't take part in games of chance. I regard the lottery as a stealth tax on people who aren't good at maths. I also think it is a small jump from studying the statistics of chance to believing that every coincidence helps build a case for the fact that we are all just participants in some giant arcade game. Albert Einstein said that coincidence was 'God's way of remaining anonymous', but it is sometimes hard to imagine why the good Lord would bother, unless he's just having a laugh.

There is, for example, the strange tale of Anthony Hopkins and his part in the film *The Girl from Petrovka*. The movie was based on a book written by George Feifer, and when Hopkins got the part he went to Charing Cross Road, in central London, to buy a copy. Unable to find one, he headed home. At the station, he noticed a book abandoned on a bench. It was the missing tome.

Two years later, while filming in Vienna, Hopkins was visited by Feifer. The actor apparently told his story to the author, who said he had lent his own copy of the book, complete with annotations in the margins, to a friend who had lost it in London. Well, yes, it was the very book Hopkins had found.

*

I can move swiftly from tales of curiosity to full-blown celestial conspiracies. You have only to examine the deaths of Presidents Lincoln and Kennedy to begin to see a curious pattern – they were both assassinated on a Friday while beside their wives, one in Ford's theatre, the other in a Ford motor car, they were elected 100 years apart, they both had seven letters in their last names . . . OK, it's getting silly but you catch my drift.

What does it all mean? Probably very little. We know that life is 'a tale told by an idiot, full of sound and fury, signifying nothing', so why do I care about all this? Well, here is a strange thing. I am hoping to move house by Christmas, but was recently told I had as much chance of that as a camel has of being hit by lightning. My question is: what are the chances of someone using that bizarre expression to me, the only person I can think of who might know that particular statistical possibility?

The real New Year starts now

3 September 2006

I FEEL THAT I KNOW you well enough to tell you that I spent the Millennium New Year's Eve in Sir Ian McKellen's bed. Now, before you decry the tabloid turn this august paper is taking, or you have to rethink hastily what you know about both Ian and myself, may I just explain that I was extremely unwell. I had that fatal combination of raging flu and a partner who insisted on partying.

We arrived at the event, my dearly beloved departed for high jinks on the roof, I went to lay the coats on the bed and laid myself there instead. The sound of midnight merriment echoed through layers of duffels, several military muffs and a rogue fox fur. I didn't mind. I loathe New Year's Eve parties. Inevitably, some gushing alcoholic will attach themselves to my hip, exuding happiness until the stroke of midnight, whereupon I will be treated to a roller-coaster ride down into their sense of failure over the past twelve, never entirely fruitful, months.

1 January never feels to me like the beginning of anything. I reserve that sensation for now – the first week of September. In Denmark we refer to it as the time when the rowan berries appear, and any Danish school child will tell you that that is when the new academic year begins. How I loved that time when everyone moved up a class; a graduation to higher status that suggested, if not proved, increasing age and wisdom. I left higher education twenty-six years ago, yet each autumn brings a curious urge to rush out, buy a new pencil case and think about wrapping brown paper around textbooks. How superior this new beginning is to the hideousness of 31 December. A

time of fresh starts – new children, new teachers, new subjects and new shoes.

I think it would do us all good, once a year, to sit somewhere different, approach the serious a little more seriously and even change the odd friend without everyone getting in a tizz. I like learning, which is just as well because education is supposed to be good for you. American research indicates that people with degrees live longer than those without. The fact that they may also have a higher standard of living and gym membership is not mentioned.

I liked school enough to wish I had been born a fish but, sadly, not enough to turn up every day. I discovered pretty early on in my American high school education that every subject on my timetable had a book written about it. This volume could be read quickly in private and thus leave the rest of your day for jollier activities. Unfortunately, this was not how either my parents or the staff viewed my schooling and, after a rather spectacular 'failure to attend', I was packed off to a British boarding school with high walls and a contract with a keen installer of barbed wire.

Locking children up during their formative years is nowhere near as popular as it used to be. Even today I marvel at the money my family were willing to spend in order to leave me hungry and cold. I was not in the least bit surprised, some years ago, when a British hostage was released from a fairly desperate confinement in Libya and declared that anyone who had been to boarding school would not have found the conditions the least bit troublesome.

Having trouble with learning establishments, rather than learning, seems to be a common trait among those in show business. The great Italian film director Federico Fellini was sent away to school when he was seven and promptly ran away to follow a travelling circus. The genius comedienne Lucille Ball was kicked

131

out of drama school in New York City, accused of being too quiet and shy; Peter O'Toole attended a Catholic school where the nuns tried to beat his left-handedness out of him; and, when he was fifteen, Sylvester Stallone's school chums voted him the one 'most likely to end up in the electric chair'.

In 1998 a retired Swiss teacher, who was 105 years old, was ordered to attend infant school in his home town of Echallens. It seems a computer had read only the last two digits of his birth date and cut a century off his age. I love the idea of him trundling along with all the town's five-year-olds to start all over again. I wouldn't mind such an error in the slightest. In fact, this time I'll even promise to turn up every day. Happy New Year everyone.

A bad ad? There's no such thing

10 September 2006

WHEN I WAS A KID in the States there was a television ad that made the briefest of appearances but in our house was never forgotten. It began with what seemed to be a close-up of someone's bottom. Slowly the camera pulled out as a deep voice announced, 'This is a peach.' A hand came into shot with some sandpaper which was then rubbed down the longitudinal crease of the round fruit. 'Would you do this to your peach?' asked the voice and then cheerfully recommended a brand of toilet tissue.

We thought it was hilarious. The authorities thought it was scandalous and the ad was never shown again. We were also fond of a doll called 'Growing Up Skipper'. She had long blonde hair and her breasts grew when her arm was turned.

Personally, I like old ads. There is an innocence about my March 1950 copy of *Housewife* magazine (price 1s), in which smiley women recommend Amazing Oxydol to give 'sparkling new life to your whites'. There are ads for the Prestige egg-beater, which 'lasts a lifetime', and cartoons of the 'cheery Welgar Boy', who apparently 'stands for Shredded Wheat'.

My favourite is a small cartoon strip called 'Mrs Crisp' in the Weetabix cereal ad. Mrs C is an older lady chatting to a young housewife called Sally.

Mrs Crisp: I called to return your pastry bowl. Having elevenses?
Sally: No, this is my lunch. I can't cook on Mondays: the washing fags me out so.
Mrs Crisp: But why not have a Weetabix? There's no cooking at all – I've a packet here . . .

133

The ad raises many questions. What kind of woman is so kitchen-equipment poor that she has to borrow a pastry bowl yet happens to have a packet of cereal about her person? Why would you ever cook elevenses?

Further back in time, I have a delicate copy of the April 1914 issue of *Housewife* from the States. Apart from explaining that 'The best friend of a hostess is the Victrola', the magazine also has whole sections entitled 'Unusual Uses of Ivory Soap'. If you ever worried about how to clean a lace door panel, you can at last relax.

With the advent of the modern digital system on television I find I rarely watch anything at the time of broadcast. I tend to tape things or store them or digitise them and then view later. The upshot is that I whizz through the adverts and it occurred to me recently that I might be missing another great peach paper or Skipper moment. Sadly, I don't think it's the case. Women on television still seem to be stuck in a 1914 or 1950 *Housewife* timewarp of worry about the stains their kiddies get on white tops. Personally, I feel that rather than asking 'How on earth will I get this blood out?', these mothers might want to question what kind of day little Johnny must have had at school in order to end up like that.

The interesting thing about ads is that they tell you something about the age and it isn't always modern. Archaeologists have discovered a 3,000-year-old ad from Thebes calling for the recovery of a slave: 'For his return to the shop of Hapu the Weaver, where the best cloth is woven to your desires, a whole gold coin is offered . . .' Hapu wants his slave but he doesn't mind making a pitch in the process.

Sometimes, of course, advertising happens unintentionally. There was a gruesome television series in Japan called *Shitsurakuen*, or, if that's not a name you want to put on your

134

T-shirt, 'Paradise Lost'. In this 1997 middle-class mid-life crisis drama some of the main characters killed themselves by mixing poison with Château Margaux. The upshot was not a surge of realisation about the fundamental good things in life but an explosion of demand for red wine. According to advertising agencies, the death by claret not only pushed up red wine sales but wine glasses as well.

Apparently advertisers don't like clever or insightful television programmes because such fare encourages people to discuss what they've seen during the ad breaks. This would explain much about the current state of broadcasting.

Perhaps intelligence will have to be done by stealth, as Alfred Hitchcock did in the film *Lifeboat*. He is famous for making a cameo appearance in each of his movies, and here he surpasses himself. Someone on board the boat is seen leafing through a newspaper and there is a glimpse of a weight-loss advertisement. Hitchcock is in both the 'before' and 'after' photos and the pictures are exactly the same.

Bitten by the travel bug (literally)

17 September 2006

I HAVE BEEN TO SUDAN and have returned a stone lighter and breathtakingly sober. The country is gripped by temperance laws. Indeed, the weight loss and sobriety suggest the entire place could be marketed as next year's ethnic alternative to a stay at The Priory. I also have sufficient mosquito damage on my legs for a Braille reader to spell out: 'I went to Sudan and all I got were these lousy bites.'

Apart from operating as a walking blood bank for our malaria-infested friends, I worked hard to try to stay healthy. This, I have to tell you, was not easy. Suffice it to say, the largest country in Africa is not quite tourist-ready and I stayed in what can only be described as challenging circumstances. I think the closest I have ever ventured to contracting a disease that would pique the interest of the School of Tropical Medicine was while staying in a shack in the town of Kadugli, owned, ironically, by the World Health Organisation.

I was travelling with an all-male film crew. It's not the first time I've spent weeks on end journeying as not only the solitary female but also the only person with a passing interest in hygiene. Bouncing along mud tracks in a mist of bromohidrosis (the correct term for smelly sweat, in which bacteria chomps away at dead skin cells making odourless sweat suddenly less fragrant) brings out the nanny in me. I am heard relentlessly booming from the back of the Land Rover, 'I've got moist towelettes for everyone and let's not forget our crevices.' We ate what was mouth-wateringly described as 'cow and rice', keeping our heads close to the plate so as not to catch a glimpse of the kitchen.

*

At another time, I shall write about my experiences in this extraordinary and neglected nation, but I returned thick with grime to an extraordinary coincidence. It was on this very day, 17 September, in 1683, that a Dutch scientist first reported the existence of bacteria. I arrived, as it were, just in time for bacteria's birthday. Antony van Leeuwenhoek had been fiddling with his teeth and thought he'd take a peek at his plaque under the microscope. Here he discovered a host of living things – indeed, a single drop of liquid may contain fifty million of these tiny free-living cells. Van Leeuwenhoek opened up the entire world of miniature wiggling life to science but it is here that I separate myself from the scientific mind. I have been cleaning my teeth for years and have never once been tempted to have a closer look.

I discovered that we are awash with the stuff. If you could count all the bacteria on your skin, the number would be roughly equal to the population of humans on earth. We are all vast colonies of microscopic life in which, just like the tribes of Sudan, some are friendly and some are not.

On the whole, I think it is something most people prefer not to think about. The first ever British demand for film censorship occurred in 1898. Far from being about what the butler saw, it was to do with what he served. A scientist named Charles Urban made a film showing the bacterial activity in a piece of Stilton. The cheese industry (presumably known as the Cheese Board) was outraged and demanded that the horror flick be banned. This was not something people wanted to spread on their crackers.

Finding clean water was a challenge on the trip and consequently I, like my Dutch science friend, have developed a greater interest in my teeth. I usually clean them assiduously because I have a deep loathing of the dentist. I once read a curious account of dentistry in eighteenth-century Paris, which I think scarred me for life. It seems that early French dentistry

137

was pretty barbaric and even the king, Louis XIV, received brusque treatment. He had several teeth pulled by an over-zealous dentist, which left him incapable of eating soup. This was a shame, for the king liked soup, but every time he tried, it cascaded out of his nose. There is a lesson here about never sitting opposite bouillabaisse-eating royalty and about checking your dentist's credentials before you say 'ahh'.

Thinking of the king, I was immensely careful not to swill my mouth in the brown waters of either the Blue or the White Nile that dripped from irregular taps. I purified the water and used iodine to kill the bacteria that remained. The only thing I forgot to do was put away my toothbrush. I returned one afternoon to find our guard happily brushing away at his own teeth with my brush and smiling at its efficacy.

As a quietly pleasing aside – the food-poisoning bacteria, *Salmonella*, was named after an American pathologist, Daniel E. Salmon. I don't know where the 'ella' part came from – perhaps a quiet homage to his wife.

My odd socks taste delicious

1 October 2006

WHEN I WAS AT BOARDING school, there was a particularly repellent dish served monthly which consisted of sausage meat baked with a potato topping. It was a meal that made even the youngest participant grieve for the wasted life of a pig. The headmistress called it 'Chef's Special', but to those of us sitting below the salt it was 'Muck Up'. I think the names of foods are very important. On my last great African sojourn, I spent a month eating what was perpetually described as 'cow and rice'. Somehow, this moniker did nothing to heighten the appetite, particularly as any actual connection to a cow could never be verified. Perhaps if it had been named 'Dinka Delight' or 'Sudan Surprise', I might have approached the meal with more salivation.

Some years ago, a famous *smorgasbord* restaurant in Copenhagen named an open sandwich after my late father, Claus Toksvig, a distinguished Danish broadcaster. Here, at last, was fame for the entire family. While our forays into the world of television and radio will inevitably fade into the ether, no one will ever be able to take away our claim to a fine smear of liver pâté with a bit of a gherkin garnish on pumpernickel.

Often the names of dishes act as a wonderful reminder of people from the past. There is Chicken Tetrazzini, named for the amazing operatic soprano Luisa Tetrazzini, who warbled her last note in 1941. Tetrazzini was a substantial girl. Indeed, if the phrase 'it ain't over till the fat lady sings' were taken to heart, everything would have shut up shop each time she performed. Unlike today's girth-obsessed performers, Luisa revelled

139

in her rolls and often spent time before performances eating buckets of pasta with her friend Enrico Caruso.

There was a celebrated evening when she had prepared to sing the role of Violetta in *La Traviata* by eating vast quantities of spaghetti. Come the pivotal tragic death scene, when her co-star John McCormack attempted to raise the dying Violetta in his arms, he found that not only was she immovable, but her body had all the sensual appeal of a pair of Michelin tyres. His inability to raise her off her deathbed sent Luisa into fits of giggles. The curtain descended on Verdi's masterpiece with the two principals unable to stand as a result of hysterical laughter.

Then there is the Margarita cocktail that reminds us of the Tijuana bartender Enrique Bastante Gutierrez, who invented a drink for a dancing girl called Margarita Cansino, who grew up to be Rita Hayworth, and there is a story about the Peach Melba and Dame Nellie that, sadly, I can't repeat.

The sandwich itself, of course, was named after John Montagu, the Fourth Earl of Sandwich. He spent much of his time as a plenipotentiary, not a career path that was ever suggested to me at school. He didn't devise the meal; he was just partial to keeping meat juice off his fingers. The invention of the sandwich is credited to the ancient Jewish sage Hillel the Elder, who was said to make a mean matzo and lamb combination.

Thinking of him always reminds me of a Jewish friend of mine from New York, who once explained to me that all Jewish festivals come down to the same three elements – they tried to kill us, we survived, let's eat.

I mention all this because, the other week, I was in Silverdell, a wonderful independent bookshop in Kirkham, Lancashire. The shop manages to attract every writer in the world to visit – the secret is ice cream. In addition to the literary offerings, Silverdell offers home-made ice cream and takes the time to invent a new flavour for each visiting scribe.

140

I was invited to sign my books and sample my signature dish. At last the Toksvigs would have a pudding to go with their main course. What might it be called, I wondered? Sandi's Sundae? Toksvig Tutti-Frutti? No. Sandi's Odd Socks, based on a column I once wrote about my inability to match my footwear. It was meant to be humorous, not the starting point for a culinary creation. Nevertheless, the rich vanilla ice cream shot through with lime and strawberry was delicious and I was thrilled to bits.

I also felt better about my African cuisine after I read a story that made my trip seem like a picnic. It seems that, in January 1950, Victor Biaka-Boda, a former witch doctor who represented the Ivory Coast in the French Senate, decided to tour his nation's hinterlands to reach out to the electorate and find out what they lacked. He quickly discovered the answer was food. His constituents ate him.

A toast to the absent bridegrooms

8 October 2006

I EXPECT IT IS COMMON knowledge but I'll tell you anyway – the current top price for a good-looking Dinka bride is 200 cows. I know this because I recently happened upon two families and, frankly, a lot of cows, hammering out a wedding contract in the African bush. Neither bride nor groom was present, which I suspect was just as well. There is nothing more likely to kick-start a marriage in the wrong direction than the knowledge that the starting price your beloved sets upon your head is two Friesians and a goat.

The absence of the lovebirds reminded me of Ingrid Bergman, probably the most beautiful woman ever to grace the silver screen and someone with an obvious large herd price-tag. Miss Bergman (she'll never be Ingrid to me) shocked Hollywood in 1949 with the revelation that she was expecting a child through her affair with the film director Roberto Rossellini. This led to one of my favourite broadcasting moments, when the gossip columnist Louella Parsons was heard to wail: 'Ingrid, Ingrid! Whatever got into you!?'

The idea that some people had sex before marriage used to be kept pretty quiet. Imagine the shock, for example, when in 1915 President Woodrow Wilson's second wife, Edith Bolling Galt, inadvertently let slip her premarital indiscretion with the American leader by declaring, 'When Woodrow proposed to me, I was so surprised that I nearly fell out of bed.'

In 1950 Bergman married Rossellini in Mexico and neither one of them attended the ceremony, for they married by proxy. 'We were very sorry not to be present at our own wedding,' she declared, 'but that doesn't make it count any less.' I don't know

142

who played Ingrid's part at the wedding but I do know that in 1957 two male attorneys stood in as actress Sophia Loren and producer Carlo Ponti when they married by proxy in Juarez, Mexico. It has left me with a delightful notion that somewhere in the world there is a Mexican lawyer who spent much of his career as a wedding stunt double for impossibly good-looking women.

Despite the rise of the cynical gene in society, it would seem that these days divorces are decreasing and marriages are on the up. I don't know if there is a worldwide trend for romance but apparently this month there have been so many weddings in Beijing that the chauffeur business has run out of cars.

Last week a dear friend announced that he had become engaged. His girlfriend was now sporting an obligatory diamond and being referred to as that short-lived item, the fiancée. They came to my house bearing a jar of Portuguese marmalade that showed a line drawing of the castle where he had popped the question.

They were so happy that it should have been nauseating and yet somehow the old-fashioned nonsense of it all was immensely engaging. I smiled, I got champagne out, we toasted, we gooed over the ring – in a nanosecond I had turned from thinking that the fastest way to a man's heart was through his chest with a sharp knife to being a drooling girl happy to discuss pageboy numbers. I was, of course, thrilled that she had found a sensitive, caring, good-looking man to marry, because usually these days those men already have boyfriends, but more than that I loved the idea that for a brief moment two lovely people were intensely happy.

Not that I am without some reserve. Give me another week and I will have moved from soppy sentiment to issuing the odd storm warning. As usual I draw the lessons from history. I think of Juliette Gordon Low, the founder of the American Girl Scouts. When she got married a grain of good luck got stuck in her ear, caused an infection and destroyed most of her hearing. Attila the Hun, a man whom many had tried to bring down, died of a nosebleed on his wedding night in AD 453, and to this day a bride stands to the groom's left at a wedding, leaving his sword hand free in case anyone tries to make off with his girl.

We live in a great cycle of repetition. Today would have been the seventy-first wedding anniversary of the American bandleader Ozzie Nelson and his wife, Harriet Hilliard. They became famous through a radio and then a television series called *The Adventures of Ozzie & Harriet*. The show starred the entire family, and America watched Ozzie and Harriet raise their boys. The idea that a musician called Ozzie could become more famous for his private life than for his talent is, of course, absurd.

The eunuch musical – director's cut

22 October 2006

YOU DON'T GET MANY EUNUCHS these days, or if you do they don't seem to advertise. It is, perhaps, the snip that dare not squeak its name. However, if films and novels of yesteryear are to be believed, there was a time when there were positive bands of these boys squeezed into tight trousers and singing songs high-pitched enough to disturb the livestock.

In the 1920s one Charles Pettit wrote a book called *The Son of the Grand Eunuch*. It's ostensibly a comic novel in which a young man, Li-Pi-Tchou, runs away with a woman called Chee-Chee in order to avoid losing his personal parts and thus having to follow his father's career path. Now I don't have the details of castration at my fingertips and I would question how the Grand Eunuch had a son in the first place, but that is not the thrust, as it were, of the piece.

Pettit's book is unusual in that the jokes emanate from the curiously untapped comedy areas of adultery, rape, flogging and obligatory castration. Even more curious was the decision by Richard Rodgers, the composer of such saccharine stalwarts as *The Sound of Music*, to turn the book into a musical. *Chee-Chee* opened in 1928 and not surprisingly closed shortly afterwards. You need to be a musical theatre nerd like myself to know that the show had a fine sideline in sniggering jokes about decapitation, which allowed Lorenz Hart to pen the lyric, 'We bow our heads in reverence, Lest we should feel their severance'. Rodgers clearly had his tongue in his cheek throughout the entire composition. There is, for example, a marvellous moment when Li-Pi-Tchou is taken away for the dreaded operation

145

and Rodgers quietly inserts several bars from Tchaikovsky's *Nutcracker Suite*.

The great choreographer Bob Fosse once said that the wonderful thing about musical theatre is that you can have a good time even in the crying scenes. I defy anyone to watch *West Side Story* and not sob wholeheartedly before leaving the theatre and declaring what a great evening it was. In the past few weeks two new musicals have opened in London and they are both good examples of how it is impossible to predict what will make a suitable show with songs. *Spamalot* premiered this week and is described as a 'new musical lovingly ripped off from the motion picture *Monty Python and the Holy Grail*'. It has stormed New York and is expected to do the same here. The story is loosely based on King Arthur, the Knights of the Round Table and quite a lot of women wearing very little. The ushers for the show wear T-shirts asking the question 'What happens in Spamalot?' and the answer is almost nothing. Fans of the film cheer mentions of shrubbery and killer rabbits, and I think it tells you everything you need to know when I explain that my twelve-year-old son thought it was 'well good' and I slept through the second half. I'm a big fan of having a plot and there was none. Indeed, I was so bored I even considered eating one of the Spam sandwiches offered in the interval.

At the other extreme is *Wicked*. It's based on a great novel by Gregory Maguire which explores the back-story to the characters from *The Wizard of Oz*. It has music by the genius Stephen Schwartz and a performance by the American Idina Menzel as the Wicked Witch of the West that is up there with any of the greats I have been lucky enough to see. It is spell-binding and Fosse's words ring true.

There's something about good musicals that gladdens the heart. Having said that, I do need to make a confession: I also have a passion for very bad shows. I don't mean boring. I mean really terrible. I collect them like a fan of roses who can't resist the thorns. Among my favourites is a show called *Out of the Blue*. Unbelievably, this was a musical about Hiroshima. It opened in the West End in 1994 and closed after seventeen days, leading the backstage crew to rename it *A Flash in Japan*. It had some lyrics that left me eating my cardigan with delight. There was, for example, the man seeking his daughter who was told by a singing doctor – 'She's alive and well and working as a nurse in my hospitell.'

Inspired by the notion that anything can be turned into a tap number, I am currently working on *The Three Sisters: The Musical*. Imagine how much jollier Chekhov would be if we added a mirror ball and a soft-shoe shuffle. I've already penned the opening number: Moscow, must go, I must go to Moscow. I will let you know how I get on with the rest.

Going up? I'll take the stairs

29 October 2006

I GOT STUCK IN A lift the other day and had to be rescued by the writer and former deputy chairman of the Conservative Party Michael Dobbs, a fellow passenger, a coat-hanger and some fairly intensive Anglo-Saxon invective.

Up until then, I'd rather liked lifts. Amusing things happen in them. Alan Coren and I used to ride in one to the BBC studios in Birmingham that was made by the Schindler Company and Alan never tired of tapping the sign and saying 'Ah, Schindler's Lift.'

The great funny man Jack Lemmon was born in one, Marlon Brando had a brief career as an elevator boy, and how pleased I once was when I read a sign in a French hotel lift that asked me to 'Please leave your values at the front desk.'

Since my enforced stay between two floors, however, I have been rather more inclined to take the stairs. I even took the time to check out Elevator World, which is a less-than-gripping website for the building transportation industry. I don't know if you're busy in mid-November, but if you are at a loss then I can tell you that America will be holding National Elevator Escalator Safety Awareness Week from the 12th to the 18th. Along with a rather scary-looking cat in dungarees called Safe-T-Rider, people from the Elevator Escalator Safety Foundation (EESF) will be teaching 'children ages 8–10 how to safely navigate elevators, escalators and moving walks'. Personally, I wonder which particular Amish county you would need to live in to require lessons in the mounting and dismounting of lifts and escalators.

Moving walks, I will admit, are rarer. The last one I went on was to Dove Cottage in Grasmere for Wordsworth's birthday, but I don't think that's what the safety people have in mind. There is more to the world of vertical transportation than I realised because not only does the EESF sell a two-hour instructional video (two hours?) but there has been a rush on for safety week and the tape is out of stock.

The original escalators were known as 'inclined lifts' and when the first one was unveiled in 1898 in Harrods in London, staff stood at the top offering brandy to anyone who had been made faint by the experience. Early escalators were made of wood and the London Underground was among the first to find a use for them. Urban myth has it that the clerk of works for the installation at Earl's Court Tube station was a one-legged man called Bumper Harris, and that on the opening day he rode up and down all day bumping about with his wooden leg to show it was safe. It is also said that he later retired to Gloucester to make cider and violins, although presumably not at the same time.

Escalators were popular because they did not require any attendants to assist the public. I am old enough to recall lift attendants. I liked the little conversations you had with the man in a peaked cap who knew just where the cambric handkerchiefs could be found.

A lift-boy would have been handy the other night. I had had a fine evening and was heading to the library in a rather ancient London club. Michael Dobbs, who is by way of being an old chum, was holding court in the foyer and we waved companionably as I entered the lift with a woman friend.

The size of an old phone booth, the *ascenseur* required the closing of both a wooden door and a metal gate. I gave no thought to our transportation until we came to a juddering halt between the first and the second floor. After some pressing of the alarm button we witnessed, through a small glass pane, the arrival of the porter carrying a coat-hanger. He waved it in a threatening and ineffectual manner at the moribund elevator for some time until I called out for him to get Mr Dobbs. Michael appeared cheerfully waving a screwdriver and soon the inner gate was open and the outer door was ajar by about two inches. Michael and the porter then did what boys do – they stopped to discuss the matter. I had bought a shoe-cleaning kit and sat on the floor having a spit and polish (at the height of a crisis I do at least intend to be smartly turned out). Meanwhile, my companion asked for the screwdriver to be passed to her. While the men debated and I cleansed, she quietly took a hinge off the door and let us out with no fuss whatsoever. There's a lesson there but I have no idea what it is.

Based on my experience, I'm thinking of starting a campaign to bring back lift attendants. Once again, let us all rejoice as an elderly man calls out 'Fourth Floor, Ladies Lingerie and Freudian slips' as if it had never been said before.

Jokes that go off like a rocket

5 November 2006

IN THESE DAYS OF HEIGHTENED religious sensitivity I thought it worth mentioning what a marvellous time of year this is for so many different faiths. There's Samhain, where fires are lit for the health of pagans; Guy Fawkes, where fires are lit for the health of Protestants; and Hallowe'en, where fires are light for party-shop owners. According to the Celts and Catalans, this is the time of year when the spiritual world is most able to make contact with the physical world. So, if you're expecting Granny back from beyond, now would be a good time to start leaving a light on. It's a time for fancy dress, jack-o'-lanterns and apple-ducking, all of which sound to me like a description of a disastrous date. I just wondered if anyone wanted to have a word about bonfire night and the Catholics?

I know that, generally, we like to think of 5 November as just a jolly day for a bit of a bonfire and a chance to get food-poisoning at the village fair, but the day does have a slight anti-Rome frisson. Let's not forget that Guy Fawkes, a good-looking ginger-haired fellow, wanted to blow up Parliament with King James I inside so he could start a Catholic rebellion and replace those pesky Protestants.

Up and down the land tonight, *The Bonfire Prayer*, which begins 'Remember, remember, the fifth of November, gunpowder, treason and plot . . .' will be boomed out by some ill-dressed town crier, whose voice will no doubt be lost as he gets to the bit that goes:

A penny loaf to feed the Pope. A farthing o' cheese to choke him.

151

A pint of beer to rinse it down. A faggot of sticks to
   burn him.
Burn him in a tub of tar. Burn him like a blazing star.
Burn his body from his head. Then we'll say ol' Pope
   is dead.
Hip hip hoorah!

Call me a liberal namby-pamby, but I'm not sure these words
provide the best route forward for inter-faith relationships.

You can see why Mr Fawkes had become annoyed. James I
had had a Catholic mum and everyone thought he was going to
be nice. 'Things,' they claimed back then, 'can only get better,'
but sadly James let himself be pressured by outside interests,
and by 1604 things had gone sour for the English followers of
Rome. Soon Guy and twelve chums had shoved thirty-six bar-
rels of gunpowder under the Houses of Parliament and
prepared for the big bang.

Betrayed by his own people, Guy was stopped in his tracks
and eventually hanged, drawn and quartered, which really is the
belt-and-braces system for dealing with undesirables. (A method
Dick Cheney has so far failed to endorse only because, I assume,
he hasn't heard of it.)

The nerves that ensued from this near-assassination rever-
berate today. 401 years later and the British monarch still visits
Parliament only once a year – and then only after someone has
checked the cellar.

There are bits of the celebrations that I enjoy. I love the fireworks, although each rocket reminds me of an incident I recall
from my childhood in America. There was a writer called
George Plimpton who, among other things, was a great fan of
pyrotechnics. In 1975, he determined to set the record for the
most spectacular Roman candle ever ignited. He helped to
create a 720 lb firework known as Fat Man which, it was predicted, would soar several thousand feet in the air. Plimpton

ceremoniously lit the fuse, at which point Fat Man gave a high-pitched whistle and blew a 10 ft crater in the ground.

That is, of course, nothing compared with the extraordinary stand-up comic Chris Lynam, who used to conclude his act by dropping his trousers and sticking a firecracker up his nether passage, before lighting what can only be described as an explosive finish. None of us on the comedy circuit could compete with his fiery finale, but then few of us had scorch marks in that area, either.

Today, of course, everything comes with a health-and-safety issue. Indeed, Ilfracombe Rugby Club, in Devon, this week held the first virtual bonfire, in which they showed a film of a previously lit bonfire where only people in hard hats were present. The film was projected onto a giant sheet strung between the rugby posts. The irony of people who play rugby being worried about health and safety seemed to have been lost on them.

Of course, I have my own safety issues now that I've brought up religion, and risk having the world's first *fatwa* issued against me by a Pope. To calm things, here is a quick joke that can offend no one at this time of year – did you hear about the policeman who found two men, one of whom was drinking battery acid and the other eating fireworks? He charged one and let the other off.

Just don't call me a lady

12 November 2006

I WAS AT KENSINGTON PALACE last week for dinner, when the Guy Fawkes fireworks were going off. Standing in the King's Retiring Chamber for State Secrets and Canapés, or whatever it was called, listening to distant bangs, gave a slight sense of what it might be like to be present at the onset of revolution. Indeed, non-royalist that I am, I had a brief moment of sympathy with Charles I's wearing of two shirts to stop his shivering as he waited to be separated from his head, or even Louis XVI wishing that his wife would stop banging on about cake.

I'm not a great one for titles, partly because I happen to recall that the epithet 'lady' comes from an Old English word *hlaefdige*, which literally means 'one who kneads bread' (from *hlaef* 'bread' plus *dige* 'knead'). It's an etymological history that to me takes a slight shine off the prestige. We Danes long ago dispensed with distinguishing the distinguished by title, yet the palace reminded me quite how much responsibility my native peoples bear for the British aristocracy.

Charles I was the son of Anne of Denmark and today we mark the passing of a significant Danish royal in British history: 12 November 1035 is the anniversary of the death of King Cnut, a name worryingly easy to misread. Cnut, or Canute, was the Danish king of England, Denmark, Norway, part of Sweden, Schleswig and Pomerania, thus making him the most significant Dane in Britain until Peter Schmeichel signed for Manchester United.

Canute was the son of King Sweyn Forkbeard of Denmark, a paternal name that would make any son determined to make his own mark on the world. Canute is best known for the story of his commanding the waves to stand back. It is a story with a typical sense of Danish social equality in it.

Canute was tired of court fawning and flattery and sat by the ocean to prove that he had no real power. He could not, he demonstrated, stop the power of nature. Less well known is that Canute was a bigamist.

Rather pleasingly, sex has played a large part in royal life for generations and the tour of Kensington Palace was full of titillation and innuendo. Who could fail to have been excited when, in 2003, the Public Record Office released papers that gave us a thrilling insight into the life of Wallis Warfield Simpson, who led Edward VIII to decide being King was not for him. She was, we discovered, a busy woman. Far from being the love-sick puppy so often portrayed, Mrs Simpson was also having an affair with a car salesman called Guy Trundle. Hard to imagine that while Ed was thinking of chucking in the crown, she was in the fast lane fiddling with another man's gear stick.

I don't know what Canute's English can have been like but it was, no doubt, better than George I's, who lived at Kensington Palace and never bothered with anything except his native German. George always reminds me of the one disastrous occasion that I met the Queen Mother.

The late royal visited my former university to celebrate the institution's 100th birthday. Her Majesty asked to meet a range of students, but foreigners were thin on the ground, so the authorities decided that I would do. I lined up in my academic gown and awaited the moment of introduction. But, busy entertaining my fellow undergraduates, I failed to notice the arrival of the royal party behind me. Tapped on the shoulder by the college principal, I turned to find myself face to face with this legendary woman. The principal announced me as Danish and, completely discombobulated, I put out my hand and produced a sentence of utter gibberish. 'What beautiful

English you speak,' the Queen Mother declared and moved on.

Her passing away led to yet another misunderstanding with my imperfect grasp of the language. I was unfamiliar with the word 'catafalque', the name for a platform that displays a casket. I thought the reporters covering the funeral said 'catapult' and, for a moment, could imagine it only as the quickest way to avoid the traffic between Westminster and Windsor.

Today, of course, is Remembrance Sunday and much nobility will gather to pay homage to the war dead. At Kensington Palace, I sat next to a gentleman who helped lead Britain into the war in Iraq. He has since been ennobled. He was charming and highly intelligent, but I kept thinking about Lance Corporal Allan Douglas. In January, the twenty-two-year-old was killed in Iraq while serving with the Highlanders. Is it me or does it make you wonder who ought to be getting the titles?

How do you solve a problem like Maria?

19 November 2006

IT'S THE ANNIVERSARY TODAY OF St Hilarius becoming Pope in 461. I don't know what he did to deserve such a fine moniker, but I do know that if modern congregations were led by hilarious bishops, chortling rabbis and the odd stand-up imam, then not only would the world be a cheery place, but I would also spend less time shouting 'lighten up' at the radio during 'Thought for the Day'.

Sadly, I lack the foresight to know which direction I shall head in when I finally go full length, but I do know I'm not going anywhere if no one is having a laugh. Existence, whether temporal or spiritual, ought, if nothing else, to be a source of amusement. It should be a place where, upon tasting a familiar mustard, one declares a sense of Dijon vu, and where one instinctively knows that serving 'fondant fancies' will always be funnier than plain cake.

I went to the opening night of *The Sound of Music* in London this week, which is as close as I get to having a religious experience and a good laugh at the same time. I first saw the film in Copenhagen with Danish subtitles on my seventh birthday. English-Danish translation being the tricky devil that it is, I may have missed out during the initial viewing, as the Mother Superior's line, 'Wherever God closes a door, somewhere he opens a window' was translated as 'Don't worry'.

I have since seen the film innumerable times – on one occasion I watched it backwards when Maria fell back down the hill and into the arms of the Nazis. I don't know what makes it so appealing. Perhaps it harks back to a simpler time when having seven children wasn't viewed as an obvious attempt to achieve a larger council house and where women taking the veil were none of Jack Straw's business.

On reflection, sing-along religion has featured heavily in my life. At the age of eighteen, desperate to work in the theatre, I got a job as a follow-spot operator on the musical *Jesus Christ Superstar*. The show, for its time, was a grand affair, bar the one evening when the Good Lord had consumed a liquid lunch and fell rather spectacularly off his cross at an inopportune moment.

I loved my job. Eight times a week I would crucify the poor man and then come home to what I grandly called my flat and what the council eventually called uninhabitable. It was a genuine garret, costing £9 a week, which consisted of a single attic room with no heating.

In my youthful dreams, I imagined that I was following in the footsteps of other fledgling writers. Indeed, I recall scribbling the word 'fireplace' on a wall as a tribute to Balzac. When he lived in a similarly unheated garret, he decorated his place by writing 'Gobelin tapestry with Venetian mirror' on one wall and over the fireplace 'Picture by Raphael'.

I longed for a fireplace and this week, rather thrillingly, I bought one from Alan Bennett. He wasn't, except presumably to himself, *the* Alan Bennett, but the spelling was the same and it reminded me of a story about Alistair MacLean which, were I giving a sermon, would provide a salutary lesson in the absurd nature of earthly fame.

Mr MacLean disliked giving interviews, so it was with some excitement that the production staff of *Desert Island Discs* in the early seventies learnt that the author had agreed to be interviewed by Roy Plomley.

Plomley arranged to meet MacLean for lunch so that they might sketch out possible questions based on the novelist's eight chosen records. During the meal, Plomley asked about

MacLean's writing. 'Writing?' replied MacLean, who turned out not to be the author of *The Guns of Navarone* at all, but the head of the Ontario Tourist Bureau. (Apparently, the show was recorded but never broadcast, which I consider a great shame all round.)

Anyway, I am hugely excited about what I shall always think of as my Alan Bennett fireplace. Before you imagine me sitting before glowing embers reading *Hilarius* and other improving texts please know that my ambition is to pretend to be George Craft's mother.

'Who he?' I hear you cry. Well, I can tell you that George Craft was one of the all-time great professional tobacco-spitters. (Anyone who thinks there is no such thing clearly missed this year's Spitoono Festival of the Redneck Performing Arts in Clemson, South Carolina.) At the age of seventy-five, George retired after setting fourteen world spitting records. 'I learned all I know about tobacco-spitting from my mother,' he once declared, proudly. 'She could hit the fireplace from any spot in the room . . . and never got a dab on the floor!' Hilarious.

An adulterer's guide to angling

26 November 2006

DO TRY NOT TO BE impressed by my versatility but, on paper at least, I am having an affair with myself. I am between homes at the moment, which suggests either a rather forlorn plea to Madonna for adoption, or familiarity with eviction procedures. In fact, I have sold my former house and am a considerable time away from moving into the next one.

Anxious not to get tied into a lengthy lease, I booked a 'serviced apartment' for a few months and paid up front. Some time later, I was rather shocked to find a bill for a substantial sum listed on my credit card as 'fishing equipment'. I know fishing is wildly popular but it's not for me. It's not that I think we should all rush to liberate the chaps from the chippie into a home for battered fish, I just don't like any activity that involves wellingtons. The boots are fine, but I have yet to find a pair of socks willing to play the game.

Confused by my alleged purchase, I made some enquiries and discovered that my new residence is often used by businessmen who, how can I put this … dip their rods in fresh waters? Anxious to keep this fact from their loved ones, they list the payment as a massive sporting outlay which wives and partners presumably accept as the piece of cod which passeth all understanding.

Apart from feeling as though I should have thought through my underwear every time I arrive home, there are some definite benefits to my new life. I have discovered, if only briefly, how liberating it can be to live somewhere where you have no chores. Nothing needs fixing or sorting, most of my clothes are in storage and someone else does the cleaning. The place is, however, not in a locale where anyone not plunging into the delights of the deep sea would want to linger. Washed up in central London with no washing-up to occupy me, I have become something that never occurred to me – a tourist.

I've always loved a good cemetery. How easily I can wile away the hours, as I did once in Ealing pondering an epitaph for a woman who 'died unexpectedly in Bournemouth'. (Which bit do you suppose was the more unexpected – the death or being in Bournemouth?) Today being the anniversary of the death of that Scottish man of the cloth, John Spottiswoode (1639), there can be no better place to spend the afternoon than his final resting place – Westminster Abbey. John had had a tricky life, having at one time been accused of incest, adultery and sacrilege all at the same time – a feat achievable only by the most dysfunctional of families. In the end, Charles I came through for him and he was buried with great pomp and circumstance and 'at least 800 torches', which suggests a cracking game of hide-and-seek.

The first King Charlie was responsible for a number of Westminster interments. He was the benefactor of the poet Ben Jonson who, despite being a rival to Shakespeare, concluded his life in penury. Jonson humbly asked Charles if he might have a square foot of burial space in the Abbey. The king obliged and exactly one square foot was provided, requiring Jonson to be buried standing up.

The last time I was at the Abbey, a security guard, also called Ben (Hamlin), and I stood looking at the display of poppies marking Armistice Day. We reflected what an ecumenical place the Abbey is. Indeed, the burial of Thomas Hardy there should give heart even to agnostics. Tom was devoid of religious belief and his wish was to be buried in his beloved Wessex. Someone in Baldwin's government, however, felt the Abbey was the only place for so distinguished a man.

161

It was agreed with Mrs Hardy that the writer's ashes would be interred at Westminster, but his heart would be laid to rest in the country. The heart was removed at Hardy's home, Max Gate, in Dorchester, by one Dr Nash-Wortham and the body sent by train to London. The lonely organ, not due to be buried until the next morning, was said to have been placed in a biscuit tin overnight, but local rumour suggested it was 'got at' and consumed by the cat in the small hours.

The free giving of one's heart in life can occasionally require a gap between existence and memorial in the Abbey. It took the naughty Oscar Wilde ninety-five years to get recognition there, while Lord Byron had been dead 145 years before he was forgiven and given an inscription in Poet's Corner. How wonderful to have such literary talent that it deserves even a square foot of Abbey space. Sadly, I lack even the racy love life. I wonder if I should try to spice things up a bit? I never thought I'd say this, but does anyone think I ought to take up fishing?

Death by falling pigs and tortoises

3 December 2006

I'VE BEEN AWAY FOR A week in a log cabin. It's a place I go when I need to escape. The small, rather basic hut is in Scandinavian woods by a small, still lake. It is, if you like, the sort of place Laura Ingalls Wilder might live if she were being filmed by Ingmar Bergman. It has no phone and it would never occur to anyone to deliver a newspaper. Consequently, I always return to the world like a bear, blinking from the cave of hibernation, bemused to discover what is being considered news.

The story on everyone's lips was, as far as I understood it, that a Russian spy might or might not have been killed using radiation in a sushi bar. While, of course, I have deep sympathy with the gentleman in question and hope there is a speedy conclusion to the investigation, I have to confess it's the sort of tale that brings out my dark side.

Many years ago, when I was a law student, I discovered a perverse fascination with uncovering civil and criminal cases where the victim had met death in an unusual manner. Nothing intrigued me more than someone's unexpected demise at the hands of a criminal wielding a chapati pan, or a company clumsy enough to allow one of its employees to reach a crease-free end in a dry-cleaning press.

Coming across a new and unexpected route to the next life always makes me think of the wonderful Graham Greene story 'A Shocking Accident', in which a boy's father is killed by a pig falling from a balcony in Naples and landing on his head. The poor lad goes through life unable to tell anyone about his father's untimely end without finding them sniggering.

While there is much to be said for ending one's days sitting quietly in a chair repeatedly asking whether you've had your tea yet, I do think there is also something rather thrilling about the grand finale.

Restaurant-based radiation strikes me as being in the same sort of league as using arsenic in wallpaper to kill Napoleon Bonaparte. The former French national hero died on the island of St Helena as a British prisoner. There ought to be a sense of the spy thriller about the story when you learn that his wallpaper contained a colouring pigment that released arsenic gas when it became mouldy. It seems St Helena is a damp place and wallpaper is given to mould but, sadly, no one knew this and it was all a horrible mistake. Death less by intrigue than by poor interior design.

Among my favourite departures are those where, to paraphrase Mr Shakespeare, nothing in the victim's life became them like the leaving of it. Take, for example, Pope Johann XII who, in 963, went in a manner that the Vatican probably prefers to forget. He was just eighteen and was beaten to death by the husband of a woman with whom he was having an affair.

Other deaths are tricky to classify. Strictly speaking, King Henry I of France went as a result of 'accidental defenestration'. In 1197, the king was reviewing his troops from a balcony window when a delegation arrived in the room behind him. He turned to greet them and, rather foolishly, stepped back at the same time. Losing his balance he reached out for his companion dwarf, Scarlet (honestly), and took the small fellow with him over the edge.

Even some of the great writers would have been hard pushed to have invented their own exit. The father of Greek tragedy,

164

Aeschylus, died when an eagle dropped a tortoise on his head. He had once been told he would meet his end by having a house dropped on him and, considering the value of the shell to the tortoise, the prediction may not have been far from the mark.

Another playwright, Tennessee Williams, a man who knew more about emotion and passion than most, died in the most mundane of accidents when he choked to death on a nose-spray bottle cap. Williams once said, 'Don't look forward to the day you stop suffering, because when it comes you'll know you're dead.' It probably never occurred to him that the suffering in question might be a common cold. The American short-story writer Sherwood Anderson has the words 'Life Not Death Is the Great Adventure' on his Virginian tombstone. He went after swallowing a toothpick at a cocktail party on an ocean liner.

In the Greene story, the son of the dad with the porcine death struggles all his life with others' grins as he tells his tale. When at last he falls in love, he realises that a test of his relationship will be telling his girl. He knows he has found true love when, instead of laughing, she quietly asks: 'What happened to the pig?'

Give traffic signals the red light

10 December 2006

JUST IN CASE YOU HAVEN'T had the time this week to keep up with the latest from the Environmental Audit Select Committee (well, it's heading for Christmas and we've all got a lot on) – allow me to assist. To precis its latest gripping report, I think it's fair to say that, regarding climate change, matters are neither good nor likely to get any better. Indeed, if you are able to read this without simultaneously choking then you're probably already on some form of artificial respiration and I wish you well. The committee of MPs accused the Department of Transport of not appreciating 'the magnitude and urgency' of the need to cut CO_2 emissions. Clearly, the report demonstrates a tragic ignorance of the work of the D of T, which frankly has better things to do than to start worrying about the future. Take this week, when no doubt staff were busy preparing birthday celebrations for the traffic light.

Yes, indeed, it was today in 1868 that the world's first traffic lights were installed, ironically enough, outside the Houses of Parliament. They resembled old semaphore-style railway signals and, rather like many of the nearby parliamentarians, were powered by gas. The device was operated by a policeman who was injured when it exploded three weeks later.

I've never been much of a car buff and, indeed, as a child, concluded from my father's driving that red meant stop, green meant go and amber meant go as fast as possible. My Papa, on the other hand, adored cars. When I bought my first one I phoned him in excitement. 'What kind is it?' he enquired. 'A yellow one,' I replied.

I suppose one's choice of car says something about one's personality. Being short, my selection has been limited to cars so small that putting on the seatbelt might make people think I'm wearing a rucksack. Arnold Schwarzenegger, the governor of California (the job of the satirist is truly redundant), declared in 2003 that he wanted 'a car that says I'm a man of the people'. He bought an Austrian Pinskower tank and had indicators and a cup-holder fitted as his concession to city driving. The present Pope might have ordered the same but, instead, he has a million-dollar Fiat that can withstand machine-gun fire and presumably enables him to go out and wave at the poor.

Of course, there is a need for some form of traffic calming. Who was it who said: 'I want to die peacefully in my sleep like my grandfather, not screaming and yelling like the passengers in his car?'

Yet, I do begin to wonder whether we shouldn't do what London cyclists already do and dispense with obeying traffic signals altogether. The Dutch town of Drachten has spent the past few years getting rid of every red and green light in the place. They've discovered that if you don't tell people how to behave en masse, then they start being more careful on their own.

Drachten was never the Formula 1 of urban movement but, like any other town, some people lost their lives to road death. In the past seven years, without stop lights, however, there hasn't been a single fatality. The huge success of this social experiment no doubt means that we'll never hear any more about it. The only time I can think of similar instruction-free streets was the time when yet another failed attempt to assassinate Fidel Castro resulted in a swathe of exploding shells missing the leader and melting all the street furniture in down-town Havana instead.

I'm not saying I am against all traffic lights. There are a few that I am keen on. The American basketball legend Wilt Chamberlain was said to have 'Love/Don't Love' traffic lights above his bed. While in the Danish town of Odense, the birth-place of Hans Christian Andersen, each pedestrian-crossing illumination bears a silhouette of the great man, complete with top hat and cane.

Then there is the traffic light installed in the Tipperary Hill area of Syracuse, New York, in the 1920s. The population was primarily of Irish descent and bands of boys religiously destroyed the light until one was installed upside down with the Irish green on top of the despised British red.

Like the burghers of Drachten, paying closer heed to others would be good for all of us. We might all slow down, start walking and start breathing again. Still, I doubt much can be done about some people's innate stupidity.

There is the old story of the man being pulled over by a police-man for doing 50 mph in a 40 mph zone.

'I was only doing 40!' protested the driver.

'Not according to my speedometer' replied the officer.

'Yes, I was!' the man shouted back.

'No you weren't!' the policeman said, beginning to get annoyed, at which point the man's wife leant over toward the window and said, 'Officer, I should warn you not to argue with my husband when he's been drinking.'

Why I love the pencil people

17 December 2006

ABOUT THIS TIME OF YEAR I often recall my favourite *Punch* cartoon. It is of a man in a Christmas paper hat chasing a cooked turkey that is running round the table. The exasperated man yells, 'Why didn't you tell me your brother was a faith healer?' It was, of course, the late, great *Punch* magazine that gave us the present-day meaning of the word 'cartoon', implying a humorous drawing. Before Mr Punch, the term applied solely to preliminary art sketches, which is good to know if you're heading for the current Holbein exhibition at Tate Britain expecting a lot of laughs.

I rarely go to look at art. I once left several perfectly good sangria bars in Barcelona to check out the Joan Miró exhibition, only to find Joan was a man and mostly he'd done the sort of pictures my kids used to put on the fridge.

The Holbein collection is amazing, not just for the art but also as a parade of portraits of people who had the misfortune to know Henry VIII. Holbein's work is remarkable, but even more astonishing is that he managed to work for the old King long enough to die in his own bed. OK, he died of the plague, but he did still have his head attached to his body. The show is a mix of 'cartoons' and full oil paintings and, of the two, I prefer the former. The fact that you can see that both Sir Thomas More and, frankly, Anne of Cleves could've done with a shave shows just how intense a line-drawing can be.

I love the skill involved in drawing and the simplicity with which an idea can be put across. In modern cartoons there is also such pleasure in the neat packaging of irreverence and the ability to deflate the over-inflated. As chance would have it, today presents a curious link between Henry VIII and my current favourite people of pencil, The Simpsons.

It was 17 December 1538 that naughty old Henry finally blew it with Rome, was excommunicated by Pope Paul III and forever made English church services less fragrant. The first episode of *The Simpsons* was aired in America 451 years later to the day. Homer and his gang have done more to prick the pomposity of modern life than anyone living and, despite being a few years too late, have had a go at King Henry as well.

There is a glorious episode called 'The Margical History Tour' in which Homer plays Henry, and his wife, Marge, plays Margerine of Aragon. Much misunderstanding ensues as an instruction to canonise Sir Thomas More leads to the poor fellow being shot out of a large weapon on a cliff top.

It is entertainment that my twelve-year-old son and I can watch together with equal pleasure. So often the script works on many levels. It reminds me of a cartoon that was popular in the 1980s called *Roger Ramjet*. Roger has saved the world and is meeting the American President. 'You've made a great impression on me,' says the leader of the free world. 'Thank you, sir,' replies Roger earnestly. 'I also do Ethel Barrymore.'

There is something about cartoons that has a universal appeal. Which of us can fail to be unnerved by the knowledge that, in 1979, when the tyrannical president, alleged cannibal and all-round bad egg of Uganda, Idi Amin, was deposed, his house was found to contain cases of old film reels of *Tom & Jerry*.

All this brings me to my recommendation for holiday viewing. Not everyone can get to the Holbein exhibition, and it may be that you just want to pull up the drawbridge and take a break. One of the glories of the internet is that it provides a canvas and exhibition space for the modern, unheard-of artist. If you are not already familiar, allow me to introduce Jennifer Shiman.

Ms Shiman is a cartoonist who, in her 30-Second Bunnies Theatre Library, recreates famous films in half a minute with a cast of cartoon rabbits. *Star Wars*, *Titanic*, Frank Capra's essential holiday film *It's a Wonderful Life*, *Brokeback Mountain*, and many other classics are all parodied by bunnies. Available free on angryalien.com, they are some of the funniest things I have seen and remind me how much we could do with a laugh in these dark months. It led me to think that I might hold a cartoon party, although one does need to be careful . . .

When Walt Disney wanted to celebrate the 1940 premiere of *Pinocchio*, he hired eleven vertically challenged people to dress up as the wooden boy and dance on the roof of the theatre. To keep the cast happy, they were given food and free beer. Sadly, they became so happy that the entire group stripped naked and began shooting dice on the theatre marquee. In the end, the police arrived, climbed onto the roof and took away all the puppet pretenders in pillowcases.

Just pass me that jubilee clip . . .

31 December 2006

I'M NOT SURE IT'S BEEN a good year for world peace. Reflecting on this, as another twelve months shuffle off into memory, conjures a curious Kafkaesque image of giant cockroaches and sanitaryware. It is said that, should there ever be a nuclear conflagration, it is likely that cockroaches will be among the sole survivors. Add to this the great architect Frank Lloyd Wright's suggestion that the post-holocaust horizon will be littered with that essential and astonishingly heat-resistant modern artefact – the china toilet bowl – and you see a poor future ahead for the picture-postcard business.

There is a curious connection between the two survivors – apparently cockroaches taste terrible because their fat is packed with uric acid. How ironic that the only living creature left on an earth with no queue for the loo would be one that didn't need to use the facilities.

Bearing this in mind, I feel I must be quick if I wish to start my new business. So, without further delay, allow me to announce that, come the new year, I shall be hanging up my quill and becoming a plumber. Yes, you will shortly see me zipping about town in a white van with the words 'Up and Plumbing' emblazoned on the side. Why this life change? Well, at the risk of doing myself out of my new-found work I have a secret to impart – plumbing is not that difficult.

There are not many who make the jump from show business to plumbing. The only example I can think of is the blonde actress from *Charlie's Angels* who was immortalised by having a tap named after her – the gold-plated 'Farrah Faucet'. My unusual career move has been born out of frustration: getting a plumber to call over Christmas was a task akin to getting erudition from John Prescott.

I've been doing up a flat with a friend. My dad taught me carpentry and my first foray into theatre was as a stage electrician, so putting in a kitchen is not a nightmare. Over the holidays, however, I reached a stage where water needed to flow. I made phone calls, I wrote begging letters, I took out small ads offering an exchange of services that would make my old Mother Superior blanch, but to no avail. No plumber would plumb, not even for ready money.

Years ago, I was inexplicably given charge of my school house junior netball team. I have had a lifelong zero interest in sports and absolutely no knowledge of how, or even why, they function. Aged eighteen, I led a group of intensely keen eleven-year-olds whose house had never won anything. They were a motley, mainly bespectacled crew in ill-fitting navy games uniforms, but they had hope in their hearts and I knew I couldn't let them down.

In the library I found a book entitled *Netball – Know the Game* and my crew and I resolutely went through it, chapter by chapter. The eleven-year-olds learnt the basics, I mastered shouting certain key phrases from the side, such as 'mark up' and 'go wide' with no real knowledge of when would be an appropriate time, and the rest of the story is frankly cup-carrying triumph. Since then, I have been confident that anything can be learnt from a book.

The Reader's Digest Plumbing and Heating Manual has changed my life. After just a few sessions with my printed mentor, I found myself waking up thinking I must pop to the shops for some jubilee clips, an olive and a 15 mm push-fit connector valve. Water flows both in and out of the sink, the washing machine sustains a cheerful hum over spinning suds and I have not had to deal with anyone sighing and moaning

173

while wearing their trousers low enough to think about parking your bike.

Oddly enough, I find myself in good literary company. It's a little-known fact that the poet Henry Longfellow was the first American to have indoor plumbing; and Sir Arthur Conan Doyle first earned a writer's crust by translating a German article for the *Gas and Water Gazette* entitled 'Testing Gas Pipes for Leakage'. OK, they didn't do the work themselves but they took an interest.

Misspending my youth in libraries means that I know that NASA once experimented with tilapia, a sewage-eating fish also called the 'toilet trout'. There was a notion that the fish could live in a space station swimming in waste water and eating the product before finally being eaten themselves. This year, someone gave me a Delia cookbook. The first recipe I came to? Oven-roasted Tilapia with Mango and Pawpaw Salsa. I just can't bring myself to cook it, but maybe as an unusual sideline in my plumbing work . . .
Happy New Year!

Magic moments in sign language

7 January 2007

FOR THOSE OF YOU WHO think that show business is a constant round of champagne and canapés, allow me to share with you that I spent a splendid New Year's Eve drinking beer in a working men's club in the small town of Padiham in Lancashire. At the top of a narrow cobbled street, we paid fifty pence to sign in as guests at the karaoke/bingo evening. A small mirror ball spun over the haze of smoke from a barrage of untipped cigarettes.

Shrouded in unmentholated mist, men sunk pints of Good Elf, while women in sparkly tops sipped at wine glasses of dry ginger. Jim, a hospital porter and a vision in beige, kicked off the singing by whipping off his bifocals with a flourish to dazzle as Perry Como. This was quickly followed by the Dean Martin of a portly fellow, clearly wearing a Christmas jumper to please a relative in the crowd. Mary, touted as 'quite the singer', was next, belting out a bygone hit that to my ears was made up entirely of vowel sounds.

It was another world for me, but what made it so extraordinary were the conversations that proceeded apace amid the cacophony. Although the mills are long gone, pretty much the entire club membership consisted of folk who had once toiled among the noisy looms. As a consequence there was not a soul in the room, apart from myself, who wasn't adept at both sign language and lip-reading. No need to turn down 'Magic Moments' in order to exchange news, take a drinks order and see if a dance later on was out of the question. It was like being in some foreign land, where I lacked even the rudiments of speech.

*

I can never go anywhere new without needing to know every-thing about the place, always using the excuse that I might pen a word or two about it. The neglected African-American writer and folklorist Zora Neale Hurston once wrote that 'Research is formalised curiosity. It is poking and prying with a purpose', and I found myself poking and prying into this unfamiliar life in the rolling fields that surround the majestic Pendle Hill.

There was much that baffled me. In the neighbouring town, I checked into a hotel where the parking spaces nearest the front door were reserved 'For Lady Guests Only'. I grew up staying in hotels, yet I have never seen such a sign before. Was this an old-world courtesy to make you smile or a taunt to motoring feminists? On the surface, so much seemed to echo a bygone era when the ploughman homeward plodded his weary way and, appropriately enough in the cradle of the Lancashire textile industry, I was reminded that today would have been Distaff Day.

The distaff was a sort of stick used for hand-spinning by women. The day after the twelfth day of Christmas was tradi-tionally when women returned to their household chores, while the ploughmen, presumably needing longer to recover, waited until the following Monday to head back out to the furrow. The term 'spinster' derives from women's preoccupation with their distaff duties, and it was common to refer to the female branch of a family as the distaff side. Apparently, it was a day of much spinning-related hilarity as the boys spent the day trying to set fire to the women's flax while the girls retorted with buckets of water.

Today would have been Zora Neale Hurston's birthday. She would have loved Distaff Day, for she spent her life document-ing folklore. She was probably best known for writing down African-American colloquialisms as near to actual speech as she was able. How I wish I had that skill with the splendidly straightforward Lancashire people I met. How intoxicating that there are still parts of the world where people don't speak Estuary English or conclude each sentence with the rising cadence of an Australian soap star. In the club, a woman mimed that she had seen me on television and then confided that she had read one of my books. 'Did you like it?' I foolishly enquired. 'It were all right,' she replied.

I was reminded of a story about King George VI and Queen Elizabeth visiting Lancashire during the Second World War. It was a time of great food shortages and their majesties were rather taken aback to be presented with a vast lunch. The Queen said rather tartly to the local mayor, 'You know, Mr Mayor, while food is so short in this country we don't have any more food on the table at Buckingham Palace than is allowed to the ordinary householder according to the rations for the week.'

'Ah well,' the mayor is said to have replied, 'then thou'll be glad of a bit of a do like this.'

A half-baked tale beats the truth

14 January 2007

THERE ARE STORIES THAT I want to be true and then there are stories that are true – making the distinction sometimes as tricky as finding those pesky weapons of mass destruction. It was hot news this week that a loaf could soon cost more than £1. Apparently, the world wheat harvest has been poor and wheat is the 'new gold' for some commodity traders, which must at least be a relief for the pit ponies.

In my local baker's, a farmhouse loaf is already £1.75 which suggests a village not awash with people living by the stuff alone. Bread is probably the only food substance that in some form or other is eaten by every race, culture and religion. Indeed, if you wished to bring all the factions together, then some new faith in which good news comes from a Star in the Yeast might be the way forward.

I grew up eating the dark rye bread known as pumpernickel, and here is where I prefer a good story to actual fact. It is said that the word 'pumpernickel' derives from the French sentence '*bon pour Nicole*', spoken with a German accent. The legend goes that a French cavalry soldier taking part in one of Napoleon's military day trips to Germany found that there was nothing to eat but heavy black bread. By chance, our hero had arrived in town on a horse called Nicole. Disgusted by the lack of baguettes, the gentleman of the cavalry is said to have declared the available bread good enough only for Nicole, or '*bon pour Nicole*'. The phrase stuck and became corrupted into 'pumpernickel'. There are several problems with this story, not least of which is the idea that a ninteenth-century French soldier would think Nicole was an encouraging name to shout when charging the Hun.

These days, bread has come a long way from horse fodder. How often in a restaurant have I been exhausted into silence by the choice of a range of breads baked with everything from sun-dried tomatoes to the truly organic brown stuff that contains small pieces of actual fieldmouse? Gone are the days when an English meal out was accompanied by two slices of white bread cut on the diagonal and lathered in margarine.

Ordering was easy in those days. I recall visiting my grand-parents in the 1960s for their annual holiday at the Lansdowne Hotel, Eastbourne. Each year, we went for one obligatory meal where the choice of starters consisted of a glass of tinned orange juice served in a tumbler on a doily-covered saucer or half a boiled egg, flat side down, covered in salad cream, or half a grapefruit with a single maraschino cherry. The main course was inevitably gammon with a large ring of pineapple on top, followed by a slice of Black Forest gateau.

Occasionally, my mother would go off piste and order a salad, consisting of half a lettuce, tomatoes cunningly cut into water lilies and a single spring onion the size of a truncheon. Anywhere serving prawns in Marie Rose sauce or melon and Parma ham, and the family had suddenly gone that bit upmarket.

Human beings have been eating raised bread for more than 6,000 years, and the word itself is part of our everyday existence. We still talk about the breadwinner, and even the word 'companion' means one with whom bread is shared (com: with; panis: bread). The bread referred to in the British news this week is white sliced – a foodstuff that both the French and the Danes find incomprehensible as a concept.

Why would you eat plastic when the baker will make you something nutritious? I prefer unleavened breads such as chapati and nan, although the former did cause the only bread-related mountaineering accident that I know of. In 1997, the British climber Alan Hinkes spent a lot of time and effort having a go at climbing the 26,000 ft-high Nanga Parbat mountain in Pakistan. About halfway up, he took out a chapati to eat. The bread's dusting of flour blew in Hinkes's face. He sneezed, causing a disc to prolapse and he had to go home.

These days, bread and menus in general have become catalogues of culinary choice that make my head spin. I long to whisper to the waiter, 'I don't eat lentils, otherwise just feed me.' I remember meeting a young Welsh singer, fresh from the valleys, who was going out to her first smart London restaurant. Anxious about what she should order, she called her mother, who advised her to order the special. Seated at a fine table in a fine restaurant with stellar company, she duly pointed to a box on the menu marked 'Special Today' and declared to the maître d', 'I'll have that'. 'I'm afraid you can't, Madam,' he whispered. 'That's the band.'

It's all downhill from here

28 January 2007

I'VE NEVER BEEN KEEN ON feet. They seem to me to be the frayed edges of the body and it is rare that one comes across anyone who immediately gives a favourable pedimental impression. It is therefore with some reluctance that I draw attention to the secret life inside my shoes, but I've got a stress fracture in my tarsal navicular. It's paying me back for my rather cavalier attitude in carrying it around all these years without a mention.

There are 206 bones in the human body and this is one I didn't even know I possessed. My medical DIY book tells me it is a 'small accessory bone', which makes it sound like something that ought to be teamed with a handbag. From the pain, I can tell you that the tarsal navicular hangs about in the middle of the foot near the navicular bone which is (and I feel even the orthopaedic geeks among you losing interest) the bone that goes across the foot near the instep.

Two things about this breakage annoy me: 1) It is an injury normally associated with running. Considering the pride I take in a slavish adherence to a sedentary life, this is terribly irritating. The next thing you know, people will be suspecting me of owning a tracksuit. 2) I am about to go skiing. Being Scandinavian, I do not consider skiing to be a stressful physical activity. You simply point your skis downhill and stop where it says *Glühwein*. It is something I can do as naturally as changing channels, but in more than four decades of skiing I have always used both feet.

I go skiing each year with a large party of family and friends, which includes my three children. Jesse, my eldest, has been

181

skiing since she was a few months old, when I would strap her to my front and whiz down a mogul field. She loved it. Indeed, one of her first words was the German for 'faster!'.

Teaching kids skiing basics is easy. There are, for example, three principal ways of stopping, of which the use of a tree is the least favoured. Safety, too, is not difficult. You shout 'ski' if a loose ski is coming down the mountain and 'avalanche' if the mountain is coming down the mountain. I love this time with my kids and am deeply annoyed to have broken a bone before I can legitimately shout 'Alp!' and have some wag reply, 'What's Zermatter?'

Today is the anniversary of the first ski lift in America (1934). It was a rope tow installed by Bob and Betty Royce, the proprietors of the White Cupboard Inn, in Woodstock, Vermont. They had seen something similar in Quebec that was run off a Dodge car, jacked up on blocks, with a rope looped around a wheel rim. Bob and Betty managed to create the first American mechanised method for mountain-climbing by using an engine from an old Ford Model T.

I can remember those rope lifts that shredded your mittens and yanked your shoulder out of its socket. In Austria, as late as the 1980s, they were powered by giant horses, who left a trail of unmentionable material that did nothing to speed up your skis but did warm up a chilly day.

The horses felt free to deposit at will such materials as can cause the skier endless trouble. Every female skier will tell you that there is nothing convenient about Alpine ladies' conveniences. I have a friend who refused to avail herself of the formal facilities and insisted on heading into the woods when nature called. Here she would pull down her *salopettes* and squat while still wearing her skis. How vivid is the picture in my mind of the day her skis failed to come to a complete rest. I was waiting on the slope when she suddenly reappeared, shooting out of the woods in a crouch position with her bare bottom flashing off downhill like a rapidly descending full moon.

I love everything about skiing. I love the swagger of the ski instructors. (Q. What's the difference between God and a ski instructor? A. God doesn't think he's a ski instructor.) I have seen great skiers with one leg and wonder whether it is too late to learn. I don't see why. There was the legendary mountain guide, Ulrich Inderbinen, who took up ski-racing at the age of eighty-two. He won every event that he entered. Of course, there were no other competitors in his age group, but I don't think that's the point.

Yes, stress fracture or no, I shall take to the slopes. Any bets on me breaking the other foot?

February is the cruellest month

4 February 2007

WHAT ARE PENGUINS CALLED IN the Arctic? Lost. They live in the Antarctic. I throw this in to try to cheer up a friend who is suffering from SAD. I don't mean she's sitting around feeling anxious about the state of the world. (Not that there isn't plenty to bring a furrow to the brow – has anyone considered the lack of privacy igloo-dwellers will suffer with global warming?) No, my friend has Seasonal Affective Disorder, otherwise known in this country as RMWIDLM (Remind Me Why I Don't Live in the Mediterranean). She hates the month of February because it's dark, grey and comes straight after January.

I'm not sure about February as a month. There was a newspaper story a couple of years ago about a Nepalese man who, having nothing else on in February, married a dog, hoping it would bring him good luck. Three days later, he was dead. It may be that the dog was particularly demanding (I hate to say it, but a real bitch), but it could also be that he failed to choose a propitious date. The Anglo-Saxons used to call this time of year Solmoneth (mud month) or Kale-monath, named after cabbage. The first suggesting the weather and the second the lack of excitement on the 'specials' board in local pubs at this time of year.

There are things of universal significance that have happened in February. Unfortunately, the only one I can think of was on 28 February 1983 – the day the final episode of the American television series MASH was aired. Hawkeye and his gang said goodbye at 11 p.m. Three minutes later, the use of water in New

184

York City rose by a record 300 million gallons, as an estimated one million New Yorkers flushed their toilets together.

Mostly, I think it's a month to avoid. Even the Russian February Revolution took place in March. Of course, that was due to everyone at the time working from different calendars. The Russians carried on with the Julian calendar long after everyone else had gone over to a daily Gregorian chant. Indeed, in 1908 (the last time the Olympics clogged up traffic in London), America won gold in the shooting competition because the Russians thought they still had another two weeks to show up.

I'm not one for the winter blues, but I would have no objection to harking back to the days when February didn't exist at all. That's before my time – in about 700 BC. Blame it on Numa Pompilius, the then King of Rome. According to legend, he succeeded Romulus, the feral lad who founded the Eternal City after being brought up by wolves (a method for raising world leaders that we might want to revisit given the disappointing performance of the current system).

Presumably, Romulus had been too busy fending off jokes about his hirsute mother to deal with almanac issues and so, for a while, the calendar jumped from December to March. I doubt that 3,000 years ago January and February were any more exciting than now, but Numa felt no toga-pocket diary was complete with a sixth of the year missing, so he spent a lot of time looking at the sun and moon, and came up with a 365-day lunar calendar. He popped in Jan and Feb with the only good news being that to make the maths work, February got only twenty-eight days.

So the good news is that the month is short, but for people with seasonal depression it can seem endless. There are drugs to relieve the worst symptoms, but my friend won't go to the doctor. She's a writer and dislikes the fact that the medical profession call what they do 'practice'. In order to combat the effect of the dark winter nights, she has a light box that provides, and I quote, 'dawn simulation'. I think being awakened by slowly brightening light must be pleasant, although I imagine that the cockerel must make a mess of the bedsheets.

My way out of dark times has always been humour and reading. There are many self-help books for depression sufferers, of which the most curious has to be a volume by Hiroyuki Nishigaki, called in its entirety (and I kid you not) *How to Good-Bye Depression: If You Constrict Anus 100 Times Everyday. Malarkey? or Effective Way?* Mr Nishigaki claims that tightening your posterior and 'denting' your navel will kiss depression goodbye. He says: 'You can do so at a boring meeting or in a subway. I have known 70-year-old man who has practised it for 20 years. As a result, he has good complexion and has grown 20 years younger.'

I'll give it a go, but I doubt it'll get to the bottom of things. I still prefer jokes. Two cannibals are cooking a clown in a large pot and one of them asks the other: 'Does this taste funny to you?'

Feel like death? Press button two

4 March 2007

THERE IS A JOKE IN our family that you can tell our local hospital is no good because it has a sign over the front door saying 'Guard Dogs Operating'. Mind you, give it five years and it won't be the sign we remember but the fact that we used to have a local hospital. I'm recovering from a bout of illness that has left me a stone lighter, with a profound admiration for the simple act of breathing and wistful for an age where medical help arrived with a kindly smile, a large black bag and sage words about poultices. Indeed, I reached a stage where I even became wistful for the kind of help the turkeys got from Bernard Matthews. Unable to walk or move my head, I made the mistake at the height of my delirium of ringing the emergency doctor helpline.

'Have you got a fever?' asked the woman on the end of the phone.

'Yes,' I said as my body released enough heat to power a small town in Wales.

'Are you coughing up phlegm?'

'Yes.'

'Does it have blood in it?'

'Yes. A lot.' My chest wheezed as if required to pluck air through cauliflower soup.

'Are you having trouble breathing?' she continued down her checklist like a small plane being cleared for take-off.

'I'm asthmatic and I can't manage my inhaler at the moment.'

There was an uncomfortable silence at the other end. Clearly it was as though I had merely phoned in to clear the paperwork that would allow me to die. At last the doctor summoned her

187

many years of training and spoke. 'You've got flu. Take paracetamol and go to bed.'

Here at last was the wisdom I had been seeking. 'Take paracetamol and go to bed.' Why, the advice had arrived just in time to stop my own course of action, which was to take methylated spirits and go to a salsa class.

A kindly friend arrived and heaved me to the doctor's surgery where I generously spread my infection and was instantly whisked onto an emergency nebuliser to reintroduce the notion of breath to my life-support system.

On reflection, I wonder if I wasn't rather irresponsible at the time of my call to the helpline. At no point did I ever ask whether the person answering my call was in fact a doctor. She could, for all I know, have possessed the same skills as the call-centre operative who advises me that turning my television off at the wall will restore an entire cable network. What I had, as it happens, was not flu but an acute chest infection for which I now have the great wonder of antibiotics. (I'm supposed to take them every four hours, which works out as being roughly as often as I can get the cap off.)

In the two years after the First World War, influenza killed more than twenty million people in Europe and the United States. This was a tragedy but I do feel that at least they didn't have to go through the charade of telling an anonymous person on the phone that they were heading towards expiration.

Dying because of someone else's lack of interest seems a poor way to go. It reminded me of the man who went to his doctor's office, sat down and took out a packet of cigarettes. He removed one, unrolled it and stuffed the tobacco up his nose. The doctor looked at him and said, 'I see you need my help.' 'I certainly do,' said the man. 'Have you got a match?'

Toady is the anniversary of the martyrdom of St Adrian of Nicomedia. This happened somewhere around 303 or 304. No

188

one can be entirely sure because you had more martyrdoms to the month in those days and it was hard to keep track. Adrian was killed by first having his limbs struck off on an anvil; he was then beheaded and burnt. Legend has it that he died in the arms of his wife and I have to confess that his rather protracted death leaves one wondering what she had left to hold at the time. I mention him because he is the Protector Against the Plague and probably someone we could do with in the present health system.

Spending on the NHS has almost trebled in the past ten years and many people are hard pushed to see where the money has gone. I only came close to meeting the present Health Secretary, Patricia Hewitt, once when she nearly ran over my foot in north London. She was parking outside a florist's in Camden Town and nearly came into contact with my person by taking the novel driving decision of coming to a halt on the pavement. I've treasured the idea of having a Health Secretary-related accident ever since. I can't say it would speed your treatment, but if the emergency doctor bothered to ask how the injury had occurred it would at least be a great story to tell while you were dying.

Too risqué for the cook to read

11 March 2007

I ONCE MISREAD A SIGN that said 'Happy Reading' as a description of the emotional state of the town in Berkshire. In fact, it was a campaign for people to smile while being literate.

I have to confess to feeling rather cheerful today. After nearly five months of middle-class homelessness, I at last settled into my new abode and can finally spend a Sunday devouring the papers. And I shall not be alone. The best estimate I can find is that about sixty per cent of all British adults read a Sunday paper. Of course, with some publications 'reading' involves a lot of pictures, which makes it easier.

The British public's continuing love affair with a daily paper is a curious phenomenon because, on the whole, we can't be searching for the news. Current affairs are served up twenty-four hours a day through a variety of media, which are generally impossible to escape. Gone are the days when victory at the Battle of Waterloo on 18 June 1815, didn't make the Fleet Street press until 22 June.

Even when news does arrive, it may seem to have a cyclical feel to it. If you read a newspaper from 11 March 1917, for example, you would learn that General Maude had just marched British troops into Baghdad. *Plus ça change.*

Despite this, the British remain avid newspaper consumers and I couldn't be more delighted. Today marks the anniversary of the first regular daily newspaper to be published in the UK. There is a marginal fight here with the *Norwich Post*, but the *Daily Courant*, which first ran off the presses on 11 March

1702, was probably the first successful daily paper in Britain. It was published by Edward Mallet from rooms above the White Hart pub in Fleet Street.

These days papers are a voluminous affairs (indeed, I must congratulate you for getting this far into the *Sunday Telegraph*) but the *Daily Courant* consisted of just one page with two columns – a hopeless publication for lining the cat tray. It contrasts rather starkly with an Ohio newspaper from the mid-nineteenth-century, which was seven-and-a-half feet long, and five-and-a-half feet wide. It required two people to hold it up for reading and, I imagine, quite a lot of co-operation for filling in the crossword.

I love newspapers, even the comic ones, and have spent more days unpacking my house contents than I should: I kept stopping to read articles wrapped round my china. Past headlines stay in my mind: 'Ability To Swim May Save Children From Drowning' or 'Steel-Eating Microbes Threaten To Devour Britain's Ports' and my favourite following Pope John Paul I's death after just thirty-three days in office – 'Pope Dead Again'.

The Vatican has provided a number of memorable newspaper moments. When Benedict XV was dangerously ill, a New York newspaper prematurely announced his death as a front-page lead in a special edition. The story read 'Pope Benedict XV is no more . . .' The report was later denied and a second edition hit the streets declaring: 'Pope has remarkable recovery.'

The British seem to have a general love of paper. For reasons I can't fathom, the average Briton uses almost two and a half times as much toilet paper as their average European counterpart (39 lb a year). Indeed, newspapers were once cut up into squares for this purpose – my grandmother insisted on using only tabloids – which reminds me of a wonderful story about Frederick Greenwood, the editor of the *Pall Mall Gazette* in the nineteenth century. He once met Lord Riddell who had just acquired the *News of the World*, which, even in the early 1900s, had a rather sensational reputation. Riddell offered him a copy and later asked for his opinion. 'I looked at it,' Greenwood said, 'and then I put it in the wastepaper basket . . . and then I thought, "If I leave it there the cook may read it" – so I burned it.'

Newspapers still give us something not provided elsewhere, such as obituaries. I like nothing better than trawling through the life of the man who invented the milk-float, or the Air Force commander who inadvertently saved Paris.

The *Daily Telegraph* is famous for its death notices and, for a while, had Hugh Montgomery-Massingberd as its obituary editor. He once reminisced in the *Spectator* about an injunction from on high that all obituaries should include the cause of death. The edict coincided with the demise of a celebrated gentleman who, sadly, had passed on after a penile implant had exploded. The cause of death was duly noted. Happy Reading.

A wake-up call for all L mothers

18 March 2007

IT'S THE FOURTH SUNDAY IN Lent, so if you forgot to give up something comfort yourself with the thought that it's probably too late now. I have to confess to having a problem with lateness. I think it's to do with my early years in the theatre. I simply don't understand not being on time. I suppose theatre is not the sort of job where you can turn up twenty minutes after everything has started and hope to catch up.

My paranoia about time means that I tend to wake up before the alarm, just to check that it is working. I mention this because I was bemused to learn that it was today, in 1944, that alarm clocks went back on sale in America for the first time since the Second World War began. The reason for the ban was that the necessary parts constituted war materials, but one has to question the logic behind a law that means an entire workforce is unable to get up and get to the munitions factories in the first place.

As far as I can find out, the first alarm clock was invented by those damned clever Greeks in about 250 BC. Some Grecian horologist with time on his hands built a water clock whose aquatic contents rose over a period of time and eventually hit a mechanical bird, which began to whistle. I normally wake up to the sound of John Humphrys and don't know if the bird wouldn't be preferable.

I had a friend who was so hopeless at getting up that he was always late for work and risked being sacked. Desperate to turn his tardiness around, he went to the doctor, who gave him a pill and told him to take it before he went to bed. My friend slept so well that he woke up an hour before the alarm and got to work before anyone else. 'I'm early today!' he boasted to his boss. 'Excellent,' she replied. 'But where were you yesterday?' His story is not as bad, of course, as the one about the woman who confused her birth control pills with her valium. She has fourteen children, but she doesn't care.

This brings me to Mother's Day and the fact that for one day in 365 there is no need to get up at all. Mothering Sunday is celebrated in many countries, but only Britain seems to select the fourth Sunday of Lent (exactly three weeks before Easter Sunday) as the commemoration date. The practice appears to have originated in a sixteenth-century Christian tradition of making an annual pilgrimage to one's mother church, usually located in a neighbourhood where often one's actual mother was still residing. For me, it is a day on which I don't have to peel the potatoes for Sunday lunch and can linger in bed contemplating the joys of having children.

My three are all teenagers and life is a little easier. Gone are the days when I hid in the bathroom in order to be alone. I've loved every minute of it, even though it hasn't always been easy. I think back to my attempts to cling to the moral high ground on toy weapons while my son took pot shots at me with an empty loo roll. How I instilled religion into them with the words, 'You had better pray that stain comes out of the carpet', and how I almost persuaded myself that tomato sauce was a sort of vegetable. I've learnt that no woman should have more children than she has car windows and to remind myself that things are worse in the animal world. For a start, whatever my track record, I've done better than a female rabbit who, if frightened or threatened, may either abandon or ignore her young or, if push comes to shove, eat them. Did you know that a female lobster, or hen, can lay 100,000 eggs at a time? Suddenly, the issue of giving quality attention to each offspring seems a little less daunting.

*

As I head for my fiftieth birthday, my own mother continues to parent me as if the notion of growing up is somewhere around a futuristic corner. She still warns me that coffee is hot and that I need a coat in the winter, and I am confident that I shall be doing the same with my mob when they reach a half-century.

There is a wonderful story about the Marx Brothers who, for years, toured America with a vaudeville act. Although they were well into their twenties, their mother, Minnie, continued to buy half-fare tickets for them with instructions to tell the conductor that they were thirteen. One suspicious train official approached Minnie and complained that one of her 'young' boys was smoking a cigar in the dining-car, while the other was shaving.

Apparently she sighed, saying, 'Don't they grow up fast?'

Happy Mother's Day.

It'll be twitchers at dawn . . .

6 May 2007

DID YOU KNOW THAT TODAY is International Dawn Chorus Day? It has a website and everything. Apparently, '2007 will be the biggest and best.' It certainly will for me because it's an annual event which, up until a few days ago, I had no idea I had been missing. It's advertised as a global celebration where people get up early 'to greet the rising sun and enjoy nature's daily miracle'. Given the time-zone issue, I imagine this as a great Mexican wave of pleasurable twitching across the world.

According to IDCD (there's an acronym for everything), a typical event involves people gathering just before dawn, enjoying the birdsong with a local expert and following this with a hearty breakfast. I'm not sure it's for me. I love the early morning and I'm a sucker for a hearty breakfast, but I don't think I want to share it with a local expert who can name each of the forty muscles in a warbler's wing and tell you with confidence that the bird-watching term for a pied-billed grebe is a peebee-geebee. I'd also be anxious about the etiquette. Is binocular-sharing frowned upon? Is yelling 'I can hear one' considered a faux pas?

I was thinking about etiquette this week because it was my birthday and I've been telling people that I'm forty-nine. This has caused a lot of frowns. Not because it seems a word of a lie, but because, despite generations of feminism, a lady is still not supposed to reveal her age. I like getting older and revel in each extra notch on the timeline.

The lovely thing about ageing is that you have to worry less and less about what is and isn't acceptable. My notions of correct behaviour have been reduced to a few critical points – I know that anything prepared by a taxidermist rarely makes a successful table centrepiece, that livestock is a poor wedding gift choice and, as I recently discovered, racing the hearse to a funeral will not amuse everyone.

I suppose the only area where I bemoan the loss of manners is in speech. The other day a young man, confident that the Old Kent Road had been built solely for his benefit, took the time to stop and eff and blind at me in a rather impressive, if unpleasant, torrent. Bring back the days when, if someone said, 'Gordon Bennett', there was a slight intake of breath from the shock of it.

It was today in 1835 that James Gordon Bennett Sr published the *New York Herald* for the first time. He was the father of James Gordon Bennett Jr, about whom the expression was supposedly coined. Junior knew how to scandalise. His engagement to the socialite Caroline May, for example, ended suddenly when he was said to have arrived intoxicated for a party at the Mays' family mansion and proceeded to urinate into a fireplace in full view of the guests.

He was also the man who paid for Stanley to find Livingstone in the jungle, where presumably the dawn chorus was second to none. I was always fond of Livingstone and spent many hours in Africa searching for the spot where he, rather ignobly, died from burst haemorrhoids.

I may not have missionary zeal, but I do understand the desire to get away from it all. My favourite American non-fiction book is *Walden; Or, Life in the Woods*, by Henry David Thoreau, who died today in 1862. It supposedly details a year spent living in a hut on the shores of Walden Pond, near Concord, Massachusetts.

In fact, it represented more than two years of coming and going to the place, but to many Americans it is the iconic work for anyone wanting to get back in touch with nature. The irony is that, visiting the place today, you can stop at a shop selling mugs, fridge magnets, bumper stickers, sweatshirts, hats, etc., all emblazoned with the Thoreau motto: 'Simplify, Simplify.' Thoreau's last words were 'Moose . . . Indian . . .' which either suggests a last-minute desire for an ethnic pudding, or that you really can't predict who will be standing to greet you when you finally cross to the other side.

On the subject of last words, it seems that, this week, our beloved Prime Minister will finally bring to an end the longest goodbye in politics. He may not actually go, but he will tell everyone when he plans to go, which is at least one step closer to actually going. It's his birthday today. I don't know what to make of it, but he shares the day with the inventor of psychoanalysis, Sigmund Freud (1856). It reminds me of the man who went to a therapist because he thought he was a dog. 'Lie on the couch,' said the therapist. The man shook his head. 'I'm not allowed on the couch.'

The naked truth about statues

13 May 2007

I WAS HOSTING A CONFERENCE about writing the other day. The audience was almost entirely female and the discussions wide-ranging. There was much debate about language, and the subject of acceptable terminology for the male member came up. It was generally agreed that 'manhood' was rather coy, yet other euphemisms were often either too clinical or smacked of the playground.

The Victorians, when confronted with nudity in art, referred to such depictions as a 'pity', presumably because it was a pity that the subject at hand had failed to be properly attired. Over the past week or so, thirty-one life-sized 'pity's' have appeared on the South Bank skyline, standing on the edge of the roofs of such buildings as the Shell Centre, the National Theatre and King's and Imperial Colleges. They are by Antony Gormley, the sculptor best known for his giant *Angel of the North* in Gateshead. According to Gormley, half of the world's population now live in a city, 'a totally constructed humanly made environment', and he wanted to make people think about what that means.

I love them. Maybe it's because I'm not really a city person. As Londoners surge across Waterloo Bridge, I look up and find comfort in the notion of the individual standing out from the madding crowd. The statues are all identical naked men based on a cast of Gormley's own body which, boys being what boys can be about their dimensions, must have taken some courage. At least the matter didn't have to go before a committee.

*

199

Each time I pass below the statue of Prospero and Ariel suspended above the main entrance to the BBC's Broadcasting House I can't help but think how our sensibilities have changed. Ariel was chosen as the spirit of broadcasting, based on the character from Shakespeare's *The Tempest* who lures visitors with beautiful songs to stay on Prospero's magical island. The sculptor Eric Gill undertook the commission and duly produced his statue, which was made public in 1932.

Sadly, it wasn't the spirit of the nude boy, Ariel, that caught people's attention, but rather his private appendage. There was immediate outrage. According to the *Daily Herald*, 'Maidens are said to blush and youths to pass disparaging remarks', and the MP for St Pancras declared that the figures were 'objectionable to public morals and decency'. Lord Reith, the first BBC director-general, who, one would have thought, had better things to do, was ordered to investigate. Ask for an investigation in this country and you won't have to wait two seconds before someone forms a committee.

On this curious panel were the Shakespearean scholar, Sir Israel Gollancz, and the writer, Israel Zangwill. Between them they decided that Ariel ought to be about thirteen years old. A doctor was then called to determine the correct measurements for a lad of that age, and subsequently, much to Gill's disgust, surgery was deemed necessary.

Rather than having to resort to eye-watering scalpel wielding, I prefer the route supposedly taken by the Italian sculptor Marino Marini. It is said that Marini made a huge sculpture of a horse and rider for the American art collector Peggy Guggenheim to display in her garden at the Palazzo Venier dei Leoni in Venice. The rider was naked and in, shall we say, an excitable state.

This was a potential source of embarrassment as, on holy days, many nuns had to pass by the garden and might look in. So, to cover all eventualities Marini made the rider's, oh dear, 'manhood' fully detachable.

The study of this particular area of three-dimensional depiction once won a prize for I. C. McManus, of University College London. McManus published *Scrotal Asymmetry in Man and in Ancient Sculpture* – a study of the testicles on 107 statues in Italian museums – which, he claimed, had intrigued scientists since J. J. Winckelmann's *History of Ancient Art* in 1764. He received an Ig Nobel Prize, an annual parody of the Nobel Prizes.

I may not take the McManus interest in sculpture, but I love it as an art form. The American sculptor Gutzon Borglum, who created the presidents' heads at Mount Rushmore in South Dakota, was once making a giant head of Abraham Lincoln out of a square block of stone. A little girl visited his studio. Lincoln's face was becoming recognisable and the child stared at the piece in amazement. 'Is that Abraham Lincoln?' she asked. 'Yes,' Borglum replied. The girl shook her head and breathlessly asked: 'How did you know he was inside there?'

An armless way to relieve stress

20 May 2007

DID YOU KNOW THAT AN octopus placed under extreme stress may eat its own arms? This must make for a trying time at the annual Atlantis underwater table-tennis championships with all the finalists gnawing away until only Davey Jones is left able to serve.

Before you become disconcerted by the thought of a deep-sea world populated by anxious-looking *Venus de Milo* octopi, it's not quite as bad as it sounds. Octopuses can grow their arms back, which is good news for the calamari lover. What worries me is that stress is so widespread on the planet that you can find it several fathoms down, chomping on a tentacle beside a shivering wreck.

Last week, Britain was revealed as a nation on Prozac. Last year, thirty-one million prescriptions for antidepressants were handed out. I blame it on the pace of life. The world is in such a hurry, I wouldn't be surprised if there were people who had to have this column read for them. I'm sure that intense time pressure is propelling half the populace into some form of sedation and that the other half would follow, if they could just fit it into their schedule.

It is salutary to think that it was today, in 1899, that the first arrest for speeding in a motor car was made in America. Jacob German, a New York City cab driver, had his collar felt when he sped up Lexington Avenue at 12 mph, when he should have been doing no more than eight (four on the corners). What no one can report is how anyone was able to measure this or, indeed, what the policeman in question was driving in order to catch him. These days, you could have nabbed him on a mobility scooter.

The British, however, can beat this. Walter Arnold was given a ticket three years earlier. (He was fined a shilling for doing 8 mph in a 2 mph zone.) We are a nation at full speed and I'm not quite sure why. As I stand champing at the bit for a two-minute microwave meal to finish cooking, I wonder where all my time has gone. A lot of anxiety seems to focus on the word 'legacy'. Everyone is racing around, worried about how they will be perceived by history.

It would be easy to blame much of this preoccupation on our beloved Prime Minister. All anyone talks about is his legacy, as if he weren't fifty-four and with plenty of years left to get a proper job.

There is also the chance for history to change its mind. The world has already forgotten that the first President Bush, father of the present triumph in office, was just as likely to make a verbal gaffe as his son. While it is hard to compete with the genius of the boy George's statement, 'Rarely is the questioned asked: is our children learning?', in his time the father, too, was a verbal juggler. Asked to sum up the presidency of Ronald Reagan (for whom he served as Vice-President), Father George declared, 'For seven and a half years I've worked alongside President Reagan. We've had triumphs. Made some mistakes. We've had some sex ... uh ... setbacks.' Words that, apart from the bit about working with President Reagan, could precis John Prescott's years in office.

I've decided to deal with both my stress and my legacy anxiety by becoming an inventor. I feel that if I could just come up with one good product, then everyone would forget my past errors. It worked for Alfred Nobel who, as the inventor of dynamite, had been known as the 'merchant of death' until he came up with the idea of a peace prize, thus enabling him to go to his grave being recalled as a good egg. I may write and suggest this to Mr Blair, who has already shown his inventive side with the reasons given for going to war.

If I wanted to make money then I would need to invent something sensible like a self-washing child but sadly I prefer the eccentric line of invention. Who amongst us cannot applaud Sir George Sitwell who, although apparently a grumpy soul, invented a tiny revolver for shooting wasps and a musical toothbrush that played *Annie Laurie*.

I'd also be happy in the footsteps of the Countess du Barry. The countess was mistress to France's Louis XV. Being mistress to a king can end well, with marriage and your face on souvenir mugs. Sadly for the countess, it cost her her head in 1793. This is not how history recalls her, for the countess was the inventor of the fish bowl. Rarely do I attend a fun fair and not give her a nod as I view the piscatorial prizes at the darts stall.

The only problem with being an inventor is that you need space to think. Does anyone know of a website with free ideas to save me time?

A long haul back to civilisation

3 June 2007

I'M THINKING OF TAKING UP flying. Anyone heading for a private pilot's licence these days is viewed with suspicion, but really I have had enough. Last week I took a domestic flight from Edinburgh to Bristol. In the modern world of aviation, getting through security is only the beginning of what has become a truly challenging form of travel.

First of all, I was relieved of my over-large tube of toothpaste which, although a little too minty for my liking, I had never thought of as inherently lethal, and then I had to suffer the ignominy of taking my shoes off to pad through the metal portal. Let us all be grateful that that Richard Reid fellow didn't choose to ignite his underpants. I understand that security is vital, but one is left with the idea that there are fiendishly clever terrorists who can bring you down with a kitten-heeled pump, a pair of tweezers and a squirt of Christian Dior.

The airline (honestly too fancy a name for this particular operation. It was more like a Routemaster with wings) had decided that rather than give out seat numbers, it was much more fun to have everyone scramble in the aisles as we all tried to get away from the baby screaming on the steps.

A member of staff, who had modelled her people skills on the last few weeks of Eva Braun's life, glared at me, immobile, as I attempted to lift my case over my 5ft-high head into a 7ft-high locker. Suddenly the idea of a non-stop flight seemed like some kind of threat.

*

I took my first international flight when I was six weeks old, as my family headed off from Copenhagen to Dar es Salaam in what was then Tanganyika.

Flying was once a pleasant experience. Passengers dressed up in smart 'travel clothes' and were served by staff who seemed on the verge of being pleased to see them.

I was a member of the BOAC Junior Jet Club and often went up to the cockpit to shake hands with the captain and have my logbook signed. Today, of course, things are necessarily different, but it is sad day when passengers are seen simply as a health and safety nuisance. Even the announcements have changed. At what point did airlines decide to drop the word 'unlikely' from the sentence: 'In the event of landing on water?' Surely from Edinburgh to Bristol it ought to be 'highly unlikely' or even 'I'd lay money on this not happening but just in case . . .'? I was on a domestic flight in the States recently and the pilot began the safety briefing by announcing: 'There may be fifty ways to leave your lover, but there's only four ways off of this airplane.' And don't start me on any bag you dare to put in the hold. Did you know there are now pictures of Saturn proving the planet's rings are made up entirely of lost luggage?

My new desire to travel solo might be the answer. It also fits in with the reasons why I went into show business – I love nothing better than being in the theatre, but I dislike sitting with other people. Become a performer, and you always get a good seat for the show. Become a pilot, and you can sign your own logbook.

Flying has come a long way and I feel sure it must be possible for me to learn. It's not like I'm shooting for the moon, which reminds me, it was today, in 1965, that Edward H. White became the first US astronaut to walk in space. He took a half-hour stroll outside the Gemini IV spacecraft and lived to tell the tale. The Americans were rightly thrilled. They had been racing the Russians into space ever since 1957, when a Soviet dog called Laika became the first living creature in space. Launched into orbit aboard Sputnik 2, Laika was known to the American press as 'Muttnik'. (When the US sent its first satellite into space it rose only a few feet in the air before crashing and becoming known as 'Kaputnik'.)

If a dog can head into the atmosphere then I feel I, too, have it in me. Tomorrow, curiously, is the 224th anniversary of humans rising into the sky at all. It was on 4 June 1783, in the market square of Annonay, a small village in the Ardèche, France, that the Montgolfier brothers demonstrated the world's first practical hot-air balloon. The 500 lb balloon was made of sackcloth and paper and held together with 1,800 buttons. (I once owned a similar outfit myself.) The vast bag rose 6,000 ft into the air to a great cheer from a crowd of well-wishers. This first foray into human flight came to earth in a field several miles away, where it was promptly attacked by pitchfork-waving peasants, who tore the evil bag to pieces and whose descendants presumably went on to found budget airlines.

I still don't know what I want to be

10 June 2007

I'M NOT FEELING MYSELF AT the moment and I think it's an improvement. I met a woman the other day, who said she listened to me on the radio on a Friday evening. 'I'm always in the car at that time,' she explained, 'because I'm collecting my six-year-old from analysis.' This statement rather stopped me in my tracks. I'm a big fan of therapy and think having an internal spring-clean should be *de rigueur* for us all. It never occurred to me, however, that one might deal with a dysfunctional childhood while it was actually happening.

In my day, you prepared children properly for later analysis with several sterile years at boarding school, followed by a generous student grant to be spent in the hostelry of their choice. The result was a well-educated, if mildly inebriated, adult with the emotional maturity of a small soap dish. Indeed, the education system produced such fine pickings for therapists that one might wonder whether they weren't secretly running the schools simply to breed new clients.

All that has now changed. Hardly anyone gets locked up for educational purposes, there are no student grants to cover essential alcohol expenditure and good parenting requires that we worry about our kids' psychological problems long before the tooth fairy has paid even a single visit.

Here, of course, I may be out of date. For all I know, the mere mention of the tooth fairy is no longer acceptable, leading as it does to complex issues about the distinction between fantasy, reality and one's teeth. I once told my middle child that she had better hope the tooth fairy was not a trainee, who, in her inexperience, might take my daughter instead of the tooth. As I said it, I realised this could scare a child half to death and I have been saving for her future psychiatric care ever since.

A survey last week produced by the Children's Society suggested that we were ruining our children by not letting them out to play. Having the kids under our feet all day is not doing much for adult sanity either.

I went through a bad phase with my girls when they played continually with Barbie dolls and I began to think I might die from a rare condition brought on by over-exposure to the colour shocking pink.

Certainly, things have come to a parlous state in this country when we won't even let the kids take the bus to their therapy sessions. Gone are the days of my New York childhood in the 1960s, when our neighbour, Auntie Evie, used to shout to the assembled gang of local urchins, 'Why don't you kids go play in the traffic?'

Despite my uncertainty about the benefits of pre-school therapy, I do believe counselling would help most people at some stage in their life and that we should never stop examining who we are on the inside. My eldest daughter has been selecting her university course and she said to me: 'The trouble is, Mum, I don't know what I want to be.' 'Snap,' I thought. I still have no idea what I want to be and hope it isn't too late to find out.

So far, I don't feel I have done anything useful. I have a good brain, but it is full of rubbish. I know, for example, that it is illegal in Alaska to shoot at a moose from the window of an aeroplane and that the correct word for the sound that a camel makes is 'nuzzing'. Neither of these facts is of any practical help to humanity. How I long to crack some age-old problem and present the solution to the world before I pass on to the great comedy club in the sky. Maybe I could start by pretending I know more than I do. I read a wonderful story the other day about the German mathematician David Hilbert. He was invited to give a talk on any subject he liked. This was in the early days of commercial aviation and the venue required that he catch a plane to the lecture. Prof. Hilbert duly advised that the title of his talk would be: 'The Proof of Fermat's Last Theorem'. This caused a sensation, as the theorem was then one of the great unsolved mathematical mysteries. On the day, Hilbert arrived and spoke brilliantly, but failed even to mention Fermat. After the talk, he was asked why he had chosen a title that had nothing to do with his lecture. 'Oh,' he replied, 'that was just in case the plane went down.'

What I do know is that the world of comedy would be bereft without psychotherapy. There is the story of the chap who needs help because he thinks he's a chicken. His family won't let him to go to therapy because they need the eggs.

Locking problem? I have the key

17 June 2007

THE OTHER DAY I WAS in a shop in London that advertised itself as open twenty-four hours a day, seven days a week. It's hard to imagine how the world used to manage without being able to buy pop-socks and milk in the early hours, but that may be a subject for another day.

Two men were busy fitting a new lock to the front door and I stood and watched them work for some time. If a shop is open every hour that the good Lord provides in a given year, at what point would they need to lock it up? Surely this was a place for which no one ever need worry about losing the key.

No doubt the lock-fitting exercise was some sort of insane insurance requirement. It reminded me of the story a few years ago when Beefeaters living at the Tower of London (presumably one of the most secure locations in the country) couldn't get home contents insurance because, technically speaking, they lived in a dodgy postcode area.

It is while considering things like the locking requirements of a permanently open establishment that I most miss my father. He passed on to the great snug bar in the sky more than eighteen years ago yet I still find myself storing little nuggets of curiosity for us to examine together later. He was a man who liked to ponder. 'Why, do you suppose . . .' he would often begin, and then go on to muse at nature's caprice in making armadillos one of the few animals besides humans that can get leprosy. Surely the loss of any part of their nose was unjustified in the great scheme of things. He could happily cogitate for hours on what the results might be if you tied buttered toast to the back of a cat and dropped it from a height, or ask us: 'If it's zero degrees outside today and it's supposed to be twice as cold tomorrow, how cold is it going to be?'

My dad was born in 1929 (two days after the great stock market crash for which, he would often say, he could hardly be blamed). We had in the house an *Encyclopaedia Britannica* from that same year and he would often tell us that any information on events before 1929 was in those books and we could look it up. Everything after was in his head and we had only to ask. He had a voracious appetite for information yet very little patience with standard schooling. Watching me struggle with French homework he once remarked, 'The thing to remember is that in French *cheval* means horse and it's like that all the way through. They have a different word for each one of ours. It's very annoying.' He then returned from a trip to Paris with a pen bought at the airport which he felt might already know how to write in French.

My father shaped much of my personality. He was known throughout Denmark as a distinguished writer and broadcaster. Following him into the family business was no problem. Imagine if, instead, he had been known as Vlad the Impaler. I might have hesitated in his footsteps. It was today in 1462 that Vlad attempted to assassinate Mehmet II. Mehmet survived as sultan of the Ottoman Empire but he lost heart when he saw how many thousands of Turks and Bulgarians Vlad had impaled on the way. The old Impaler had three kids of his own and cannot have cut much of a dash as an inspirational father figure. When a couple of foreign ambassadors refused to appear bareheaded before him, Vlad had their hats nailed to their heads. This surely is not the example you want to set for impressionable young minds. Of course a modern analysis would blame his own dysfunctional childhood. Vlad's dad was assassinated in some marshes and his older brother was blinded with hot iron stakes and then buried alive, which is the kind of thing that would have a lasting impact on anyone.

A friend of mine is about to become a father for the first time and he is anxious to get it right. At a loss as to what to advise him I've suggested a 'groaning cheese'. I can't seem to find the exact details but as I understand it this was a medieval practice in which instead of pacing outside the bedroom door waiting for a new infant to arrive, the father would sit and eat from the centre of a special cheese until a large hole had been gnawed. Later, his newborn infant was ceremoniously passed through the hole. I have no idea what effect this had on anyone except that it kept the men busy at a time when frankly their work was done.

Today is Father's Day and I miss my old papa hugely. I shall drink to his health and know that we would have passed a happy hour contemplating how deep the ocean might have been if sponges didn't grow in it.

It's enough to make you weep

24 June 2007

I'VE BEEN THINKING ABOUT THE phrase 'or I'm a Dutchman' as an expression of incredulity. Apparently, it comes from an ancient rivalry between the good clog-wearers of the Netherlands and the brogue-shod peoples of the UK, when to the British all things Dutch were decried as false and hateful.

I think this is a little harsh. These are, after all, the people who gave us encouraging alcohol when we were afraid (Dutch courage), the ability to have both members of a couple pay for a date (going Dutch) and a small cap which, over the years, many women have been grateful for.

It arose in my mind because I discovered the other day that the CEO of our national telephone provider, BT, is a Dutchman called Bernardus Verwaayen. I like the Dutch. My native Danes and the Dutch have been on each other's sides both in conflict and in applauding the mutual desire to sell herring and chips on every street corner. Both nationalities tend to be frank in expressing their opinions and I realise over the years I have possibly become rather too British in my manner.

I never thought I'd say this but I have decided that I am too polite. I have spent years believing that 'manners maketh the man', or, indeed, the miss, but I fear the only upshot of my adherence to civility will be death in some hideous maelstrom as I utter my final words, 'No, please, after you.' The sad truth in the modern world is that I am beginning to learn that bad behaviour begets results. I find myself in a position that I don't doubt almost every reader will identify with – my telephone and broadband system are not working properly. Indeed, they have not worked for so long that the very phrase 'service provider' can now induce an involuntary tick in my left eye. The idea of any large company providing 'service' these days is as outmoded a concept as being able to buy a tray of toffee complete with miniature hammer.

I live in a small village where the choice, as far as the telephone is concerned, is either to have one or not. Involuntarily, I am tied to the old apron strings of BT and since March have been trying to get them to mend my faulty system. I have spoken to dozens of people, I have patiently answered the same questions over and over, I have removed screws from faceplates, I have turned power on and off, I have been, if you like, an engineer by proxy, endlessly confirming that the system does not work.

Finally, this morning, I did two uncharacteristic things – first, I lost my temper with a perfectly charming man in India and, secondly, I burst into tears. The result was almost instantaneous – I was put through to a hitherto unknown department which claims to be sending an engineer within the week to sort matters out.

Perhaps diva behaviour is the only way forward. It was today in 1880 that the actress Sarah Bernhardt was sentenced to pay costs and damages of £4,000 for breach of engagement with the Comédie-Française. Bernhardt was not only the most famous of actresses in her lifetime, she retains a mythical status in the pantheon of badly behaved divas.

I expend a great deal of energy behaving well and not crying. It is, after all, the behaviour that was drummed into my generation. I recall a British man who returned home from years in prison in some God-forsaken hell-hole, remarking that really it had been no worse than his time at boarding school.

Although crying is often seen as a woman's final defence, on the whole I am not in favour. I prefer the attitude of the Italian composer Gioacchino Antonio Rossini, who once declared that he had only ever cried twice – once when he heard the diva Adelina Patti sing and once when he dropped a wing of truffled chicken into Lake Como.

I've never done either of those things, but I like to think that no *aria* or even the loss of the finest prepared poultry would reduce me to lachrymosity. The trouble is – tears work. It is, in fact, a crying shame how successful they can be in moving mountains or call-centre employees. I've since discovered that the BT CEO is a former board member of Endemol, the television company behind many reality television shows such as *Big Brother* and the recent practical joke in which a quiz show sought a kidney donor. It occurred to me that perhaps we were all engaged in some giant version of *The Truman Show*, where secret cameras record our every move and only bad behaviour makes you a winner.

Anyway, the engineer is due in a week. I am sure he will make everything better, or I'm a Dutchman.

There's no biz like showbiz – official

1 July 2007

I WAS CHATTING TO THE rock legend Alice Cooper the other day, the way you do, and he was telling me he had recently performed in front of 153,000 people in Brazil and how noisy it was. 'I know what you mean,' I replied. 'You've never heard real uproar until you've made 600 people chortle in Cheltenham.'

I'm in the middle of my theatrical tour (Short and Curly – coming to a theatre near you but hardly any tickets still available), bringing mayhem and merriment to the masses, and it has coincided nicely with a pat on the back from the Department for Culture, Media and Sport. A report just out commissioned by the department has concluded that the entertainment industry is now as valuable to the British economy as the financial services sector. As a consequence I have taken to wearing a pinstripe suit, awarded myself a million pound bonus and bought a small golf course in the Algarve.

Apparently the creative economy is a 'great unsung success story' employing 1.8 million people, making four billion pounds a year and generating more 'cultural goods' for export than any other country. Now, I can't take all the credit but I like to think I'm out there doing my bit. A member of the Government applauded this flow of finance but looked anxious and concerned. 'We need to think about what we can do to help the creative industries,' she mused. Clearly this is a woman who, despite being charged with our cultural health, has never been backstage in her life. If she really wants to help she could turn up at almost any local hall with an entertainment licence, bringing along a dustpan, a brush and a course of penicillin.

*

In general, the state of theatres in this country is parlous. I was asked recently by a member of the audience how I prepared for each night's performance. I suspect she wanted a tale of show-biz excess involving caviar, champagne and a small entourage of minions wafting fans from a respectful distance. I didn't like to tell her that it was more often than not on my knees with a roll of gaffer tape trying to seal the holes in the stage with the dual purpose of keeping the mice down and the actors up.

None of this is, of course, new. Years ago I was one of the first, if not the first, female follow-spot operators at the Adelphi Theatre in London's West End. In those days the theatre was home to a pair of cats called Plug and Socket, who lived entirely off locally sourced rodents. Access to the lighting booth was via a wall ladder that ran up beside the gentlemen's urinals in the upper circle. In my time there I lost any delusions of grandeur and had a view of boys' personal habits that few women will have been privy to.

I do wish it were all a bit more glamorous. Today is the birthday of the Academy Award-winning actress Olivia de Havilland. She is ninety-one and in my book one of the last of the great Hollywood leading ladies. She is a woman to whom the whole of Hollywood should bow down, for in the 1940s she took on the might of the studios in a lawsuit that successfully gave actors control over their own careers with a court ruling still known as the de Havilland law.

Pictures of de Havilland epitomise glamour but she, too, knew that show business has another side to it. While playing the part of Melanie in *Gone with the Wind* she was subjected to the director George Cukor twisting her foot under the covers in order to make her wince during supposed labour pains.

Vivien Leigh famously played the starring role of Scarlett O'Hara and was famously difficult. In one scene, a tattered Scarlett seeks food in the garden of the damaged and desolate Tara. She finds only a radish, takes a bite and retches. Miss

218

Leigh did not enjoy making retching noises so Olivia did them for her and it is her professional gagging you can hear in the film.

Despite the health and safety issues of touring in this country, I do think it is worth it. A wonderful old lady came up to me at the stage door one evening, patted my arm and said, 'It's better than watching telly, isn't it?' and she was right. There is something wonderful about a room full of people generating health-giving endorphins as they emit a united laugh. Personally I think jokes should be available on the NHS.

Today would also have been the birthday of the American comedian, Myron Cohen. He died in 1986 but still makes me laugh. Here is a classic Cohen gag. A businessman gets on a plane. Sitting next to him is an elegant woman wearing the largest diamond ring he has ever seen, so he asks her about it.

'This is the Klopman diamond,' she says. 'It is beautiful, but it's like the Hope diamond; there is a terrible curse that goes with it.' 'What's the curse?' the man asks.

'Mr Klopman,' she replies.

I'm not Callas, just clueless

8 July 2007

MY SISTER WRITES MUSICALS FOR a living so I tend to start emails to her with 'La La La' in case that is helpful in kick-starting a song. It is one of the great tragedies of my life that I am not musical. In my head, my singing has all the resonance of Maria Callas in the shower but something inexplicable happens to the noise on the way to my throat, and in the end I sound like the final moments of a frog in a blender.

It's not that my tuneless singing makes me depressed but I do think of following in Ellen Naomi Cohen's footsteps. Ellen had a pleasant voice but she lacked range and couldn't hit the high notes. She wanted to join a band called the New Journeymen but was rejected. The story goes that some time later she was walking past a building site, got hit on the head by a pipe and when she came round she could sing as high as you please. She became Mama Cass, the band became the Mamas and the Papas and the rest is pop history.

Given the right blow to the head I don't think I would mind what kind of music I could sing. I love it all. (Well, with the possible exception of what is known as New Age music – you know, the sort of stuff that can be played backwards and still sound exactly the same.) Nothing, however, is more calculated to start a disagreement than a discussion on the competing merits of different types of music. There are those, for example, who think the best thing jazz musicians could do is club together and buy a tune. I have also heard disgruntled folk define perfect pitch as the tossing of a ukulele into a skip and having it hit an accordion.

220

Whatever your particular musical tastes, however, I suspect there are few people in this world who don't enjoy some kind of melodic noise. Sadly, we don't tend to reward those who provide this great pleasure as well as might. I'm not talking about the pop divas but the average workaday musicians who scrape or blow for our benefit. Hence the old joke – what's the difference between a pizza and a musician? A pizza can feed a family of four.

Today, I should warn you, I intend to sing out whatever the consequences. It is the last day of the Sing London festival which for the past ten days has been encouraging the capital to open its throat and bellow. On this day alone you could learn to sing 'Handel in a Hurry', join a Magical Mystery Tour on a London Routemaster bus filled with musicians, take a singing tour of the National Gallery or join the mass finale outside the Royal Festival Hall. Surely this is an idea that should be spread across the nation? What a glorious thing to have Britain unite in song. How much more interesting would our politicians be, for example, if they had to deliver their pomposity in the form of a light *aria* or a sea shanty?

Today would have been the birthdays of both the American jazz singers Billy Eckstine (1914) and Louis Jordan (1908). Eckstine was the first romantic black male in popular music while Jordan provided the link between the birth of jazz and rock 'n' roll. How great would it be if we all decided to down tools in our inevitable Sunday visit to a DIY superstore and sing *Ain't Nobody Here But Us Chickens* instead?

If I could choose then I would learn to sing opera. I love the theatricality of it and certainly I have the physique. The American operatic baritone Robert Merrill once said that opera 'is the toughest art of all'. Not that he didn't have a sense of humour. In his book *Between Acts, an Irreverent Look at Opera and Other Madness*, Merrill tells a story about playing Silvio, the lover of the diva Nedda in *Pagliacci*. Nedda was being played by a substantial woman who weighed considerably more than he did. For their passionate duet, the director wisely decided to place Nedda in a chair and told Merrill to put his head in her lap. 'But she doesn't have a lap,' he whispered to the director who told him to do the best he could. Merrill knelt down and appeared to put his face straight into the good lady's private parts, which caused the entire cast to giggle. The baritone and the diva then began to sing but it wasn't long before Merrill's voice began to wobble. 'What's the problem now?' yelled the director. 'I think I'm getting an echo,' quipped Merrill.

Whatever your musical preference, sing out today. It's good for the soul. Tone deaf or not I intend to boom to the nation and follow Merrill's advice to all fledgling vocalists – 'When in doubt, sing loud.'

Rain? I've had it up to here

15 July 2007

THERE'S AN OLD SAYING: 'Mackerel skies and mares' tails make tall ships carry low sails.' Even though I'm quite old myself, I have no idea what it means but I intend to learn. It's something to do with the weather, which for many in Britain is proving a current obsession. So far this summer I feel we've all been badly let down by global warming. There's been enough rain to suggest that Gordon Brown ought to announce a plan to pair up the animals and start building a large boat. Next weekend we're holding a huge family party which, complete with marquee, has been months in the planning and while it is, of course, not in the same league as those who have suffered flooding, it is occupying my mind.

I have become one of those old duffers who stand in the hall tapping the barometer and muttering, 'Good Lord, look at the state of the humidity.' I've tried to be modern about it all and checked out the Met Office website, but frankly they hedge their bets. All I've learnt is that all the heavy rain 'may be partly a consequence of the expected development of moderate or strong *La Niña* conditions in the tropical Pacific Ocean'. Standing in a Surrey garden holding my finger in the air, I find this is quite hard to get my head round. As I understand it, this is all part of what is known as the 'butterfly effect', which roughly sketched seems to state that a Red Admiral having a quick wing flap amongst my buddleia can cause a tornado in Texas.

The truth is, I don't think anyone knows what they're talking about. This week I woke up to the usual dulcet tones of the

223

Today programme, only to find John Humphrys talking about flatulence and belching in cows and what it is doing to the climate. Surely something is wrong somewhere? If Radio 4 wants hot air as a topic it ought to be running to the House of Commons to find it. Spied from a distance, the bucolic view of cows and sheep in a field seems about as environmentally friendly as it gets, but apparently up close you will hear more damaging air expulsion than Jeremy Clarkson on a salt plain.

Apparently, there are ten million cows in this green and pleasant land, each producing about 100–200 litres of methane every day. I had an Uncle Edward like that and the only answer was not to let him near the beans.

In many aspects of life we seem to have come full circle. My grandmother carried a basket when she went shopping. For a while that seemed old-fashioned, but now I bang my thigh with wicker as I attempt to lower my carbon footprint in the supermarket.

There is the same regression with weather prediction as people turn back to the old folklore methods. The simplest one is to get a rock and put it in the garden – in the morning if it's dry, then the weather is clear; if it's wet, it's raining; white, snowing; and if it has gone, there was probably a tornado. Insects are, apparently, great diviners of weather. The old calculation was that you counted the number of chirps that a cricket makes in fourteen seconds, add forty and you get the temperature in Fahrenheit. Sadly this is not working in our garden, as most of the crickets are too busy doing the backstroke in large puddles to chirp at all.

Meteorologists in Reading have discovered that the air is full of tiny aphids. They float like so many summer balloons about two kilometres up and are great indicators for airflow. Guess the airflow and you can tell where a shower might erupt. This is all very well, but even standing on the roof I can't see the blighters and it's not long before I'm back in the hall tapping the barometer.

I live in the country, so there ought to be other indicators. There is, for example, an old saying that bubbles over calm beds of water mean rain is coming. I could have guessed that, as we have beds of water where the roses used to be. They say that if a dog pulls his feet up high while walking, a change in the weather is coming. This is hopeless for me. I have a shih-tzu. He's such a lapdog he pulls his legs up high when walking just in case there might be a morsel of mud to sully his rather fine coat.

Despite this, I still think my best indicators will come from the animal kingdom. I know that horses run fast before a violent storm, that pigs gather leaves and straw and a bull leading the cows to pasture almost certainly means rain. (I also know that wolves howl more before a storm, but if that happens in Surrey things are worse than I thought.) The party is next Saturday and I predict we shan't hear the disco for the sound of horses running, pigs leaf-gathering and a distant bull shouting 'this way' to a bunch of belching cows.

Genius: I know it when I hear it

3 February 2008

I HAVE IN MY TIME been fortunate to meet a large number of the great and the good of this world. Most, if truth be told, were not as great as they would have you believe. My few brushes with Hollywood glitterati, for example, on the whole confirm a suspicion that the most necessary component of an international movie career is not talent but luck wrapped in an impenetrable ego.

Being in the presence of true talent is rare but it does happen. I once had the privilege of doing a short double act with the Canadian writer Margaret Atwood and was annoyed to discover she not only writes a mean book but was able to be funny as well. I don't know exactly what it is that marks some individuals out as unique: I just know you can feel it the moment you are in their presence. I only had a two-minute conversation with former US President Bill Clinton, yet in that moment even I could see what it was that had brought Monica Lewinsky to her knees.

The word 'genius' is over-used in the media. People talk about Jonny Wilkinson having a genius for tossing a pig's bladder up between two posts or the Labour Party having a genius for finding trouble where no one else had thought to look. Neither description is an accurate use of the word. Genuine genius is so exceptional that, in these days of hype, I suspect we have almost forgotten what it looks like.

This week I was in the presence of a double whammy of talent so overwhelming that it was enough to make all those who aspired to creativity hang up their hats of endeavour with a sigh

226

of shame. The words on my ticket for the Festival Hall in London said simply 'Daniel Barenboim, piano'. That was all. One man, one man of sixty-five, sitting at a keyboard with no modern amplification playing for an hour and a half on his own. It was the opening night of Barenboim's eight concerts to play the entire Beethoven piano sonata cycle. So many people had wanted to hear him that the stage itself was crowded with seats and there were those who could almost have reached out to turn his pages. Except that there were no pages. There was no support whatsoever and no need for any. Daniel Barenboim has been playing the Beethoven sonatas for forty-seven years. They seem to run through him in places where the rest of us merely transport the cells of daily living.

He first played the Festival Hall at the age of thirteen. He was a *wunderkind*, a child prodigy. Such creatures are rare. Today marks the birthday in 1809 of the German composer Felix Mendelssohn, probably regarded as the greatest musical child prodigy after Mozart. There must be something about the German gene, for there was a German boy born in 1720 called Christian Heinrich Heinecken, who was said to be able to speak within a few hours and who, by the age of one, had a perfect knowledge of the Old Testament. I can only think that that kind of precocity must have led the odd relative to think that Herod might have had a point. Sadly, Heinecken died aged five. Barenboim has gone from strength to strength.

Being feted by the world from an early age could lead to a galloping case of narcissism but Mr B seems to be an exceptional man in many ways. Possibly the only person to hold joint Israeli-Palestinian citizenship, he has used his talent to try to broker some form of understanding in that troubled section of the world. Take his genius and place before it the music of arguably the greatest composer of all time and the effect is almost unbearable.

At the end of the concert Barenboim was presented with the

gold medal from the Royal Philharmonic Society. It is an honour rarely given and the connection with Beethoven is splendid. In 1817 the society commissioned Beethoven, for £50, to write his ninth symphony. Probably, as the chairman of the society said, the best fifty quid ever spent in musical history.

Today is known in America as 'The Day the Music Died' because of the deaths in 1959 of Buddy Holly, Ritchie Valens and J. P. 'The Big Bopper' Richardson. It is, I am delighted to tell you, a misnomer. Music is alive and well and moving the hearts, spirits and minds of the lucky few at the Festival Hall. How I should have loved to have met Beethoven, the man once heard shouting in the street at the top of his voice – 'I will take life by the throat!' You only have until 17 February to hear Barenboim do just that: please, I never suggest exercise to anyone, but run, do run to get there.

I'm as old as the LEGO brick

10 February 2008

THIS YEAR, IF THE GODS are willing and there is a following wind, will mark the completion of my first half-century. I say 'first' as if there were many more to come. The truth is that, without massive future medical intervention, I am probably also entering my last half-century. The upshot is that I feel I should finally decide what I want to be when I grow up.

I have lived through a life of many changes. It was exactly fifty years ago that (while my parents splashed out on a second-hand cot for me) Prince Charles was given Wales as a present, instant noodles finally arrived in our lives and BOAC became the first airline to fly passenger-jet services across the Atlantic. I am as old as the European Union, as ancient as the peace symbol and sadly the same age as the British parking meter.

All good stuff, but nothing pleases me as much as the thought that I am of an age with the LEGO brick. This week that pinnacle of moulded plastic turned fifty and I am delighted to tell you that I shall be spending the weekend practically in the shadow of the toy's home. The small neck of Danish woods where the Toksvigs first climbed out of the primeval ooze lies not far from the town of Billund, birthplace of the birthday brick. I have headed home for the weekend and by chance arrived just in time for the celebrations.

It won't surprise you to learn that as a Dane I have had a long association with the humble toy. (Indeed, if you have the average British person's knowledge of Denmark, you might be equally unmoved to learn that I was also brought up by herrings and once met Hamlet's father.)

When I was eight I took my first driving lesson in a car made of eight-studded bricks and, at ten, I rode in a multi-coloured train made of the stuff, dressed as a Danish soldier in the annual Macy's Day Parade through New York City. Since its birth at the hands of a Danish carpenter, called Ole Kirk Christiansen, 400 billion stackable plastic pieces have been produced. Divide that up and it would provide sixty-two bricks for every person on the planet or, annoyingly, not quite enough to make anyone a decent model house. You could also, if so minded, stack all the pieces into ten giant towers swaying from here to the Moon. Although, with my luck, this would collapse just as my mother was announcing bedtime.

I like toys. I have rarely had more fun than I did at Christmas, playing on my daughter's new air-guitar computer programme. Britain's first playground for pensioners has opened in Greater Manchester and old folk are encouraged to become swingers once again. How marvellous. I can't think of anything more soothing than a quick dash down a slide, but until recently it was an adult activity often rewarded with having your collar felt.

As a child, I was never keen on those dolls with the large chests and impossibly small feet, who seemed to suggest that being a stewardess represented the zenith of female achievement.

I can't recall whether it was urban myth or truth but, during the Christmas of 1989, the Barbie Liberation Organisation supposedly managed to switch the voice boxes of several hundred talking Barbie dolls with those of talking GI Joes. The militant action was said to leave macho boy toys lisping, 'Let's sing with the band tonight', while Barbie rather pleasingly used her new *basso profundo* voice to declare that 'Dead men tell no lies'.

The Australians, of course, went one better and produced a plastic doll called Feral Cheryl who came complete with dreadlocks, tattoos, piercings and even a bit of what was politely called 'natural body hair'. Her only accessories were advertised as 'a bag of home-grown herbs, a sense of humour and a social conscience'. Here at last was a doll any child could take along with pride to an anti-nuclear demonstration.

Sadly, I think Cheryl has gone out of business, but not so HeroBuilders, an American company that will supply any action figure, including Condoleezza Rice, Korea's Kim Jong-Il and your very own Middle East peacemaker, Tony Blair. There is a truly tasteless figure of Michael Jackson dangling his baby from a hotel window and a depiction of Britney Spears that suggests that no amount of therapy will ever be enough for the poor girl. On top of that, it is happy to make a doll that looks like you. Yes, you too can be a twelve-inch action figure, complete with identical miniature clothing and twenty seconds of your voice delivering a changeable message of choice. A changeable message? Why at this rate I could be an MP when I grow up.

Speculation: just think where we'd be without it

9 March 2008

IT'S BARON BLISS DAY IN Belize, which is as pleasing a piece of alliteration as I have come across in an age. Henry Bliss died today in 1926. He was a British-born fellow who made a fortune speculating in petroleum shares. The only thing I ever speculated in are thoughts such as: I wonder why the mole in my garden never holidays next door? Bliss gave a fortune to the people of Belize (hence the big day today), but that's not why I like him. It is said that he was originally disinherited by his folk in Suffolk for keeping a hansom cab waiting. How splendidly eccentric. I can't think what my kids would do that might lead me to such a dramatic decision, but I doubt whether a public-hire vehicle would be involved.

Despite this attachment to my youngsters I have to confess that my daughter is being sold at auction this week. The whole thing is part of her 'rag' week, but nevertheless it leaves me feeling slightly edgy. I didn't see her through chickenpox, whooping cough and a brief but annoying addiction to Pingu just to see her exchanged for a wad of cash. Apparently, in the interests of the school charity, she is to be someone's slave for the day and do their homework. I only wish I had thought of it first. I've always relied on a blend of overt charm, subtle threats and straightforward pleading to get things done at home. It never occurred to me to just offer money.

I like auctions. They are as close as I get to gambling. It is often only when faced with a rival bid that I suddenly find myself

232

wildly attracted to something. Last month I bought a 30-year-old Chevrolet pickup truck in just such a fit of enthusiasm. The truck lacks even a hint of power steering and will require me to develop the forearms of a stevedore should I ever wish to move it from the drive. Despite this, it makes me smile each time I look at it for it reminds me of:

1) My youth in New York, where everyone's dad drove a Chevy pickup with one hand while popping open a little something from a six-pack with the other;

2) Sammy Davis Jr's left eye. Davis crashed his Chevrolet in the 1950s and lost his eye on the curious cone that used to adorn the steering wheel.

When Davis died pretty much everything he owned was auctioned. Here was a man who had crooned his way through debt. As the great American comic Phyllis Diller said, 'Sammy had it all, he just never bothered to pay for it.'

My delight in auctions has its limits. I have never, for example, paid for the organs of the famous or even a DNA sample from the slightly suspect. This week the fascinating and former newspaper magnate Conrad Black checked into prison in the state of Florida. His particular penchant for collection has been matters Napoleonic. His home expenses, as stated in court, included $12,500 for Napoleon's shaving stand. Indeed, so wide-ranging was his collection that a statement was once issued, declaring: 'The proprietor of the *Daily Telegraph* would like to go on the record to say that he does certainly not own Napoleon's penis.'

Today is the anniversary in 1796 of Napoleon marrying his first wife, Joséphine de Beauharnais. One can only presume on the night in question the general was fully intact and able to hoist the flag. It is believed, however, that his appendage (not flatteringly described by anyone) was lopped off by a priest and passed on to the highest bidder. The most recent owner was a urologist, John K. Lattimer, who paid $3,000 for the unique artefact and died last year in Englewood, New Jersey. (I've been to Englewood and am never surprised to hear of anyone's demise.) Before Lattimer, the proud owner was a Philadelphian called A. S. W. Rosenbach, who took pleasure in displaying the 'shrivelled sea horse' on a velvet cushion.

It's curious to think of bits of oneself soldiering on for display purposes. It was today in 1765 that the French writer Voltaire saw success in his campaign to seek a posthumous exoneration of a man who had been wrongly executed for murder. Voltaire was a genius who towards the end of his life declined to forswear Satan as he felt it wasn't a good time 'to make new enemies'. The nimbleness of Voltaire's brain in life, however, was never as interesting as its alleged journey after death. It seems a dispute between his heirs and the government led to his brain being included in a sale of furniture and never seen again. Imagine your shock if you'd innocently bid on a sideboard and found the grey matter of French Enlightenment in one of the drawers.

I don't know how much my child will fetch this week. I have high hopes. A Francis Bacon triptych sold for £26.3 million last month and the people in that weren't even good-looking.

The dangers of unprotected texts

16 March 2008

GERALD FORD, THE FORMER American President, was said to be so intellectually challenged that he couldn't walk and chew gum at the same time. The same appears to be true of a staggering number of people in this country who can't walk and text. Why you should want to be able to do this is beyond me. Texts are effectively a modern version of the telegram. I can't believe that 100 years ago every perambulation engendered an urge to send missives via a young lad in a pillbox hat. Nevertheless, last year a staggering six million people were injured while texting and simultaneously walking into a piece of street furniture. Innocent lampposts and bollards have received the indentation of the foreheads of those people who couldn't wait to ask 'R u ok?' of someone they saw five minutes ago.

As a consequence, last week a pilot scheme of padding lamp posts in east London's Brick Lane was revealed to stem the tide of what has been described as 'unprotected text'. I've not heard a more marvellous health and safety device since the lifeguard was invented for trams. This was an ingenious basket that attached to the front of a trolley car to catch pedestrians paralysed by the sight of a tram bearing down on them. Tragically, the lifeguard worked only if the pedestrians were dead centre and, annoyingly, they often failed to comply, making them more dead than centre. As a result, the basket tended to take up only parts of people and proved far less effective than simply shouting, 'Oi, you idiot, there's a tram coming.'

No doubt the lamp-post pads are part of some elaborate publicity stunt, but they are symbolic of the death of the straightforward accident in our society. No one has an accident any more. No one says, 'Oops-a-daisy, up you get.' No, instead, people have injuries for which someone else is assuredly to blame. It was today, in 1912, that Lawrence Oates, feeling quite literally under the weather on Scott's South Pole expedition, departed the communal tent with the words, 'I am just going outside and may be some time.' For years, this has been seen as an Englishman behaving beautifully in the face of adversity. Today, it would almost certainly represent a clear-cut legal case against the tent manufacturer for negligently providing an opening through which a man might depart to his demise.

As a law student, I enjoyed those cases where life's lunacy led to legal dispute. I can't so much as smell the kerosene-like whiff from a dry cleaner's without recalling the bizarre case of a man who pressed himself to death. The splendid Royal Society for the Prevention of Accidents website has a section that I could play with for hours. If you are interested in people flirting with being sent to the next life with a neat crease down the middle, then the information is at your fingertips. (1,415 steam iron injuries per year at last count.) You input the type of accident you are interested in, the victim's gender, their age, the location, an object involved, and so on, and within seconds the RoSPA will give you the statistics. Thus, I can tell you that, in 2001, eighteen people aged 65–74 were injured on a cattle grid, but by 2002 this epidemic of bovine protection tragedies had been eradicated. Blessedly, in 2002, no one was injured in a parking area with a pig, but 964 British citizens had a cardigan or pullover-related incident they thought worth reporting.

Health and safety has become something of a straitjacket. Had I been sitting at home this morning in 1867 reading my copy of that medical mag, the *Lancet*, I should have read of Joseph Lister outlining his discovery of antiseptic surgery. No doubt it has been a marvellous thing, but the notion that we can protect ourselves against all harm has become a bit silly.

Sometimes survival just comes down to luck. In 2003 members of the Invincible Eagles circus were performing a trapeze act without a safety net (and here I think we can hear the heavy chords of impending doom). A Chilean member of the team, called Mauricio Alberto Yovanovich, missed his partner's outstretched arms at some considerable height and plunged to the floor. As it happens, a rather rotund female in her fifties, Georgina del Carmen Riffo, was sitting in the front row. Mauricio landed on her and both walked away with a mere scratch and a great dinner-party story.

Of course, one should be wary of being amused by someone else's misfortune. I was having a drink with someone I hadn't seen for a long time. He ordered a pint and drank it down in one great gulp. 'Heavens,' I said, 'that was quick.' He nodded and said, 'Well, I drink like that since the accident.' This silenced me. 'Sorry, what accident?' I managed. 'Someone knocked over my beer,' he replied and ordered another.

An Arctic delicacy? My heart was
in my mouth

23 March 2008

I ONCE WENT PTARMIGAN HUNTING in the Arctic. I'm not much of a hunter, being more inclined to the gatherer side of food provision, but I was there for the purposes of documentary filming. The hardy hunters, who were proving their intense manhood by shooting a twelve-inch sedentary bird, declared to me that I was to be the recipient of a local honour. The still warm heart of the moribund snow chicken was plucked from its nesting place, plunged into neat vodka and offered to me as a delicacy. It resembled the size and shape of the one chocolate you find left in an assortment box which for some reason no one wants.

I have spent a lifetime travelling with a desire never to offend local culture. I eyed the mini-cardiac offering as yet another challenge and swallowed it whole. At this point my noble men of the ice fell to the floor laughing at the success of what turned out to be a hilarious Arctic practical joke.

Ever since, I worry that my enthusiasm to experience local culture is slightly on the wane. I've just returned from the Tyrol, where I had as good a time as you can while skiing in the rain. Driven in by inclement weather, I headed for the hotel sauna.

The entrance door displayed a bold sign in German. It is a language that has the unfortunate effect on the English ear and eye of seeming to contain nothing but orders. I entered without giving proper *achtung* to the warning. Two feet inside the heated box I was greeted by a naked man standing with his hands on his hips smiling at me. He looked like someone doing an impression of a bowl sporting a surprisingly small pair of sugar tongs. It took me a moment to realise that I was the only person in the sauna wearing a swimsuit.

An impressive array of physical specimens of Adam and Eve's descendants were all splayed out on wooden benches staring at me. It was quite clear that I had committed a sauna faux pas and was entirely wrongly dressed in being dressed at all. English boarding school having long ago shamed the naturist out of me, I turned and departed.

I realised that what I actually like about Tyrolean culture is the bit that exists in some Disneyland manner mainly for tourists. I love yodelling, a word derived rather brilliantly from the German *jodeln* meaning 'to utter the syllable jo'. I suspect it is a very long time since anyone yodelled on an Alpine peak in order to pass on the message that they might be a touch late for tea, yet this mad tonal oscillation continues round the world. From Salt Lake City to St Moritz there are yodelling festivals with more than 15,000 professional yodellers (15,000 professionals?).

Human beings seem to need to clutch their own particular cultural curiosities with them wherever they go. It was today in 1848 that the first Scottish settlers arrived in Dunedin, New Zealand, on the ship John Wickliffe. The Maoris had been there for generations yet head there now and you can sport the Dunedin tartan, drink whisky at the Robbie Burns pub and in a couple of weeks toss the caber during the annual Highland Games. A true Scottish experience, presumably watched over by bemused antipodean sheep.

My partner comes from Lancashire and I am often berated for failing to recall whether to support white or red roses in the great War of the Roses. I think it's too long ago to take sides, but the bit I like about this critical piece of British history is that the woman who led the Lancastrians was French. It was today in 1429 that Margaret of Anjou was born. She married Henry

239

VI of England in Titchfield, Hampshire, a place otherwise well known for housing a branch of the Office for National Statistics. The daughter of an Italian king and a French duchess, she was, I suspect, a fiery foreigner not thrilled to discover that her royal husband had many bats in his belfry. Her son's inheritance was threatened by Richard, Duke of York, and her husband was unable to do much except dribble, so Margaret found herself in charge, literally. She led the army at the Battle of Tewkesbury on 4 May 1471. I can't say it all went well but I like to think she wore her armour with the kind of elan only a Frenchwoman might achieve.

In July a Tewkesbury tourist can witness a re-enactment of the battle at one of those medieval festivals that convince Japanese tourists that all British people live in half-timbered homes and like nothing better than to morris dance. Mead will be sipped and pig roast gnawed upon, ignoring the fact that Margaret probably favoured a light *confit de canard* with a splash of Burgundy.

I've got American friends coming to stay for Easter. They want to go out to afternoon tea and stay somewhere with a butler. I've no idea what to do with them.

I prefer to make my point with a pencil

30 March 2008

IT'S A CURIOUS THING THAT I know a quote from Stan Laurel, a man perhaps more noted for his silence than his pronouncements. It's not brilliant but it probably got a laugh in his day when he declared, 'A horse may be coaxed to drink, but a pencil must be lead.' I like pencils. The ratio of pencil to rubber suggests an optimistic tool and yet one that allows for the possibility of error.

I spend a great deal of time in the British Library, where pens are banned and pencils reign supreme. They were the instrument of choice of so many writers. Hemingway wrote only in lead, as did Anna Sewell, born today in 1820, who wrote *Black Beauty*. (Mind you, she also claimed that the book was an autobiography translated from the equine.) I sit in the library with a fresh wooden stylus or 'portable, hand-held communications inscriber' as a Pentagon audit once described them, knowing that, given an average seventeen sharpenings per pencil, I could write about 45,000 words or, when inspiration fails, draw a line thirty-five miles long. Indeed it is these very thoughts that stand between me and the writing of the great modern novel.

Today, and heaven knows we need something to celebrate, is Pencil Day. Yes it was exactly 150 years that Hymen Lipman patented the first pencil with an attached rubber. Hymen Lipman? Among the many names we considered at the birth of our son I don't recall Hymen even being brought up for a laugh. You might as well name your daughter Candida while you're at it. It makes my suggestions of Abattoir for a boy and Avarice for a girl seem rather tame.

241

Little is known about Hymen Lipman except that he lived in Philadelphia and probably spent his spare time in therapy bemoaning his parents' sense of humour. Considering he clearly had a penchant for writing instruments you would think he might have jotted down the odd *mot juste* about himself, but no. As ever, the chance stumbling upon one of life's incidental characters led me to some curious searches.

Late home from my garden office I defended my tardiness by explaining I had been 'looking up great Hymens in history'. It was true. Ever idling in the brackish waters that are the swamp of online knowledge, I had pursued Hymen on an ancestral investigation site and was rewarded with the unfortunate sentence: 'Request to have your Hymen site listed on this page.' I declined.

I wonder what Hymen would have made of Pencil Day? Would he have sent an e-card sporting a smiling pencil wishing you 'a frolickin' good time' while dancing to the sort of music you imagine only Rolf Harris (seventy-eight today) could wring from a stylophone? (Available from www.123greetings.com.) I once had my portrait painted by Rolf Harris, using a four-inch paint brush and three tins of house paint. I can't say it brought out the best of me, overcome as I was by emulsion, and I wondered at the time whether a pencil sketch might not have been more pleasing.

My grandfather was a painter and he worked for a while as an animator for Disney Studios, bringing to life with his pencil the characters created by others. People like Marc Davis, who was born today in 1913 and was one of Disney's Nine Old Men, the core animators of some of the greatest cartoons ever made. Without him Thumper might never have slipped on the ice or Tinker Bell been quite so naughty.

It is said that Picasso's first word as a child was the Spanish for pencil and I have always preferred his simple sketches to the final portraits of people painted with oils and a school geometry kit. Van Gogh was born today in 1853. Here was a man not famous for being a laugh a minute but he knew the value of this splendid tool when he wrote to his brother: 'I shall set to work again with my pencil, which I had cast aside in my deep dejection, and I shall draw again.'

The pencil is such a wonderfully simple device. I met a woman who told me she was going to move to Peru because she wanted to be a writer. 'Why don't you save some money and just get a pencil from Smith's instead?' I suggested. I like the way you get a sense of the physical labour of writing as the pencil shortens by the hour. The legendary Hollywood studio boss Jack Warner used to insist his writers wear down their pencils by a certain amount each day, and I have a wonderful image of F. Scott Fitzgerald doing coin rubbings just to whittle down his pencil to his daily quota.

I remember a poorly thought-out anti-drug campaign about ten years ago that issued pencils with the slogan 'Too Cool to Do Drugs'. Unfortunately, when sharpened, the pencil next read 'Cool to Do Drugs' and, later, 'Do Drugs'.

Did you know that the Number 2 pencil is the most popular? Surely it's time it was renumbered to reflect this?

Is that a reptile in your trench coat?

6 April 2008

ON THE WHOLE I AM a fan of the unexpected. It is, after all, the unforeseen that helps to weave the predictability of daily life into a rich tapestry of experience. As a consequence I rail against routine and hope I shall never be heard to utter the words: 'Have lunch out on a Tuesday? But that's my day for the chiropodist.'

The unpredictable is, of course, not always pleasing. There was a wonderful story this week about a German woman called Ingrid Bruelling who checked into a hospital in the city of Kassel to have some wrinkles removed. I say wrinkles. Ms Bruelling had recently lost sixteen stone on a crash diet and must have had folds in her flesh akin to the lower reaches of the Grand Canyon. She awoke from her tightening procedure to find not only did she have firmer skin but a new set of breasts as well. The Kasselian doctors had taken it upon themselves to be liberal with silicone implants and increase her bra size from a C cup to a D. The medics said making her chest larger was the best way to iron out the wrinkles. Having gone to great lengths to be smaller in the first place, what Ms Bruelling said was presumably unprintable.

Then there was the story last Tuesday of the 2 ft 3 in crocodile in Norway which a visitor carried out, unnoticed, from an aquarium in Bergen. The aquarium director was quoted as saying, 'I think whoever did this knew what they were doing.' One can only hope that he's right. The reptile, a smooth-fronted cayman, may not be the sort to try to part you from your liver but it could certainly chomp a few fingers and make practising your piano scales tricky.

Out of the blue, boob jobs and crocodiles going walkabout under someone's trench coat represent little peaks in the flat line of predictable daily experience. I know that whatever pension scheme I buy into and however much I invest, I will spend my twilight years trying to suck life out of £10 a month. I know that whatever I write about I will receive at least one letter a week that begins 'Dear Ms Toksvig, Surely a deliberate mistake . . .' and I know that whatever airport I turn up at, I will have a miserable experience.

Why anyone was surprised that the new Terminal 5 at Heathrow was anything other than a new circle of hell is beyond me. The chaos was marvellously British. BA (who are British) were arguing with BAA (who sound British but aren't). BA versus BAA – why, it has the makings of a new children's nursery rhyme in which a sheep attempts to go on holiday and finds someone has lost his sack of wool. I may have got the numbers wrong (Dear Ms Toksvig, Surely a deliberate mistake), but I think BA said there were 19,000 bags missing and BAA said there were 28,000. A spokesman for the Department for Transport suggested the discrepancy might be due to BAA and BA using different counting methods. This only makes sense if one of them is using base eight instead of base ten.

Back in the days when I was a member of the BOAC Junior Jet Club, flying was fun. People dressed up for it and the flight itself was an enjoyable experience. Today it is hell. Security is necessarily tight but it has also become marginally incomprehensible to the average passenger. These days I'm not allowed to do in-flight sewing because, as I understand it, some fiendishly clever fellow has worked out how to hold a plane to ransom using an embroidery needle and two lengths of DMC cotton. The old joke that a man was arrested at an airport with a ruler, a protractor, a set square, a slide rule and a calculator because he was believed to be a member of the Al-gebra movement carrying weapons of maths instruction no longer seems entirely absurd.

Early aviation was fun and romantic. It was full of wonderfully named pioneers such as the aircraft manufacturer Anthony Fokker (born today in 1890), whose first plane was destroyed when his business partner crashed it into a tree. This suggests an early lesson in piloting things yourself and recalling that the best place for planes is somewhere above the tree line.

Then there was the aviator Hudson Fysh, who died today in 1974. Fysh founded the Qantas airline and once attempted to fly from Australia to Great Britain in 720 hours, roughly the time it now takes to pass through Terminal 5.

Still, BA and BAA should keep hope in their hearts. Robert Goddard, the inventor who developed the first successful liquid-fuelled rocket, had many hiccups on his way to triumph. Determined to create a 'moon-going rocket', he kept experimenting. Not everyone was impressed. In 1929, his launch of a new missile was greeted with the local newspaper headline: 'Moon rocket misses target by 238,799 miles.'

Let's hear it for rousing applause

13 April 2008

EVER CONFIDENT THAT IT'S NEVER too late to educate oneself, I have been trying to get to grips with classical music. This is not as easy as it sounds. Oh, the music is lovely, the musicians seem delightful, but some of the audience can, frankly, be a bit of trial. There seem to be so many unwritten rules about how I am supposed to behave that, were I a different type of individual, I might be tempted to stay at home and listen to the record instead.

Last week I went to hear the pianist Mitsuko Uchida. I'd never heard of Ms Uchida and, indeed, before she popped out onto the stage I rather thought it was going to be a chap at the keyboard. I was enraptured by her playing and at the end cheered lustily. This caused the people in front to turn around and look at me as if they were worried that I was present on some day-release scheme from a secure unit.

I thought I had done rather well by saving my response to the end. I had wanted to whoop and holler long before we finally got permission. Knowing when to clap and not to clap is complex for the musical philistine, and I don't know why it causes such anxiety. It's not as though great musicians in the past all wanted reverential hush. There is a wonderful letter written by Mozart, in 1778, to his father, in which he revelled in the applause he received throughout a concert: 'I was so delighted, I went right after the Sinfonie to the Palais Royale – bought myself an ice cream.' An ice cream? What a party animal he must have been.

Someone told me that the silence between movements (not a pleasant word at the best of times) was all Wagner's fault.

Apparently, the preparatory silence before a performance is known as the 'Bayreuth hush' and it dates from a personal request from Wagner for the audience to be quiet during a performance of *Parsifal* at Bayreuth. The whole thing rather backfired when the maestro, moved by one of his own scenes, called out 'Bravo', and was promptly hissed by the audience.

For symphonic silence there are those who blame Leopold Stokowski, the conductor perhaps most famous for conducting Disney's orchestra in *Fantasia*. Apparently, he believed that clapping in the middle of a symphony spoilt the sanctity of the experience. He described applause as 'a relic from the Dark Ages' and even held meetings to try to get the wretched noise stopped. Surely we can't allow someone who was Mickey Mouse's friend to set the tone? It must be time for a change.

It was today in 1742 that George Frideric Handel's oratorio *Messiah* made its world premiere. Given its subject matter, you might have thought that this was a piece designed for the reverential silence of the church or chapel. In fact, the first performance took place in Neal's Music Hall, on Fishamble Street, near Dublin's Temple Bar district. I like Handel. He seems to have been a man given to both temper and fisticuffs, and I can't believe he wanted the whole thing conducted with a funereal overtone. Nor, indeed, does Fishamble Street sound the place for it.

The world needs more applause not less. How much jollier would waiting in a bus queue be if everyone applauded when the Number 36 finally turned up.

Today marks the birth in 1899 of Alfred Mosher Butts, the man who invented Scrabble. My family and I play a variation of this game in which you choose a general accent, such as French, as the theme for the game. Words can be spelt any way you like, but you have to be able to say them confidently in the accent in order to get points. Anything outrageous gets not just good marks but wild applause. It's a good sound.

I went this week to a preview of the new musical *Gone with the Wind*. It is a lengthy affair. (Margaret Mitchell took nine years to write the book, and you certainly get some sense of that.) At one point the heroine shoots a 'varmint Yankee'. The young man playing the part was enthusiastic and dived to his death with unbounded energy.

By chance, his demise coincided exactly with the late return from the lavatory of a woman in the front row. She was wearing a rather spectacular ensemble in fuchsia, and for one brief moment was perfectly illuminated in a spotlight.

Startled by the light, she looked up to see the civil war combatant flying towards her. His head landed just short of the lip of the stage and inches from her nose, causing her to fall backwards into her seat with surprise. No cannonball could have been more effective. It made you think the whole war could have been over so much quicker if they had simply fired bit-part players at each other. No one applauded, but they should have. Oh, they should have.

Help! The market's being squeezed again

20 April 2008

I ATTEMPT TO WAKE EACH morning rident. Smiling. Beaming. I don't quite manage cachinnation (guffawing), but certainly there is a trace of the sort of smile that could have made Mona Lisa a mint. Then, someone on the *Today* programme decides to consult an economist. Any economist – and instantly my *joie de vivre* sinks with the speed of a Zimbabwean dollar.

The news agenda tends to run in cycles in which all politicians repeat the same phrases as if they might eventually mean something. For some time we were berated with the notion of 'family values'. I don't know what it meant, but it conjured up an image of Britain divided into units of relatives, all bearing the same 'two for one' price sticker. Then we had 'robust' (a chest condition developed by oarsmen). No one dared give a response that was not robust. It was enough to make you long for the flaccid answer of yesteryear.

At the moment, the phrase of the month is 'credit crunch', which sounds like an economist's breakfast cereal. I like words and I am bored with the constant repetition of the same ones. Were any one of the wretched broadcasting financial experts to declare not that the housing market is 'being squeezed' but that this dapocaginous (mean-spirited; heartless) rigadoon (lively baroque period dance) of fiscal ineptitude that has elumbated (made weak in the loins) every homeowner to an abapical (at the lowest point) financial state is made no better by the rodomontade (bluster) of politicians yarling (howling), why then I might again pay attention.

*

How thrilling therefore to wake up one morning and discover Barack Obama, a man who so often speaks like a Hallmark greeting card, being had up over semantics. He got himself into trouble for declaring that people in small Midwestern towns of America 'cling' to guns and religion because they don't have anything else. This was clearly a mistake. I grew up in the States. I know that the word 'cling' should only be used in conjunction with the word 'film'.

It seems to me that in order to stay out of trouble politicians should go one of two ways. The first is to stay quiet like 'Silent' Cal Coolidge, a former and taciturn American President. He was a man of so few words that when he died Dorothy Parker asked, 'How could they tell?' Silence can be a fine thing. It was today in 1893 that the great silent movie clown Harold Lloyd was born. Here was a man could make people weep with laughter without even opening his mouth. (Boris Johnson has the same effect on me today.) Lloyd's 'glasses character' was the inspiration for Superman's identity as Clark Kent, proving, as it did, the notion that a man could hide his identity simply by taking his glasses off. Sadly, Mr Obama doesn't wear glasses and can't seem to keep quiet.

In that case, the second option is to use words no one else understands. This has the effect of making people think you are clever when in fact you are still just a politician. There was a senator from Wisconsin called Alexander Wiley who once declared, 'I think the country is entitled to know he is young, vigorous and full of spizerinctum.' I have no idea whom he was talking about, but would guess no one pursued the matter once they hit the word 'spizerinctum'.

Wiley came from the small town of Chippewa Falls and said 'spizerinctum' was a word coined by a local banker to describe someone full of pep and vitality. I've been to Chippewa Falls and the need for such a word is not immediately obvious. Check out the activities available this weekend and you'd be hard pushed to choose between the Wilderness Medicine & First Aid in the Wild course today or tomorrow's Cold Climate Grape Management Workshop. Of course the fact that the local theatre is named after Fanny Hill suggests there must be more to the place than first meets the eye.

This is a great day for Wisconsonians for it was today in 1836 that the US Congress passed the act which created the Wisconsin Territory. Who knew that this fine state would go on to produce the first Barbie doll, claim the town of Somerset as the Inner Tubing Capital of the World and be home to the Hamburger hall of fame? These are the sorts of things Mr Obama still has time to focus on in Pennsylvania in order to triumph on Tuesday. Stop worrying about people clutching their Remington rifles on the way to church and highlight the important stuff.

Take the town of Hazleton, which maintains a law prohibiting lecturers from sipping carbonated drinks while speaking to students in a school auditorium, or Kennett Square, self-proclaimed Mushroom Capital of the World, or Punxsutawney, whose world-renowned weather forecasting groundhog, Punxsutawney Phil, helps make them the weather capital of the world. Bring these things to the stump, Mr Obama, and the keys to the White House will be yours.

How to stage a polite invasion

4 May 2008

THEY SAY WISDOM COMES WITH age, but I wonder if age does-n't occasionally arrive unaccompanied. I have long accepted that the accumulation of years means accepting certain changes. On the downside, my arms are now too short for my eyesight. On the upside, the spreading of my *derrière* means that I can check it in a mirror without turning round.

The compensation for these decrepitudes was, I thought, that I would grow more certain about matters of importance. That I would have viewed the world long enough to have clearly formed ideas about right and wrong, about good and evil. Yet, the truth is I find myself less and less confident about almost every subject you care to mention. Would that I had the blind-ing certainty of the astonishing number of people who were appalled by my light-hearted suggestion that classical music could do with a bit more spontaneous clapping. Why, I might as well have suggested hot-drink juggling by nudists as suitable Saturday night entertainment.

This week, I was astonished to discover myself in the unique position of being in agreement with a member of the Iranian regime. Here is a political entity with which I have so far had some intellectual dispute. However, the Prosecutor General, Ghorban-Ali Dorri Najafabadi, has declared that the importa-tion of Barbie dolls is having a destructive effect on the culture of his country.

Despite the fact that his job title makes him sound like a throwback to the Salem witch trials, I have to say I concur. Barbie did not stand alone in Mr Najafabadi's firing line. (This is just as well. Were her proportions translated into human measurements she would be about 7ft tall with size one feet and unlikely to withstand even the mildest breeze.) The Prosecutor General also singled out Batman, Spider-Man and Harry Potter as the work of the Western devil, and here I find a counter-argument tricky to come by.

It made me realise that there were many more ways to invade a country than had ever occurred to me. All the while I thought Ms Rowling was simply a marketing miracle. I had no idea that she had in fact launched a bespectacled schoolboy wizard, packed with decadent influences, as a modern Trojan horse. Perhaps I have less clarity because the world is increasingly complex. I long for the old-fashioned system of invasion where you just openly packed a knapsack and headed across a border to take over.

It was today in 1855 that William Walker, an American adventurer, strolled out of San Francisco with fifty-seven chums to conquer Nicaragua. Mr Walker was a professional filibuster. I use the word not in the sense of hijacking debate, but in pirating an entire nation.

As with George Walker Bush, this Walker was a man not troubled by doubt, and he was confident that the world would be a better place if Latin America were run by white people speaking English. With a speed to be envied, Walker defeated the Nicaraguan national army and took control of the country in just over two weeks. Sadly, the whole thing went to his head. He held an election in the Mugabe school of democratic government and everything went downhill from there.

Nevertheless, I like the notion of the solo soldier of fortune. Today marks the birth in 1827 of John Hanning Speke, a British Indian Army officer who tramped about Africa looking for the source of the Nile. On his first outing to Somalia with Richard Burton (the explorer, not the Elizabeth Taylor fan), the pair were captured and stabbed. They escaped, but Burton had a javelin impaled in both cheeks, which, I believe, made gargling tricky. When Speke finally completed his explorations, he sent a telegram to London which simply read, 'The Nile is settled.' He was wrong, but I love the certainty of the statement.

Whichever way you look at it, invading another country without being invited is, as with, apparently, applauding the first movement of a symphony, terribly bad manners. If I know anything, it is that I like good behaviour, but I recently learnt an interesting thing. The English word 'etiquette' comes from the old French verb *estiquer* – to attach. It seems that, in days gone by, a list called *l'estiquette* used to be attached to a post in the courtyards of castles and palaces. It was a statement of the rules of the day, and it was frequently torn down and amended as the lord of the manor saw fit.

Nothing was written in stone and no rule was immutable. Thus, genuine etiquette allows for change and uncertainty.

I've got next weekend off and I'm thinking of invading somewhere warm. Anyone want to come?

I couldn't find a tartan, so a title will have to do

11 May 2008

I ONCE WASTED HALF AN hour in a shop in Edinburgh that guaranteed to find the correct tartan for any surname. I had high hopes of something subtle shot through with the red and white of the Danish flag, but inexplicably, the Toksvig tartan eluded them. All this may now change. I have attained an age where I am the target of one of two types of birthday gift. I either get plants, because I have patently reached the trug-owning stage of life, or something in the comedy line, because there can be little left to a mature woman but wry amusement.

Among the latter which fell upon my door mat recently was the gift of a lairdship in Scotland. I am now, should anyone wish to address me correctly, Sandi Toksvig, Lady of Kincavel. The accompanying certificate goes to great lengths to convince me that the title is genuine. Why, it declares, the papers have been drawn up by a Scottish lawyer, as if probity knew no greater heights. My elevation to the land-owning classes is accompanied by an assurance that I now possess one square foot of Scotland, which I may visit if I choose. I paced the dimensions out and realise I shall need to shed pounds before I decide to sit down for even the simplest picnic on my estate.

I have never been a big fan of titles and have great admiration for those who quietly decline them. Were I so inclined I might years ago have styled myself Dane Sandi Toksvig. This, I think, would have fooled only the odd dyslexic maître d', but it might have amused the children. The title 'dame' comes from the Latin *dominus*, meaning 'lord', and is also, curiously, the name of a

Danish death metal band, whatever that may be. (Don't all rush out to purchase the CDs.)

The bestowing of the DBE on an actress is meant to give women from the world's second oldest profession a veneer of respectability. Today marks, for example, the birth in 1892 of Dame Margaret Rutherford. She had had a tough upbringing with a mentally unstable father who had battered his own pa to death. It's that kind of dysfunctional upbringing that often propels people to the stage, where they can spend a lifetime pretending to be someone else. She didn't make her acting debut until she was thirty-three, but went on to raise chortles around the world.

Her life, however, is more interesting than her films. She married the actor Stringer Davis and in the 1950s they adopted the writer Gordon Langley Hall. Adoption is a commendable thing, but Gordon was twenty-five at the time and a curious addition to the family. He was the illegitimate son of the writer Vita Sackville-West's chauffeur and another servant at Sissinghurst Castle. He grew up knowing the Bloomsbury set and often claimed to be the inspiration for Virginia Woolf's *Orlando*. After his adoption, Gordon moved to South Carolina, had a sex-change operation and, as Dawn Pepita Hall, married a young black motor mechanic called John-Paul Simmons. Their marriage in 1969 took place at home owing to bomb threats on the church. The story goes on with shootings, poisonings, rape, a somewhat unexpected baby and finally John-Paul Simmons departing for a woman said to have shot and killed her first husband.

There you have a screenplay that no studio would ever have given credibility to yet it is a far more interesting storyline than anything I've seen in ages. I think anyone who takes on an honorific prefix to their name has some duty to lead a more interesting life, or at least pretend to. Here the shining example is Baron Karl Friedrich Hieronymus Freiherr von

Münchhausen. This German adventurer was born today in 1720. He did have the odd foray abroad to fight for kith and kin, which you'd think would leave him with a tale to tell, but none of it can have seemed sufficiently exciting. As a consequence the baron began to make things up and before long he was riding cannonballs, pulling himself out of swamps by his own hair, shooting a stag with cherry-stones and fifty brace of duck with a single shot. There is a marvellous moment when he saves the lives of two English spies using the identical sling that killed Goliath and I can't begin to relate the wonderful effects of the frost upon his servant's French horn.

Now that I am ennobled I feel honour-bound to lead a more intriguing life. As far as I can work out, the Dundas clan once ruled the roost in Kincavel. Confusingly, they took to naming almost everyone in the family Robert, so it's hard to know who did what. I do know that the 23rd Laird joined the East India Company and in 1792 died in a shipwreck off the coast of Madagascar, which is pretty good. Their motto is *Essayez*, which simply means 'Try', which I like as there seems no pressure actually to succeed. The tartan has a pleasing hint of red. I've ordered a waistcoat and am designing my coat of arms as we speak. Adventure will be round the corner.

Garden birds and other monsters

18 May 2008

I'M HAVING TROUBLE WITH OUR feathered friends. I have done everything in my power to encourage them into my garden – bird baths dripping in glistening water, peanuts that would make Jimmy Carter nostalgic, seeds bursting with succulence – but, it would seem, none of this is enough. Leave the door to my garden study open for a second and one of the airborne brigade is in, flapping about with all the effectiveness of Gordon Brown facing a decision.

The correct collective noun for a group of birds is a 'dissimulation' and I think that is about right. A dissimulation is a form of deception in which one conceals the truth. These fraudulent feathered fellows loll about in my garden pretending to have an eye on the ball of fat that I painstakingly created for them from the Sunday joint, when all the while what they really want to do is to cover my encyclopaedia in guano. I sit down to weave together light elements of the English language, but instead find myself recreating the facial expressions of Tippi Hedren faced with an unkindness of ravens in *The Birds*.

I've never been a fan of the horror film. My limit for experiencing celluloid pain was reached years ago when Bambi and Thumper fell over on the ice. I've never understood why people want to pay good money to have the bejesus scared out of them by a scary movie. I once went with a friend to see a film called *Seven*. It took me a while to realise that the thrust of the story was to recreate horrific crimes based on the seven deadly sins. Once it had dawned on me that we had reached only number three, I left and went out for ice cream.

*

It was today in 1897 that Bram Stoker's gothic horror novel *Dracula* was first published and I freely confess never to having seen a single frame of film with the same title. In the book, you can tell that things are not going to go well right from the start, when you find the young English solicitor, Jonathan Harker, on his way to help Count Dracula with a property transaction. Anyone who has ever had anything to do with buying and selling property knows that someone somewhere is about to have the blood sucked out of them. The story takes many twists and turns, with a shipwreck, a bad-tempered wolf and the lovely Lucy Westenra having to be persuaded to die by having a stake through her heart, garlic put in her mouth and a beheading for good measure.

No one in these terror flicks ever dies easily, and a tenacious clinging to life can be impressive. Today is the feast day of Saint Venantius. He was just seventeen when he upset someone enough to be whipped, have his teeth knocked out and jaw broken, then be singed with flaming torches, hung upside down over a fire, thrown to the lions and finally hurled off a cliff. What is clear from this ancient Italian tale is that the lions must have been having an off day.

The original title for Stoker's book was *The Un-Dead*. This is not how we like our dead and I am reminded of the Brazilian funeral parlour which, a few years ago, got into trouble for its controversial slogan: 'Our clients have never come back to complain.'

The only monster movie I would recommend to anyone is *Reptilicus*, which was made in 1961. This is a rare Danish-American co-production in which a winged, dragon-like monster attempts to eat Copenhagen. It's a classic tale in which the classic tail of a monster is found by miners and taken to a lab. Here the staff fail to follow health and safety basics and leave the lab door open. Reptilicus begins to regenerate and, before you know it, he is roaming the Danish countryside eating cows and upsetting ordinary folk trying to have their tea.

The film was made in two versions – one in Danish and the other in English. In the Danish version the comedian who first inspired me to tread the boards, Dirch Passer (born today in 1926), was given a comic song. This was cut for the Americans, who clearly thought some of the impact of reptile death and destruction was lessened by an interlude of musical merriment. The reason I've seen it (and here I present the all-time piece of horror trivia) is that my father, Claus Toksvig, played the reporter in the film who kept trying to calm everyone down. There are marvellous shots of him reassuring the nation that 'there is no cause for alarm', while over his shoulder you can see the annihilating beast eating the town hall.

If I do sit down to watch some Bram Stoker-inspired flick it will have to be *Horror of Dracula* with Christopher Lee and Peter Cushing, made the year I was born. According to film lore, there was a scene in which Lee was required to pick up a girl and hurl her into an obligatory grave. Lee took the action a little too seriously and upon depositing his victim, overbalanced and fell in on top of her. Cushing, with his immaculate diction, is said to have remarked, 'We are not making that kind of film, dear fellow . . .'

It's Rhubarb versus the Puppet Man

15 June 2008

IT'S THAT TIME OF THE year when the actors' union, Equity, holds its elections. Of all the political processes in which I take an interest, this one pleases me the most. There are votes for stuntmen, votes for people whose job title is to be an 'extra' in life, and even nods to the representation of pole-dancers. I have to confess to some bitterness over my own failed pole-dancing career (I blame the Pole. He was far too busy sending cash to Gdansk to concentrate on the act.) Despite this, I read all the candidates' statements with intense interest and am undecided between a vote for Rhubarb the Clown or someone who calls himself the Puppet Man (please don't think I am kidding).

How dull the previous battle between Barack and Hillary suddenly seems. How much more interesting would the wider world of politics be if those leading from the fore could also offer plate-spinning or unicycle-riding when matters got a little heated. Think of the Puppet Man – how refreshingly honest to have a candidate who is open about the fact that he is answering a question while pulling someone else's strings. I have to confess to a leaning towards Rhubarb, though. His website states that 'Rhubarb does not talk' as 'his show transcends language and culture'. How utterly splendid, and it suggests a possible future for Gordon Brown already. The PM has the look of a man trapped in an invisible box and might well see the value of mime.

I think it was my concentration on these theatrical contests that led me to have yet another of my endless misunderstandings the other day. I awoke to endless chatter about 'negative equity' and developed a full-blown notion that this was an off-shoot of the actors' union. Clearly, 'negative equity' was a small union sub-branch of entirely depressed thespians who did nothing all day but sit around moaning that show business was not what it used to be. Of course, the real story was nowhere near as interesting, involving as it did those harbingers of general joy to society – economists and estate agents. The thrust, as I understand it, is that we're all doomed and my house is now worth £4, but only if I include the cutlery and plates.

Numbers have figured large in the weekly news. The number forty-two, for example, has had more of an outing than its near neighbours forty-one and forty-three can possibly have thought fair. I'm sure I've mentioned before that maths to me is an entirely foreign language. Take the Ukrainian mathematician Nikolai Chebotaryov, who was born today in 1894. Chebotaryov is apparently revered among the numerate for his 'density theorem'. Check this with that fountain of all superficial knowledge, Wikipedia, and you will be told that this theorem 'in algebraic number theory describes statistically the splitting of primes in a given Galois extension K of the field Q of rational numbers'. Everyone got that? As far as I am concerned, you might as well use the theorem that proves that all cats have nine tails, which goes like this: 'No cat has eight tails. Since one cat has one more tail than no cat, it must have nine tails.'

I like the number forty-two. We short people applaud, for example, Rule 42 in *Alice in Wonderland* which states that 'All persons more than a mile high' must leave the court. There is a splendid moment in the Bible for the follicly challenged. A group of yobs tease Elisha because he is bald and God sends two female bears to maul forty-two of the reprobates. There are, as it happens, forty-two laws of cricket, a game in which maths is critical. Straightforward sums suggests that thirty-six ought to be the maximum runs possible in an over, but not so.

263

There was a game in Western Australia in 1894 when a ball struck by the batsman came to rest in a tree. The umpire declared that the ball was still visible and had not hit the ground, so the batsmen should carry on running. The tree lacked low branches for climbing, so the fielders searched for an axe with which to chop the thing down. When this proved fruitless, someone produced a rifle and they began trying to shoot the ball down. They gave up only when the visitors declared after completing 286 runs on a single ball. Splendid sums.

What saddens me is that in all the chat about forty-two this week I don't think I heard much mention of history. That, for example, it was today in 1215 that King John put his seal to the Magna Carta, which in theory stopped naughty people in charge keeping prisoners past their sell-by date. Or that today marks the death, in 1381, of poor old Wat Tyler whose followers were promised freedoms never delivered.

I suspect the discussion about forty-two is far from over. As Dan Quayle, the former American Vice-President, once said, 'I believe we are on an irreversible trend towards more freedom and democracy, but that could change.' I wonder what Rhubarb thinks about it all.

It takes more than rain to put us off a rumba

29 June 2008

IT IS AT THIS TIME of year that I find the people of these fine isles to be at their most optimistic. I don't just mean that as usual we entered Wimbledon with yet another British 'hopeful', I'm thinking of our stoic determination resolutely to ignore the weather. Despite the fact that rain is almost guaranteed there is hardly a parish in the place not about to launch some open-air festival or other.

The other night, in the name of culture, I enjoyed a particularly windswept and rain-drizzled picnic at Hampton Court Palace. It was a quintessentially British affair. Emblazered men carried folding chairs and tables miles from a car park in a field in order to become practically cryogenically preserved over an unsuitable salad prepared by sun-dressed women. Those in charge had cleverly provided the usual paucity of ladies' loos, thus encouraging us, I think, to herd together for heat. Shivering like extras in a Pingu movie, we moved post-picnic to a central courtyard in the heart of the palace to hear the Cuban band the Buena Vista Social Club.

By now the weather had worsened, but I can't say I was worried. Surely at a musical event in a thunderstorm, I reasoned, the most likely person to be hit by lightning is the conductor. The BV Social Club is made up of nine venerable old gentlemen, a couple of young men and a woman singer who moved as though she were made entirely of liquid. I was in no doubt that old Henry VIII would have had someone's head off just to get to her. Perhaps it was her sizzling sex appeal, perhaps it was irritation at the strict instructions from the organisers for everyone to remain seated, but within moments the senior citizens of Havana had this frozen Surrey crowd on their feet. It was a joyous combination of cha-cha-cha and the unique British sound of waxed rainwear trying to find the beat.

Performing in the open air used to take place in this country because no one had taken the time to invent the light bulb. Take the great Globe Theatre in London. Here the shows took place in the afternoon, not because everyone worked half-days but because it was the only time anyone could see what they were doing. Being close to an open exit was also good years ago, when health and safety was not quite the luminous-bib affair that it is today.

It was on this very day in 1613 (and curiously, during a performance of *Henry VIII*) that an over-enthusiastic stage management department managed to burn the theatre to the ground after failing to consider the impact a real canonball might have on a thatched roof. The ease of egress for the audience is reflected in the fact that only one person was listed as being hurt.

I don't know what he can have been doing, for the injury stemmed from the man's trousers catching fire and having to be put out with a bottle of ale.

I've never performed at the Globe but I did once spend a season as a member of the acting company at the Open Air Theatre in Regent's Park. Over a summer in 1981, while Princess Di was getting married, I was preoccupied, playing astonishingly minor roles in a number of Shakespeare plays and a smattering of George Bernard Shaw. It rained so hard that year that for some time there was a moat in front of the stage. Indeed, it was so deep that the first few seats could only have been sold with scuba lessons.

There were many curiosities about working there, not least of which was the audience's failure to comprehend that on a well-lit afternoon we could see them just as well as they could see us. For those of us with limited lines to be troubled with, this gave us daily shows of our own to watch. There was, for example, the time our leading man, a Lothario of some legend, espied a pretty young woman heading slowly down the many steps from the top of the theatre. She carried a camera. He paused and posed, repeating his soliloquy in order that she might get his best side, only to see her reach the stage, turn and take a picture of her friend high up in their seats.

When rain fell, as inevitably it did, the acting company was required to soldier on until an announcement was made by the company manager, requesting us to leave the stage. This had to be timed finely as no one wanted to return any money to the drenched and disappointed theatregoer. Many was the time we galloped to the end of *Much Ado About Nothing* through such a torrent of rain that only those members of the company with swimming badges made it to the curtain call.

The many festivals I am performing at this year include Henley in a couple of weeks. Here I feel I'll be on to a winner because it's by the river and they'll automatically have boats for back-up. Last year Henley had 22.61 inches of rain. You don't suppose that could all have been on the same day, do you?

With all the grace of a Papal Bull

6 July 2008

I OFTEN WONDER WHETHER EVENTS which today we regard as historic had the same impact while they were actually happening. Whether during the Reformation the *Daily Express* of the time ran headlines reading 'House Prices in Freefall as Church Splits'. Last week, conservative Anglicans issued the Jerusalem Declaration, which represents possibly the biggest Church divide since Henry VIII left Rome. The conservatives are cross about gay bishops. This week, further furore over women bishops. Soon we may have two kinds of Anglican churches – the liberal ones, where love is welcome wherever it is fortunate enough to be found, and the conservative ones, which have a rather stricter door policy. To the outsider the difference may be tricky to spot, so I've had an idea. Why not put signs outside the liberal establishments that read 'No Smoting'? We could have red circles with a line over, say, a woman with her mouth open being hit by a thunderbolt.

Smoting, or more technically, 'smiting', used to happen all the time. The Philistines were smoted, the children of Ammon had their fair share, and during the Black Death pretty much everyone in Europe had a turn with somewhere between a third and two thirds of Europe's population dropping dead from the pestilence. Things were terrible and some people blamed the Jews, so today in 1348 Pope Clement VI issued a Papal Bull explaining that it wasn't their fault. Nevertheless Jews, foreigners, beggars, lepers, anyone looking at you a bit funny were dispatched in a series of pogroms during which the sale of 'Love thy neighbour' bumper stickers was at an all-time low.

*

I like the sound of a Papal Bull. It sounds like a barnyard creature with tremendous connections and nice red shoes. Bulls and religion seem to be the *motif du jour*, for at noon today the festival of San Fermín begins in Pamplona, Spain. Saint Fermín is said to have been martyred by being dragged through the streets of Pamplona by bulls. As if that weren't a warning to everyone to avoid disgruntled bovines, the fiesta includes the famous *encierro* or running of the bulls. Young (and, I hope we can presume, mildly inebriated) men run half a mile down cobbled streets chased by a bull battalion. People have died doing this, but being gored, trampled or just badly chafed by a living piece of leather is apparently all part of celebrating the saint.

You can't fault religion on the provision of drama. How *EastEnders* must yearn for some of the storylines. It was today in 1415 that the religious thinker Jan Hus was burnt at the stake by the Council of Constance. Jan had been upset about Indulgences and said one or two words about them that clearly put him the wrong side of council care.

I always think of an Indulgence as champagne in a hot tub, but in fact it's a sort of pardon where the sinner is let off some of the hotter aspects of retribution. Jan thought some of these official acts of forgiveness were simply available for money (the very idea) and earned himself a centre seat at a council barbecue as a result. To be honest, his demise was a diversion because the council had got together for a different reason. At the time, three chaps were all claiming to be Pope. Not knowing who had been given such a top job suggests that someone had taken their eye off the ball during the interview stage and it took Sir Alan Sugar-like decisions to put the matter right.

Apart from Pope-picking, the men of Constance also ordered a book to be written called *Ars moriendi* ('The Art of Dying'). Whether Sir Thomas More read it before he died today in 1535 is unknown. Thomas would have been your man for a newspaper column on the English split with Rome. He was once Henry VIII's friend, but they stopped seeing each other when Tom lost his head over religion. You may recall Henry wanted to marry Anne Boleyn but, annoyingly, he was already married. He wanted the Pope to pretend the marriage had never happened, but the Pope wouldn't play ball and nor would Tom. A lesson there for us all not to get involved in our friends' domestic affairs. Thomas was beheaded, although the King showed his respect for an old friend by allowing a mere chop of the axe rather than the hanging, drawing and quartering he was strictly speaking entitled to.

Fortunately, we have in the main moved on from burnings, beheadings and baseless blaming. But possible schisms lie ahead as the debate rages on whether we are all created equal or in fact some are more equal than others. I would have thought in the modern climate (which is rising faster than the red paint on the fundraising thermometer for the church roof) we might have other things to worry about. Still, what do I know? At least I've got these great 'No Smoting' stickers and I'm working on a neat device to get a mote out of someone else's eye.

Where angels should fear to tread

13 July 2008

WHILE NURSING A FAMILY MEMBER back to health, I have watched more television than is good for my own constitution. Our satellite dish allows access to innumerable channels that I cannot imagine have any following. Indeed, there are broadcasters so niche in their appeal that you wonder whether it wouldn't be cheaper for them just to send a free video to anyone who expresses an interest. Skimming through the listings of these obscure offerings is like entering the undergrowth of the television jungle without a machete.

In the quest for something diverting late at night, I came across a fly-on-the-wall programme about a woman called Katie Price and her husband, Peter Andre. I met Ms Price once. She was dressed as an angel and, although we both appeared on the same television show, I cannot remember why. In the late-night offering I stumbled on, she was spending some time trying to decide what to wear, never mentioning the fact that she had a perfectly nice pair of wings in the cupboard. During the course of the five minutes I endured of this 'reality' entertainment, I learnt a great deal about the most intimate exchanges of body fluid, or lack thereof, of the couple in question. Knowing what else flies like to sit on, the term 'fly-on-the-wall' suddenly seemed astonishingly apt.

To me, it's not just one's parents whose sex life should be utterly unknown, but everyone else's as well. These days there is far too much information about all manner of things relating to anyone who might happen to be in the public eye. I know, for example, that today is the anniversary of when, in

271

1985, Ronald Reagan underwent surgery to have polyps removed from his colon. I'm not surprised he had polyps at that end, as that is mostly where he spoke from, but, nevertheless, it is a nugget of medical knowledge I could have done without.

I preferred things when details about the condition of world leaders were sketchy. I know that Julius Caesar, probably born today in 100 BC and at one time the undisputed master of the Roman world, may have had either epilepsy or hypoglycaemic fits. I don't really care. I'm more inclined to be impressed that he managed to shout, '*Ista quidem vis est!*' ('But that is violence!') when his assassin came at him with a knife – a moment when even my most ingrained Latin would have left me. I don't even care for the suggestion that he got his name from a relative born by caesarean section. My squeamishness prefers the alternative explanations – that someone in the family had thick hair (*caesaries*); or bright grey eyes (*oculis caesiis*); or, even better, had killed an elephant in battle (*caesai* – Moorish, not Latin, if you are a pedant).

Usually I feel I have enough detail. I don't need a graphic documentary to tell me that if Pope Clement X (born today in 1590) died of gout, then he probably liked a tipple. Mental matters are, I confess, a little more gripping. I am fond of the poet John Clare (born today, 1793), because he was both brilliant and patently barking. I think anyone who spends time in an Essex asylum declaring, 'I'm John Clare now. I was Byron and Shakespeare formerly', is interesting. Or even Queen Louise of Sweden (born today, 1889) who, because she was rich, was allowed to be eccentric rather than crazy. She often travelled as 'Countess of Gripsholm' or 'Mrs Olsson', smuggling her dogs with her. She clearly feared her self-imposed anonymity might also be her downfall, for she also carried a small card, reading, 'I am the Queen of Sweden', in case she got knocked down by a bus.

*

272

The trouble is I am not immune to gossip. Just when I think I have my moral compass firmly fixed I come across a curious historical titbit which leaves me gagging for more. Today marks the birth in 1527 of the great Elizabethan scientist John Dee. Dee coined the term 'British Empire', without which there would be no biannual opportunity to declare, 'Good grief, you'll never guess who's got an OBE.' Dee was also keen on maths, so I doubt that he was a hit at parties. He was once arrested and charged with 'calculating', something I have been longing to have happen to those clerks at Revenue and Customs who keep writing to me with incorrect sums.

It turns out 'calculating' means casting horoscopes, and here lay Dee's problems late in life. He concluded his years obsessed with the supernatural. Then two things happened. 1) Dee took a very young wife. 2) Dee met Edward Kelley, a man who convinced him that he could talk to angels. Soon the angels were chattering away and instructing Kelley that Dee had to share his young wife with him. Apparently, Dee believed him and the great Elizabethan wife swap was under way. Now there is a programme I'd like to see. Come to think of it, I know this woman who has her own angel costume . . .

It's summertime – the living should be easy

3 August 2008

THE GLORIOUS AMERICAN WRITER Flannery O'Connor (who died today in 1964) once wrote, 'Everywhere I go, I'm asked if I think the universities stifle writers. My opinion is that they don't stifle enough of them.'

It is summertime, the sun shines and I ought to be out supping strawberries or, at the very least, knocking someone else's croquet ball over the boundary. Instead, I am desk-bound with correspondence. I thought the advent of email was supposed to render me paper-free; that the weight of mis-sives could be lifted from my shoulders by a single 'accidental' pressing of the delete key – but no. I am overwhelmed with laudable pen-to-paper efforts and will need to employ many elves over the next few months to make even a dent in the nec-essary replies.

I had a glorious period some time ago when I moved house and the Post Office failed to take my redirection request seri-ously. Post went off into the ether and for a while no one wrote to me – other than, after some weeks, the Post Office, to say it was looking into the matter.

I suppose I should take heart from the fact that having no time for carefully composed sentences is hardly a modern phenome-non. I always had an image that those of our forefathers not actively involved in ploughing or dying of pestilence had aeons of time for quill-dipping. That, in fact, they did little else between meals other than scribe letters, compose madrigals and make up new rules for real tennis, but not so.

It was today in 1527 that the first known letter sent from

North America was penned by the English sailor John Rut. Rut had been sent by Henry VIII on an expedition to find the North-West Passage. By then Henry had fallen for Anne Boleyn and was trying to get rid of his first wife, so presumably didn't have the time himself to look up foreign passages.

By summer John was in Newfoundland where, frankly, even today there is not much to do other than fishing. Great fishing, but I'm not sure it fills a day to capacity. You'd think Rut would have had plenty of time to catch the King up on his holiday adventures, but he concluded his letter: 'In the Haven of St John the third day of August written in hast 1527, by your servant John Rut.' Indeed, written in so much 'hast' that he didn't even have time to spell the word properly.

I know that my burden is nothing new. Engraved in the stone façade of New York City's main post office is the statement, 'Neither snow nor rain nor heat nor gloom of night stays these couriers from the swift completion of their appointed rounds.' It sounds like a lot for a postal union to live up to, but in fact it is a 2,500-year-old quote from Herodotus, writing about the Persians who delivered letters on horseback. This suggests that even the great Persian poet Rudaki sighed as cylinders in Akkadian cuneiform (never an easy read) clunked onto the mat with requests to speak at the Babylonian Ball or the Caucasus's Caucus.

Please forgive me while I, in some 'hast', try to slash through a few things in one blow: no, I don't know if slouch hats were worn on the North-West Frontier in 1947; the phrase 'the gostak distims the doshes' was invented by an American head-master, Andrew Ingraham, in 1903, and I did not make it up; how I should love to open (or close, I can't recall) a Scout hut in Derbyshire in 2010, but sadly time is my enemy; and no, I don't claim to be Danish merely for comedic purposes.

*

I hate being in a hurry, for I love both receiving and sending a good letter. While I dash off a reply concerning my possible attendance at a barbecue for crematorium engineers, I leave you with my favourite piece of correspondence of all time. It was written in 1943 by the British Ambassador to Moscow to Lord Pembroke at the Foreign Office in London. It is polite and extremely well constructed, but I have to warn you it has adult content. If you are easily shocked do please look away now.

My Dear Reggie,
In these dark days man tends to look for little shafts of light from Heaven. My days are probably darker than yours, and I need, my God I do, all the light I can get. But I am a decent fellow, and I do not want to be mean about what little brightness is shed upon me from time to time.

So I propose to share with you a tiny flash that has illuminated my sombre life, and tell you that God has given me a new Turkish colleague whose card tells me he is called Mustapha Kunt. We all feel like that, Reggie, now and then, especially when spring is upon us, but few of us would care to put it on our cards. It takes a Turk to do that.

Sir Archibald Clerk Kerr

My ideal games all involve sitting down

10 August 2008

FOR THE HISTORIANS '10TH AUGUST' means only one thing. It is shorthand for the storming of the Tuileries Palace in Paris in 1792, which led, of course, to the monarchy giving up being royal and having to give French lessons instead. Anyone who has been in Paris of an August afternoon will know how easy it is to get hot under the collar. You do have to wonder if the royals wouldn't have been better off just heading to the hills until the autumn and waiting for everyone to calm down. I would have thought unseating the monarchy would have been tricky if you arrived at the palace and found no one was home.

I never want to do much of anything in August and rarely feel like storming anywhere. I did once lose my temper in B&Q in July, but even then failed to lead a much-needed coup in the wallpaper aisle. For me it is a season for games. I don't mean Olympic Games. Nothing that energetic. I know those games are off and running, or off and synchronised swimming, or off and some other unlikely event, but I have to say it's not for me. Other than enjoying watching beach volleyball when I am in post-Pimm's state, I find people in snug-fitting sportswear mildly unattractive. I also never understand why they want to compete in the summer when perspiration is likely for even the most genteel, and the chance of getting a fly in your mouth while running must surely be on the up.

This is the month for slowing down, not baton-passing. For as long as possible, my family and I retreat to the Danish shores and live in a small log cabin. It has no television or telephone. We do old-fashioned things such as speak to each other, cook food that doesn't come in a packet and, in the evenings, play games. We're not world class, unlike Shusaku Honinbo, a legendary Japanese Go player who died today in 1862. Go is an extraordinary strategic board game for two players and the Japanese take it very seriously. From the seventeenth century, state sponsorship allowed some people to play full-time.

In the West, playing full-time suggests that someone has cracked some kind of benefit scheme. On that note, there is an American game I first played in the 1980s which seems to be making a bit of a comeback. It's called Public Assistance – Why Bother Working for a Living? The object of the game is to get by entirely on welfare. You get extra cash for Out-of-Wedlock Children, Saturday Night Crime (Armed Robbery, Gambling, Prostitution and Drugs) and the trick is to avoid the 'Get a Job' block. It says something about my ingrained work ethic that I always end up fully employed and worse off than everyone else.

I also wonder if this summer the game Monopoly won't be a little uncomfortable. In these days of the credit crunch, I don't know how I'll feel knowing that the price of our British house is plummeting even as we sit pushing a small iron or top hat round the board. Monopoly is credited as the invention of Charles Darrow, who was born today in 1889. Of course, the way to make money from Monopoly is to claim you invented it. Darrow was the first millionaire game-designer in the world, ignoring the fact that he based his idea on something called The Landlord's Game created by Lizzie Magie. She was eventually paid off for $500 and no royalties. An early example of the sort of honourable behaviour we've all come to expect when dealing with real estate.

There are more than 2,000 board games available, which suggests that they are being invented all the time. There is a game of newspaper headlines called Strange But True in which you have to try to decide which of these headlines – 'Woman Raises Baby Rhino in Apartment' or 'Beaver Steals Camper's Wooden

Leg' – is more likely to be true. Then there's All Wound Up, a game with wind-up pieces in which you and your deceased friends try to be the first ones out of the graveyard. Or how about Oy Vey? A politically incorrect game in which everyone is a Jewish mother with a family of two sons and two daughters. The object of the game is to get both sons to become doctors and both daughters to marry doctors.

I've thought of a game called Rain of Terror, in which you have to get as many heads of French nobility as you can into a basket before the weather changes. It's like Kerplunk but with more blood. The family don't seem that keen. In fact, they don't always share my passion for game playing and there are evenings when I find myself dependent on my trusty book of crossword puzzles. The comic American James Thurber was also a fan and his favourite story concerning his hobby involved a stay in hospital. Puzzling over a crossword, he asked a nurse, 'What seven-letter word has three 'u's in it?' She considered the question and replied, 'I don't know but it must be unusual.'

As you read this, I am trapped in an invisible box

17 August 2008

SAMUEL GOLDWYN (born today in 1882), the legendary film producer, had a John Prescott-like dexterity with the English language. He once declared, 'Colour television! Bah, I won't believe it until I see it in black and white.' When my family moved to America in 1966, we had one of the first colour televisions produced. It was a large wooden box with a panel below the screen from which three lamps – red, green and blue – glowed. I remember green being the more dominant colour, as almost everyone on the screen had an alien glow about them.

It made me think how much entertainment has changed in my lifetime. I can remember waiting in for Channel 4 to begin broadcasting, little knowing that we would soon have 100 more channels, managing, rather cleverly, to provide 100 times less choice.

It was today in 1982 that the first CDs were released to the public in Germany. My kids cannot imagine life without them and believe such a time to be antediluvian. When we last moved house, I packed up all my long-playing records and my son asked me what they were for. Today, my entire collection has been downloaded onto a player smaller than my wallet. Not that you can always tell which of the new technologies represent the way forward. Think of all those people who invested in Betamax video recorders or thought that eight-track car stereos were the cool way of the future.

There was a story recently about a young man who went on holiday to America and was desperate not to miss his favourite television show, *Prison Break*. (I've never heard of the show and can only presume it involves career criminals having a gap year away from felony.) So the man downloaded the programme onto his laptop via his mobile phone. Clearly, his mother had failed to explain to him that it is possible to just make your own fun by the pool when you are away.

Now most of us have had that experience of finding things a little more expensive abroad. I once ordered a drink in a hotel in Taormina in Sicily that was so breathtaking in price I asked if they had any rental plans for refreshments instead. Anyway, I do hope this particular episode of *Prison Break* was a gripping one, for the young, presumably pale, techno geek returned to Britain to find a bill for the download of £31,000.

The modern desire to download makes some old-fashioned entertainment seem almost inexplicable. It is hard to imagine that the legendary sex goddess, Mae West (born today in 1893), once appeared on American radio doing sketches with the ventriloquist, Edgar Bergen, father of Candice. Ventriloquism on the radio today would seem as likely as mime in a newspaper column (pay attention now as I pretend to be trapped in an invisible box), but Bergen's show was a big hit. Apparently, the NBC executives nearly had a fit as Mae West flirted with Charlie McCarthy, Bergen's wooden dummy, declaring, 'Charles, I remember our date and have the splinters to prove it.'

My kids only listen to the radio for very loud music punctuated by inane chatter from DJs with few notions about clipping their consonants. One of the few areas of entertainment we all agree on is cartoons. The entire family are fans of *The Simpsons* and we have been known to quote lines at length. I like Homer Simpson's boss Mr Burns and was unnerved to learn that the former US Attorney-General John Ashcroft used to lighten sober post-9/11 meetings by doing impressions of the man. It's not quite the robust response to terrorism that the average

281

citizen was looking for. Ashcroft's impersonation cannot, however, be as good as my son's. Arriving at a hotel in a storm, my eight-year-old boy once startled the manager by declaring in his Burns voice, 'I must slip out of these wet clothes and into a dry martini.'

It was exactly 100 years ago today that the world's first cartoon was projected in Paris. It was called *Fantasmagorie* and it was made by a man called Émile Cohl. Cohl's father was a rubber salesman. This is never going to be a good paternal career to boast to other schoolboys about. Not surprising, then, that Cohl took to the solitary entertainments of drawing and stamp-collecting. The cartoon is wonderfully surreal, as you might expect from a man who was a member of the Incoherent Movement and once went to a masked ball dressed as an artichoke. Cohl's best-known film, *Le Peintre néo-impressionniste*, has an artist displaying a blank red canvas which he claims is 'a cardinal eating lobster with tomatoes by the banks of the Red Sea'.

Freed from human restraint by their drawings, most cartoonists seem to have an odd take on life. I think replacing sanity with sketches is splendid. As Goldwyn once said, 'Anyone who would go to a psychiatrist ought to have his head examined.'

Listen, they're playing our song

31 August 2008

SO WE SAID GOODBYE TO the Olympics with a lot of Chinese people Mexican-waving and an exciting hint of the celebrations to come featuring the unique British skill for topiary work on public transportation. Not being of a sporty inclination I can't say that a four-year wait for more of the same will drag.

Not that I am without a sense of loss. I will miss, for example, the rhythmic gymnastics. Had I known in my youth that a hula hoop could be tossed with such effect to music I would never have run down a street instead chasing it with a stick. I will miss the insight into gold medal-winning technique provided by swimmers making post-contest declarations such as 'I decided to put my head down and swim really fast'. An analysis that made me wonder whether all those years of not wanting to get my hair wet was all that had stood between me and podium success. But what I shall miss most of all are the national anthems. Where else but during the Olympics can you hear such a cacophony of cultural celebration?

Today, as it happens, is the day the great nation of Moldova celebrates its national tune. Today is Moldovan Limba Noastra or 'Day of Our Language', which is also the name of its anthem. The Republic of Moldova is one of those Eastern European regions that has shuffled about during history, with different countries all trying to have the last word on who's in charge. Since 1994 the Moldovans have had not only their own flag but a tune to go with it, and so naturally everyone takes this as a reason to down some of the local wine. And what a cracking tune it is. The sort of rabble-rousing composition in which a

283

man on heavy cymbals is absolutely essential. It's the kind of martial beat that makes even the non-Moldovan leap to his feet.

Sadly, the same cannot be said of every melody carrying the weight of national representation. Despite the fact that the Spanish anthem sounds as though it's going round a musical loop, it is said that King Alfonso XIII was so worried he wouldn't recognise it when it was played that he employed an 'anthem man' to nudge him when it was time to stand up. The fact that the tune lacked words probably didn't help. Even the most tone-deaf royal could spot the lyric 'God Save the King' as a clue.

The oldest national anthem in the world is the Dutch *Het Wilhelmus*, which was written in 1574. Today marks the birth in 1880 of Wilhelmina I of the Netherlands. While she was exiled during the Second World War, churchgoers in the small Dutch town of Hizen were fined by the Nazi rulers for singing the song on her birthday. I'm sure most of us have trouble recalling more than the first few lines of any anthem we are loyal to, but the Dutch one is particularly curious. You have to sing it as if you are yourself William of Orange and conclude the first verse with the intriguing statement 'To the King of Spain I've granted a lifelong loyalty'. Perhaps the Spanish avoided lyrics so that they wouldn't have to return the compliment.

The origin of the United Kingdom's anthem is a sort of musical mystery. Some think it derived from plainsong or possibly a tune by John Bull or Henry Purcell. Personally, I like the story put about by the French, which is no doubt untrue but pleasingly bizarre. They suggest that Jean-Baptiste Lully wrote the tune *Grand Dieu Sauve le Roi* to celebrate the healing of Louis XIV's anal fistula. How splendid. How I long for some truthful basis to this tale of tails for who among us would not want to erupt in jubilant song at such a joyful event?

Whoever did write the British tune did a good job, for it has proved a worthy representative for several nations. It was used as the first German national anthem, albeit with the words changed to *Heil dir im Siegerkranz*, which seems marginally less cheery. It is still used to represent Liechtenstein, a UK/Liechtenstein musical brotherhood that can cause confusion. In 2004, when the two countries played each other at football, the same tune was played twice, thus causing bewilderment among the more simple-minded in the crowd.

It will be four years before we are once more roused by nationalist timpani playing and I hope we shall all know what to do. There is an apocryphal but delightful story about the one-time British Foreign Secretary, George Brown, attending an official reception in South America. Mr Brown is said to have arrived in a slightly frayed state. Attempting good grace, he asked a tall, elegant vision in red to dance. The vision declined, saying: 'I will not dance with you for three reasons. The first is that you are drunk. The second is that the band is not playing a waltz, but the Peruvian national anthem. The final reason is that I am the Cardinal Archbishop of Montevideo.'

There was only one red nose, but an entire restaurant full of red faces

4 January 2009

I ONCE HAD A VERY awkward meal with a clown. She was a diminutive person (which, because of my height is not a description that I use for many people), rather round and hailed from Argentina. I met her in Edinburgh during the festival and, thinking we might enjoy some Buenos Aires banter, invited her for something to eat. I selected an extremely smart establishment where ladies of leisure lunch and arrived early. The restaurant boasted a sweeping staircase down into the dining area. Much idle chatter was flowing until, that is, my comic companion arrived – in the full uniform of an Argentinean colonel.

Other than in cowboy films when the saloon doors swing back to reveal a sinister man with a six-shooter, I have never heard a dining establishment become so instantaneously still. Had there been a piano player, he would have stopped mid-chord. She eyed us all from beneath a peaked cap and turned to subdue the stone steps. A small ball in brilliant blue, her golden epaulettes shinier than the bridge work of the open-mouthed patrons, her knee-high black leather boots beat time to a ripple of gasps.

In that moment I could only hope that I looked so aghast no one could possibly recognise me. She sat and proceeded not to engage me in the mystery of buffoonery as I had hoped, but to speak at length and, for a person whose career involved only mime, in surprisingly loud tones, about her astonishingly varied private life.

Once the meal was over she surveyed the entire shell-shocked room and announced she now fancied finding someone to make love to, but sadly did not have the necessary four hours. Four hours? I can honestly say unless the four hours included a particularly lengthy game of I Spy there wasn't a person in the room up to it.

I thought about her for the first time in years as I sat down to begin filling in my new diary for 2009. I get mine from the performer's union, Equity. It's an organisation that looks after every kind of entertainer and I noticed, in the front, it had listed useful numbers, including one for Clowns International, which is apparently the 'oldest-established clowns' association in the world'. It has an office in Essex where you can only imagine that endless cars full of a surprising number of men in big shoes constantly turn up to bemoan the falling standard of trousers.

Clowns International's website allows you to search for a local clown. According to this, there is only one in my home county of Surrey. (So many remarks occur to me here, but I'm not planning to move.) He's called Rico and is described as 'professional and reliable'.

Needing clowns to be both professional and reliable seems somehow counter-intuitive. Rico is also described as having '£10 million public liability insurance'. You have to wonder how badly wrong balloon animals can go to require such financial back-up. Apparently, he 'is happy entertaining everyone', which I would have thought was a given. It makes you wonder if there is a small section of the clown community who are unreliable, unprofessional and miserable in the face of select audiences.

Clowning seems curiously old-fashioned, though not as out of date as the kind of performances once given by the American circus star Charles Sherwood Stratton, who was born today in 1838. He was better known as General Tom Thumb, a man who never grew much above 3 ft tall. The legendary showman P. T. Barnum heard about Charles, and the boy, aged five, went into show business. He was taught how to sing, dance, mime and, bizarrely, did impersonations of both Cupid and Napoleon Bonaparte. It made Stratton an international celebrity, feted by the great, the good and Queen Victoria.

It's not an act you can imagine might wow the modern audience, but then neither is the hoofing of Daisy and Violet Hilton, a pair of conjoined English twins who strutted their stuff on the slightly later vaudeville stage. The girls were pygopagus, a curious word which means joined at the back. Their mother's landlady 'adopted' them almost as soon as they were born, for she saw money in the girls' uniqueness.

They were trained to dance and sing, played the clarinet and saxophone and, for a while, were part of a dance act with Bob Hope. In America, they found fame and fortune and, sadly, many a representative to fleece them. They eventually died of flu, aged 60, on or near 4 January 1969, having been reduced to packing groceries for a living.

These days, I hope we see all human beings in a slightly more rounded fashion. Certainly, I have seen good changes in my time. The first agency that represented me also looked after many of what used to be called 'speciality acts'. There was a fierce woman on the front desk who operated the telephone system as well as the gates to representation.

I remember sitting in her presence one morning when a tiny man entered. Without looking up, the telephonist barked, 'Circus department, fourth floor.' There was a slightly awkward silence. It turned out the fellow had come for a job in accounts.

Opera has something for everybody: tragedy, drama and the odd swan

1 February 2009

It's a sign of the times that I have been listening to a woman who is already dead singing an aria about dying. It's a neat trick if you can do it, and with the wonders of modern technology anything is possible. The Italian soprano Renata Tebaldi (born today in 1922) went off to the great encore in the sky more than four years ago but click your computer mouse in the right direction and you can still hear her coming over all tubercular in *La Bohème*.

Tebaldi's break to the big time is a lesson to us all to never dismiss fate. Renata's uncle Valentino owned a café in the Italian town of Pesaro. As well as coffee, the town sported a music conservatoire where the diva Carmen Melis taught. Carmen was a fulsome girl given to a pastry or two, which she bought from Valentino. He mentioned the niece who happened to be there on holiday, Renata sang and the next thing you knew the young girl was en route to warbling round the world.

Over the past few years I have developed a passion for opera, which has surprised me and mildly appalled my family. I have always loved theatre, but the thought of opera made me anxious. My Italian being limited to the ability to order water with gas and tutti-frutti ice cream, I felt sure I would be bound to laugh inopportunely. I imagined my guffaw at the very moment that the heroine announced her tiny hand was about to become more frozen than the doctor had hoped.

I'm not the only person to have felt uneasy about the art form. Today marks the death in 1963 of Fleetwood Lindley, the last living person to see Abraham Lincoln's face. Famously, Lincoln was assassinated during a performance of a comedy at the Ford Theatre, leading to the classic actor's question, 'Other than that, Mrs Lincoln, how did you like the play?'

Mindful perhaps of this poor presidential theatrical experience, the Secret Service was understandably anxious when, in 1953, Dwight Eisenhower decided to attend a performance of *La Bohème*, an opera about which they clearly knew nothing. The impresario, Rudolph Bing, was asked some security questions. 'We hear the girl dies,' an agent began, 'how is she killed?' 'She dies of consumption,' Bing is said to have replied. 'But it isn't contagious at a distance.'

Once I realised that opera is just a play with cracking tunes, incredibly camp staging and astonishingly long curtain calls I was off and running. Indeed, I am thinking of writing one myself and I have found the ideal story combining high drama with a nice hint of the comic. It's going to be called *Kalabaliken i Bende* (*The Skirmish at Bender*), a salutary tale of what happens when guests overstay their welcome. It's based on a true story of what happened to the King of Sweden on this day in 1713 after he had tried the patience of the Sultan of the Ottoman Empire.

Charles XII of Sweden was a confused lad. For a start he should have been Charles VI but one of his relatives had read a fictitious history of Sweden and got his numbers mixed up. In fact Charles's full title was Charles, King of Sweden, the Goths and the Vends, Grand Duke of Finland, Duke of Estonia and Karelia, Lord of Ingria, Duke of Bremen, Verden and Pomerania, Prince of Rügen and Lord of Wismar, Count Palatine by the Rhine, Duke of Bavaria, Count of Zweibrücken-Kleeburg, Duke of Jülich, Cleve and Berg, Count of Waldenz, Spanheim and Ravensberg and Lord of Ravenstein, which I think already sounds like a great opening number.

In 1709 Charles lost a war and ran off, as you would, with a thousand Swedish soldiers to Bendery, Moldavia, which was then part of the Ottoman Empire. At first the Sultan thought he was a good egg and paid for everything, giving him the nickname Demirbas Sarl which sounds like a compliment but actually means 'Fixed Asset Charles'. After four years the Ottomans got tired of the Swedes and attacked the camp – herein lies the great drama. The necessary hint of comedy is provided by Charles being captured when he tripped over his own spurs.

If you are nervous of opera *La Bohème* (which, incidentally, premiered today in 1896) may be the one for you. George V said it was his favourite because it was the shortest.

There is a wonderful story about the tenor Leo Slezak who during a performance of Wagner's *Lohengrin* missed the swan he was supposed to exit on (in itself the sort of stage direction you will find only in opera) when a stage hand sent his feathered transport on too early. As he watched the bird disappear into the wings Slezak turned to the audience and asked, 'When does the next swan leave?'

On earning badges and a piece of history
that's never likely to be repeated

22 February 2009

It's World Thinking Day. I'm in favour of thinking and, indeed, often wish those in charge dabbled with the practice a bit more often. But before you rush off and muse randomly on the subject of your choice, let me remind you that World Thinking Day is designed for contemplation 'about the meaning of Guiding and Scouting'. For some the meaning is simple. The Scouts and Guides represent an excellent occupation for hormone-filled youth to abandon the shopping malls and learn to ging gang their goolies instead. Today marks the joint birthdays of Robert Baden-Powell (1857), founder of the Scouting movement, and his wife Olave (1889), who was, in her time, World Chief Guide – which sounds like an awful lot of work with a compass.

Years ago I was in the Danish equivalent of the Brownies. We were rather more colourfully called Bluebirds and everyone was known by a nickname selected by the 'pack'. Mine was Stump, which means scrap. I was far and away the smallest in the troop and as a consequence was always the one made to stay behind and sweep out the corners. I left with a solitary badge for housework and little or no self-esteem.

The Scouts are said to be the largest youth movement in the world although anyone heading down our local high street on a Saturday night may find that hard to believe. There is no doubt they do a lot of good. They also do a lot of curious things. Troop 442 of Union, Missouri, for example, holds the record for the world's largest ping-pong ball release and retrieval. What can I tell you about Union? It was once one of the world's largest manufacturers of cob pipes and, according to the current calendar of events, the only thing to look forward to is that City Hall will close at noon on Good Friday.

Keen to make their mark, on 11 September 1999, Troop 442 released 3,055 ping-pong balls from a tractor scoop on North Church Street and successfully rolled them downhill into a wooden funnel. The first question to ask is 'Why?' and the second – what kind of badge do you get for that? Traffic calming, possibly.

I don't know whether you can get a badge for thinking but as it happens old Baden-Powell has been much on my mind. According to Scout law, 'A Scout tells the truth'. I like the simplicity of this statement but the fact is truth is a slippery fellow that even a decent bow knot won't always tie down. I am currently writing a book set in the Second Boer War (1899–1902). As a result I have read dozens of books, newspapers and pamphlets from the period. I have learnt bizarre things, including how to load a Mauser rifle, what a pom-pom gun sounds like and how to bake bread in an anthill.

Over the last year I have bought enough Boer War memorabilia to start a small museum. Magic lantern slides, original maps and a small army of miniature soldiers crawl across my desk as I try to understand what really happened. My research has led me to two possible conclusions about Baden-Powell – he was either the hero of Mafeking who enabled the garrison to withstand a 217-day siege by 8,000 Boers or he was the villain of the piece who caused a thousand black Africans to die of starvation so that the whites might not have their service of afternoon tea disrupted.

Determining the truth about what happened when you weren't there is a tricky business. Sometimes history just sounds ridiculous. Take the tale of the last invasion of Britain, which happened this very day 212 years ago. An Irish-American colonel called William Tate decided to lead 1,400 conscripted French ex-convicts and invade the United Kingdom. Tate only spoke English so giving orders was tricky. You can just imagine him striding the deck trying to think of the French for anything other than the location of his aunt's pen on the bureau.

The plan was to land at Bristol but the weather was terrible so they headed for Wales instead (and haven't we all had outings like that?). Just off Fishguard somebody spotted them and fired just about the only cannonball they had in their possession. Tate didn't know this, panicked and turned back to land on a nearby beach instead. Here a Portuguese ship carrying alcohol had recently been grounded and was quickly discovered by the invasion force. Drunk as skunks they saw a woman, Jemima Nicholas, heading towards them in a tall black hat and a red cloak carrying a pitchfork. Thinking she must be a grenadier, twelve of them immediately surrendered to her. The official capitulation was signed in the Royal Oak pub followed by a practically *de rigueur* run on the pound and George III brilliantly proving his patriotism by sacking his French chef. It is as unlikely a story as you will ever come across but the country has been safe from incursion ever since.

I've decided not to take anyone's word for what happened in the past so next month I am off to Mafeking in search of the facts. It being South Africa I thought I might try the wine while I'm there. Does anyone know if there is a badge for that?

Save money by recycling discarded words into useful little couplets

1 March 2009

I'VE BEEN TRYING TO WRITE an epigram on thrift. These days both conscience and cost require us to be frugal and it might be that a few *bon mots* on the subject could be helpful. I like epigrams because they are often jolly. I am not like the American poet Robert Lowell (born today in 1917) who gloomily believed, 'If we see light at the end of the tunnel, it is the light of the oncoming train.' We are in a time of straitened circumstances, so we might as well find a bit of fun in it.

Privately, I do my best to be prudent – I save old government initiatives to press into logs for the fire, I wrest bones from the dog to make into soup, and have started hoarding ends of yarn to be knitted later in life into grandchildren. Then the other day someone asked me what I was doing about waste products from my business. To be honest there isn't much in my line of work but it did occur to me that each week there are a number of words which I discard during the writing process. Perhaps I have been too cavalier with these pieces of text (all right, I admit it, sometimes whole, practically untouched phrases). In the interests of the environment, perhaps I could gather them together. There aren't enough for a novel but they might make useful little couplets.

Today marks the birth of the poet Martial, who was born some-where between 38 and 41 AD, which either means we're not sure or his mother had the longest labour in history. Martial is the man to whom we should pay homage for the invention of the modern epigram – short, witty poems best described in the anonymous verse:

> What is an epigram? A dwarfish whole,
> Its body brevity, and wit its soul.

They are pleasing little snippets that can warm the heart of anyone stuck on a late-running train without the benefit of a book. Martial's aren't all funny or indeed all rhyming. Some are merely grumpy notes to his landlord as in:

> I live in a little cell, with a
> window that won't even close,
> In which Boreas himself would
> not want to live.

You would need to know that Boreas was the Greek god of winter to truly get the gag, whereas John Dryden's effort is pretty clear to everyone:

> Here lies my wife: here let her lie!
> Now she's at rest – and so am I.

I like the idea of recycling words into something useful, for I love to make do and mend. I worry, however, that many of these skills are unknown to the next generation. Faced with a bicycle puncture not many moons ago I asked a young friend if she might help me. 'Certainly,' she declared, 'what do you need?' 'A bucket of water,' I replied. She nodded and then inquired, 'Fizzy or flat?' I didn't know where to begin. The idea that you might seek an escaping air bubble from a pneumatic tyre in a container of sparkling water seemed like some modern parable for the difficulties of getting into heaven.

Today is St David's Day and I'm sure the Welsh saint could easily have constructed a sermon from such a metaphor.

Goodness knows the speakers on Radio 4's *Thought for the Day* often manage with less. St David died today in 589 (it was a Tuesday in case you're wondering). His mother, Non, was said to have given birth to him on a Pembrokeshire cliff top during a violent storm, which on her part, suggests an incredibly poorly planned walk.

I was thinking about St David as I set to work restoring four old stained-glass windows purchased from a salvage yard. I'm rebuilding the porch on my house and I thought a hint of the Welsh cathedral about it was just the job. 'Do the little things in life,' the Welsh patron saint commanded. (Actually he said '*Gwnewch y pethau bychain mewn bywyd,*' but I felt I might lose one or two of you.) I was entirely happy as I scraped and sanded the frames and it soon became clear that I would need to replace the old putty. I putted off to a large establishment open at all hours for the public to buy DIY products for projects that will almost certainly need to be put right by professionals later.

Not wishing to visit every aisle of Anaglypta wallpaper I approached a young member of staff for help. 'Do you have putty for glazing?' I asked. 'I wouldn't have thought so,' she replied, 'what's it for?' I felt the expression 'putty for glazing' was pretty self-explanatory so I tried it again – 'It's putty used in glazing . . . if you're glazing a window you need . . . putty.' She looked at me so blankly that I did a quick check around the shop to make sure I hadn't walked into a cake shop by mistake and was making a complete fool of myself. As I looked back at her a complete epigram popped into my head:

She did not understand what I wanted to buy,
So all that I glazed that day was her eye.

It's not exactly learned Latin but I feel the poetry of parsimony is on its way.

Hooked on tales of feisty females and life on the high seas

8 March 2009

NOW THAT THE INITIAL SHOCK of speeding into the financial storm is settling down and the windscreen wiper of time is clearing away the debris, it is possible we can begin to see out of the window again. One thing is apparently very clear. It may be that women's micro banks, which have proved such a success in the developing world, could provide the best economic model for the future. These are small financial institutions whose security is based on the ridiculous notion of lending to people who can pay you back.

Getting back to basics seems to be of the moment. The other day my local supermarket had a display in the fresh produce section offering me a magazine and some seeds so that I might grow my own vegetables. This seemed a quick way to do themselves out of business. The next thing you know I shall be breeding chickens, fattening calves and working out how to press my own loo roll. They say a woman's work is never done but nevertheless I hadn't planned to be open 24 hours a day.

Today is International Women's Day so here is a quick quiz.

1. According to the UN, how much of the world's work is done by women?
2. What percentage of the world's assets are owned by women?
3. Why do you think it took a woman (Mary Anderson) to invent the windscreen wiper?

Before I give you the answers let me to tell you that I am cele-brating today by wearing a stripy shirt, a patch over one eye and a parrot on my right shoulder. I have drawn the line at the wooden leg on the grounds it might 1. Mark my study floor and 2. Affect my clog dancing career, but otherwise my pirate look is complete.

My reasons are several fold. First, today is the birthday of that great Irish-American pirate Anne Bonny, who was born today in 1700. Anne's dad was an Irish lawyer who became a plantation owner in South Carolina. He got upset when, aged sixteen, Anne married a sailor called James Bonny. Any parent might view with suspicion a boyfriend picked up at the docks, but James was also a part-time pirate which would try anyone's patience. Anne's father washed his hands of her.

The Bonnys moved to the Bahamas where, socialising at work, they met other pirates. Soon Anne ran off to the high seas with one Calico Jack. Much swashbuckling later, Anne was arrested and faced the noose. Legend has it that Anne's father came to the rescue and she returned to Charleston where she married and eventually died, a pillar of the com-munity, in her eighties. I love her life. It has all the elements of a great film – a rebellious youth, a passionate love affair, some derring-do, a touching paternal reconciliation – all tied up in the words of a respectable old woman who can tell the tale in flashback. With stories like this you have to wonder why so many modern movies decide instead to centre around women whose *raison d'être* is retail (*Confessions of a Shopaholic*), or an obsession with the perfect wedding (*Bride Wars*) or feature girls too feckless to come in out of the rain unless told to do so by a boy (*Slumdog Millionaire*). (If you are off to see *Slumdog* do enjoy the fact that the host seems to say, 'Who wants to be a Milliner?' Here I think is a potentially more interesting story about escape from the Mumbai slums through hat-making.) There are so many great women to choose from so why not make an epic about someone splendid like Princess Khutulun instead?

The Canadian politician, Charlotte Whitton (born today in 1896), who was the first woman to be mayor of a major Canadian city, once said 'Whatever women do they must do twice as well as men to be thought half as good. Luckily, this is not difficult.' Khutulun proves Whitton's point. She was the niece of the great thirteenth-century Mongol military leader, Kublai Khan. Khutulun went into her uncle's business of soldiering and was said to be stronger than any man in the army. She would have been quite a catch but Khutulun had plans. She bet any prospective groom that she could beat him at wrestling. If she lost she would marry him but if she won he had to present her with 100 horses. Marco Polo wrote that Khutulun never married and by the end of her life had 10,000 horses.

So why do we need to remember and celebrate these stories of feisty females? Well, it brings me to the answers to my quiz.

1. The UN estimates that women do 75 per cent of the world's work.
2. Women own 1 per cent of the world's assets.

Even those of us who struggle with basic sums and glaze over when Robert Peston speaks, might find those figures a tad on the uneven side. I have decided not to wait any longer for global matters to improve and instead take the piratical route to demanding equality.

Oh, I nearly forgot.

3. Why did it take a woman to invent the windscreen wiper? Well, I suspect up until then most men had been quite happy saying, 'Don't be ridiculous, dear, I can see perfectly well.'

Stay upbeat and be of the moment – just don't tell me about it

15 March 2009

LIFE IS OCCASIONALLY AWASH WITH delightful irony. The French geographer Élisée Reclus (born today in 1830) so loved travelling around the world that he spent twenty years writing nineteen volumes about how to get about the place. As well as having a penchant for maps, Reclus had an antipathy to government and was a rather celebrated anarchist. I like the fact that a man who didn't want to be told what to do, nevertheless was the sort of boy who wants to tell everyone else the best routes to anywhere. That, however, is not the irony. Having traversed the earth he returned to France where his political views rather pleasingly earned the wandering fellow 'transportation for life'.

These days travelling by train in the UK can have a sense of a similar punishment. Modern railway timetables remind me of the logs Christopher Columbus kept. It was today in 1493 that Columbus returned to Spain after his first trip to the Americas. Not only did he have no real idea where he had been, most likely the principal gift he returned with was syphilis. In order to keep his crew calm on the eight-month journey, Columbus kept two logs – one correct one and one with artificially reduced journey times to suggest they were closer to home than anyone thought. We have a similar system with timetables being rather notional documents and the trains actually running on something I think should be known as 'Branson time'.

I have to say, I don't mind. The other day I was travelling back from the Lake District through some of the most beautiful countryside on the planet and I had far longer to enjoy the view than anyone could have predicted. My upbeat attitude to delay stems from a long, tiresome journey I once took when I met a Buddhist monk. He advised me to stem my impatience by trying to 'be of the moment'. I took this to heart and indeed was so of the moment on the train that I failed to notice not everyone was feeling the same contentment. Happily staring out of the window, I suddenly cried out for all to hear, 'Oh, look, there's an oxbow lake!' The silent Mexican wave of disapproval that raced through my fellow passengers made it clear that they thought I was at best annoying and, at worst, worryingly unhinged. They, however, saw no hint of insanity in constantly answering their mobile phones in order to loudly reveal every nuance of their personal and professional lives to the rest of us.

I like an oxbow lake and don't see them all that often. If you are over a certain age you may recall studying them at school and, if you are not then you may need me to explain that there was a time before satnav when geography was thought to be an important part of an all-round education.

These elbow-shaped pools of water are formed when a river decides to straighten its course and leaves behind an old bend in the stream as a small lake. I identify with them. How many times has the world decided to plough on a bit faster and I've thought, 'I wish I could just stop here for a bit instead.' The oxbow lake is a wonderful metaphor for opting out of the mainstream and taking a moment to breathe.

The trouble with pointing these things out on a train is that hardly anyone has time to be interested. Being 'of the moment' is terribly unfashionable. Everyone is preoccupied tapping on a computer, shouting on a phone or, worse still, being intently challenged by a small games console in the vain hope that they might make their brain as sharp as Nicole Kidman's. The idea of journeying without a panoply of technological pastimes seems anathema to most people. It's hard to believe but in 1927 when Charles Lindbergh made the first ever transatlantic flight he hardly bothered with a thing. There was no parachute, no radio, and no brakes. In fact, and I think this was going a bit too far, he didn't even have a forward-facing window. Just a small periscope and the intention to reach Paris from Long Island by turning right at Ireland. I like his attitude. To keep himself going he packed five chicken sandwiches and a bottle of water declaring, 'If I get to Paris, I won't need any more. And if I don't get to Paris, I won't need any more, either.'

The world has changed dramatically in the last quarter of a century. It's hard to believe but it was today in 1985 that the first internet domain name was registered. The company was symbolics.com, who produced 'special-purpose computer systems for running and developing state-of-the-art object-oriented programs in Lisp'. I like the idea of a computer system with a slight speech impediment but Lisp, it seems, is a programming language for artificial intelligence. Now almost everyone has a domain name and artificial intelligence has too often replaced real intelligence.

I shall resolutely try to continue being of the moment when I journey but I do rather envy Columbus. He may have been at sea for eight months but at least he didn't have anyone shouting 'I'm on a ship! I said I'm at sea!' every five minutes.

Several wrongs don't make it right –
but they can make it funny

22 March 2009

SOMETIMES I FIND THE INTERNET frustrating. I spend my life caught up in what I call a 'chain of curiosity'. I read one thing, such as the fact that the average person's left hand does 56 per cent of the typing, and immediately I wonder what is the longest word that might occupy the same hand 100 per cent? (It's 'stewardesses'.) If I am not chasing a fact I am usually checking its veracity and this is where trouble with modern research often ensues.

Today, for example, marks the anniversary of the death of the novelist Thomas Hughes in 1896. Among other things, he wrote the novel *Tom Brown's Schooldays*. There is a famous statue of him outside Rugby School and many a website will tell you that the sculptor of this piece made an error by carefully crafting buttons on the right side of the jacket and no button holes on the left. Indeed, several sites go on to claim that the sculptor was so mortified by this mistake that he killed himself. This seemed to me to be taking anxiety over a man of marble being able to do his coat up a little too far. I started to check things out. First of all I looked at lots of photographs of the statue and couldn't see any buttons at all. Then I spent some time trying to find out who the sculptor was. It turned out to be Sir Thomas Brock, but confirmation that the man topped himself in a fastening-related suicide has so far eluded me.

I don't know why I am so keen to get things right. The truth is I rather like the odd mistake. Writers make them all the time. There is a marvellous bit in Daniel Defoe's *Robinson Crusoe* where Crusoe decides to attempt to salvage some items from his shipwreck. Robinson declares, 'I pull'd off my Clothes, for the Weather was hot to Extremity, and took the Water . . .' Naked as the day he was born, he heads out to sea, swims round the boat, gets on board and within a few moments is in the bread-room, where he miraculously manages to fill his 'Pockets with Bisket'.

Mistakes can change your life. I once met a woman who lived in the Scilly Isles. She loved the place but had only turned up twenty years earlier because she thought she was going on holiday to Sicily. Blunders add a delightful frisson of unpredictability to life. Without a relentless homage to mis-understandings the world of comedy would be a poorer place. The great Chico Marx (born today in 1887) spent his entire career not quite comprehending his brothers.

> Groucho: How would you like a job at the mint?
> Chico: Mint? I don't like mint. What other
> flavours you got?

I'm not saying all errors are good. Some fashion faux pas are unforgivable. Today, for example, marks the birth of the Flemish painter Anthony van Dyck in 1599. Tony was respon-sible for lots of fine portraits of posh people but who can forget that he also left his name to the 'vandyck beard'. This is a goatee and moustache combination that in almost every case makes the wearer appear to be parading a merkin on their face as a bet. Then there are blunders with more permanent results. It was today in 1978 that a 73-year-old man decided to walk between the two towers of the ten-storey Condado Plaza Hotel in San Juan, Puerto Rico, on a tightrope 121 ft above the ground. The fact that he was the circus daredevil Karl Wallenda should not have made this any more sensible. I am all for senior citizens continuing to work as long as possible but I think someone should draw the line at high-wire acts.

Sadly several guy ropes were not connected properly and Karl lost his life.

Mind you, I don't think he carries as much blame for his own demise as the explorer John Ainsworth Horrocks (born today in 1818). John should be famous for founding the Australian town of Penwortham but unfortunately everyone knows him for his inability to ride a camel while carrying a gun. I think John's first mistake was to decide to go hunting on camel-back. They are tetchy creatures at the best of times. The second was failing to secure the safety catch on his gun. The camel lurched, the gun went off and John managed to shoot himself in the mouth. Sadly, he died a month later of gangrene, but not before he had the poor dromedary executed.

My favourite news story last month concerned the Irish police deciding to crack down on a Polish driver with more than fifty outstanding motoring offences. It was a curious case for the man in question. 'Prawo Jazdy' had always produced his documents yet each time he had given a different address. It turns out that '*Prawo Jazdy*' is printed on every Polish driving licence because it means 'driving licence' and not because it is anyone's name.

The German writer Goethe (who died today in 1832) said, 'A clever man commits no minor blunders', which clearly makes the Irish Garda geniuses. I wonder if they can check out Thomas Hughes's buttons for me.

None of us is really in control of our lives, even when we think we are

5 April 2009

WHY IS IT WHENEVER I ASK for 'black coffee' in one of the global network of shops that infest the high street that the barista earnestly inquires whether I 'want milk with that?' Perhaps the words 'black' and 'coffee' fused together make an unclear request or maybe I don't know how to order. I stand looking at the list of the astonishing number of ways in which the flavour of arabica beans can be utterly destroyed and I find myself baffled. I hear people boldly ordering a 'skinny, wet cappuccino'. Of course it's wet. It's coffee. It's made with water. Maybe it simply upsets the staff that I don't avail myself of the endless choices.

Today, everything is about choice and I do wonder if the whole notion hasn't got a bit out of hand. I was staying in a hotel the other day which had the most complex shower I have ever seen. Without my glasses the world is a bit of an impressionist painting but I can usually work out which bit is hot and which bit cold by the telling blue and red markers. This one had about eight shower heads and a computer to regulate them individually. I had to get out and fetch my glasses to turn the thing on. Standing in the type of cubicle I imagine cryobiologists dream of I accidentally pressed the wrong button and the whole thing went into some sort of pre-programmed overdrive. Water shot at me from every direction with no hope of me ever being able to turn it off, my glasses steamed up and I couldn't find the way out. I felt like Shelley Winters in *The Poseidon Adventure*.

*

307

I'm not saying having a choice is a bad thing but sometimes it worries me. Take patient choice with the NHS. Some of this is, of course, splendid. How marvellous if you were in hospital and instead of being force-fed jelly someone in a white coat turned up with a dessert trolley. I am less clear about other decisions. Given a range of options to cure something hideous I would prefer to select the one that works. The trouble is I have no idea which one that might be because I'm not a doctor. I am about to spend the next ten years of my life paying for my youngest daughter to become a medic. I'm not spending all that money so that when I finally need my hips replacing she asks me to decide what with.

My son, who is further down the educational food chain, is currently doing what must be considered medical basics – biology GCSE. I've been trying to help him but I'm not sure he needs me. Most of it is tested through multiple choice. Gone are the days when you had to do neat drawings of the lungs with appropriate red and blue arrows. Instead you are asked to decide whether alveoli are a) air sacs or b) a Spanish garlic sauce. Perhaps I should just go with the flow and realise this is the way forward. Perhaps life is just some sort of endless quiz show where you hope you pick well. We live after all in a world where the only way to become a millionaire is to a) rob a bank, b) run a bank, c) ruin a bank or d) answer a question from Chris Tarrant.

Perhaps we have all these modern-day decisions as an illusion of control in our lives. The fact is none of us is really at the helm even when we think we are. I've been reading a splendid book called *Women of the Raj: The Mothers, Wives, and Daughters of the British Empire in India* by Margaret Macmillan. It's about that period of history when the world map was mainly pink and the principal choice many British women faced in the day was what time to change for dinner. On the surface these females seemed to hold total sway over their households but

Macmillan tells a wonderful story about a *memsahib* who is horrified to discover that her male cook is not only running a brothel from the kitchen but has also taken a homosexual lover. 'How could he do it?' she cried in horror, to which another servant replied, 'Vaseline, m'am.'

The whole subject of choice is on my mind. I am lately back from that other former colonial outpost, South Africa. In search of long-lost Boer War graves we headed off-road to villages where any path is notional, electricity unlikely and choice absurd. We met a headteacher who wanted books for her school. 'What do you need to add to your library?' I asked. 'We don't need to add,' she replied, 'we need to begin.'

We stopped at a small shop. Inside it was dark with wooden shelves ranged behind a counter protected by mesh. There was little on offer – bars of soap called simply 'Soap' and cans of warm cola. 'Do you have coffee to drink?' I asked. The woman nodded and after a while produced two cups. We sat on the dusty step outside the shop and looked across the wide plains under the brilliant blue sky. The coffee was instant and not very warm. Do you know what? It was just fine.